ZERO TO SOLD

HOW TO START, RUN, AND SELL A
BOOTSTRAPPED BUSINESS

ARVID KAHL

ISBN: 978-3-9821957-0-4 (Paperback)

ISBN: 978-3-9821957-5-9 (Hardcover)

ISBN: 978-3-9821957-1-1 (eBook)

ISBN: 978-3-9821957-2-8 (ePDF)

Version 1.3.0 (May 18th, 2021)

For Danielle, my one person.

I wouldn't be who and where I am without you.

CONTENTS

PRODUCT EVOLUTION: CONTROLLED GROWTH AND SAYING NO

BUILDING THE RIGHT THINGS

BUILDING THINGS RIGHT

CUSTOMERS: BUILDING RELATIONSHIPS THAT LAST

PRICING: SUBSCRIPTIONS, PLANS, AND OTHER FINANCIAL CHALLENGES

BUSINESS: PULLING LEVERS AND ADJUSTING SCREWS

MARKETING AND SALES

THE STABILITY STAGE

BUILDING RELATIONSHIPS: WORKING WITH CUSTOMERS

BUILDING A MATURE BUSINESS

BUILDING A MATURE PRODUCT

BUILDING A TEAM

BUILDING A BRAND

THE GROWTH STAGE

SELLING YOUR COMPANY

BEYOND BOOTSTRAPPING

All of the really successful people I know have a really strong action bias. They just do things.

NAVAL RAVIKANT

AN INTRODUCTION TO ZERO TO SOLD

Many people dream of having a business that makes money for them while they sleep. Yet, most people never turn that dream into reality. Life gets in the way, they say, and they aren't cut out to be a business owner anyway. I believe differently. I think that everyone can be an entrepreneur and create a sustainable business that will allow them to live a life of freedom and financial independence. It will require some sacrifice, as building a business will take a lot of work and time. But it will lead to a life of control, a life of choice, and a life of opportunity.

Zero to Sold will show you what the life of a bootstrapped founder will look like. It will teach you how to fill all the roles required to run a business and what you need to get done in each stage of your bootstrapped company's evolution.

No matter if you are just starting to think about being an entrepreneur, are in the middle of running a bootstrapped company, or are a seasoned founder, you will find useful strategies, thought-provoking anecdotes, and insightful concepts in this guide.

Zero to Sold will focus on examples from the Software-as-a-

Service (SaaS) ecosystem, as this is my area of expertise. Most advice will be applicable to marketplaces, eCommerce, and non-software businesses, too.

While this is a guide, a manual, and a compendium, in the end, you are the agent of your own success. Carefully reflect if the advice in this book applies to your business. Read and learn as much as you can, but treat all guidance and direction as anecdotal. You will have to find your own combination of strategies and tactics. *Zero to Sold* will help you get there.

ON BOOTSTRAPPING

THE FEEDBACKPANDA STORY

I WROTE *Zero to Sold* because I've been through starting multiple bootstrapped businesses, growing a few, and selling one of them. Allow me to share the story of the one I sold.

Within two years, I co-founded, ran, grew, and finally sold a Software-as-a-Service business called FeedbackPanda, a productivity tool for online English teachers.

What many don't realize is that this was an overnight success many years in the making. FeedbackPanda wasn't my first rodeo. I've been part of many internet businesses before, and I've had my fair share of failures. I was in businesses where we never finished building the product. I co-founded startups that fizzled out because we didn't know how to market our service. I've been involved in companies that didn't find a way to monetize their popular products, only to pivot to something completely different after many years of trying to make it work.

I'll be sharing my experiences from both FeedbackPanda and the not-so-successful startups in this book, as I believe that you can learn the most at the intersection of experience and knowledge. So, I will provide you with both.

FeedbackPanda, the business that changed my life, was a service born out of necessity. It was a product that solved one critical problem for a well-defined audience, that allowed me to experience and learn the things that I have compiled into this book.

FeedbackPanda was a collaborative effort between me and my girlfriend, Danielle Simpson, who was an online English teacher at the time. We bootstrapped the business from day one, and when we sold it for what I would call a life-changing amount of money, the Monthly Recurring Revenue (MRR) of FeedbackPanda had just reached $55,000.

Within two years, we had built a niche service from a proof-of-concept into a thriving business that was attractive enough for a Private Equity firm to take it off our hands.

So, where did this all start?

It started with a leg injury. In early 2017, Danielle suffered an injury that meant she couldn't leave the house for a while. For a trained Opera singer like her, that made regular work impossible. You can't invite an audience of hundreds into your living room for a concert.

Danielle started looking for work she could do from home, and she found something interesting. A wave of Chinese companies had emerged that recruited native English speakers to teach English as a second language to Chinese students. She tried it out and was hooked immediately: it was a fun job, it could be done using just a laptop, and the pay was alright.

Shortly after, she found that there were several large online communities of teachers who taught for various Chinese companies. Danielle joined those online social media groups and forums and started hanging out with her virtual colleagues that numbered in the thousands at that point.

A few weeks into teaching on a full-time schedule, she noticed things that started as nuisances but quickly became painful problems. The teaching part of her job was great and fun, but certain formalities took way too much additional time. The most noticeable problem was student feedback. After every 25-minute lesson, the teacher would have to write a few paragraphs of a lesson report that was supposed to inform the parents of what their child had learned, how well they learned it, and what they could practice at home. Having only five minutes between lessons to take care of this and everything else (ranging from grabbing a coffee to using the restroom), Danielle would defer this work until after she was done teaching for the day. It couldn't be avoided, as the Chinese companies would not pay teachers for their teaching work unless the feedback was provided as well.

When Danielle started teaching 10-hour days, the added feedback time would often amount to almost two hours of unpaid overtime. That meant two hours less for spending time with me, meeting friends, or reading a good book.

So she did what anyone would do: she developed a system, using Excel sheets and Word documents to track information about what her students learned, how they did, and what to suggest to their parents. She started using text templates for the content of the lesson and the preparation hints, as the Chinese schools defined the curriculum, and it could be used as a template for every student.

We found out that many other teachers did the same when they started talking about their self-built solutions in their online communities. Teachers began to share their templates through Google sheets. It was clear that this was a shared problem in a very tight-knit community.

One day, Danielle and I talked about the painful experience of student feedback, and how her system, even though it helped, was clunky and overwhelming. I looked into it, and it seemed quite possible to build a web-based application that would do this work faster and more reliably.

We also saw that this would be a great business opportunity. There was a sizeable market with an apparent, shared, and critical problem. The problem was solvable, but no one had yet built anything to make it noticeably easier. So we decided to build a validation prototype, to see if it had a meaningful impact on Danielle's day-to-day workflow.

It took me a week or two to build the system. When Danielle started using it, the workflow impact was obvious: she transferred her Excel and Word files into the system, and the automation kicked in immediately.

Instead of two hours of extra work each day, it would take her less than 10 minutes altogether. We knew we were onto something big from that very moment.

I had built the software with potentially turning it into a SaaS in mind. It had an authentication system built on Auth0 that would allow users to log in using their social media accounts—after all, that's where we knew they hung out. It had a rudimentary subscription system built on Stripe that allowed us to charge from day one.

So, we released it to the public, built a landing page, and waited. Nothing happened. One or two people signed up for the free trial, but there was not much else. We hadn't done any marketing, and we hadn't made any sales. The service just sat there, idling.

And then, one day, everything changed. In a comment to a Facebook post about how teachers dealt with feedback, Danielle dropped the link to our product with an explanation of how she used it. Teachers started to respond, asking for more details, they checked out the program, and came back to share their newly found discovery on social media.

Our growth was almost entirely organic since that day. This one comment released an avalanche of word-of-mouth marketing that fueled the growth of our business from its first few users to thousands of customers a couple of months later. It was surreal, but we had tapped into a highly active tribe. Once we understood that, we didn't need to do much when it came to marketing our product: our users would do most of that for us.

Signups surged on that day, and there has not been a day without at least a few dozen new subscriptions ever since. Online teaching influencers discovered the product, talked about it through their channels, put links on their blogs, and our landing page started to receive more and more visitors.

Danielle was at the helm of product and design, while I managed the technical and infrastructural parts of the business. We shared most other jobs, particularly customer service. Over time, we automated the company as much as we could. We documented our internal processes so we could easily outsource or take over each other's activities. We built the business as if we were to eventually sell it, even though that was never our goal. The only goal we set was to help teachers do their jobs better and pay our bills.

We had noticed that teachers loved to share, so we added a collaboration system where they could help each other out by sharing their templates. All of a sudden, we had a product that developed a strong network effect overnight.

And that feature made the business grow beyond our wildest expectations. Every day, new teachers would sign up, and since we provided a service that solved their problems well, we had incredibly high retention and conversion rates.

For many of our customers, teaching from home was a side hustle. Using our product enabled many of them to turn this into a full-time source of income. We priced our service to be affordable and easily justified. We even increased our prices by 50% a year into running the business, and it continued growing nevertheless.

So we coasted along, adding new customers every day,

building features and making the service more reliable, and integrating deeper and deeper into the web-based teaching software our customers were using. Everything looked and felt awesome.

And then, things started to become stressful. The customer service load increased with more and more new teachers signing up. Maintaining integrations took time out of my feature budget, as the boom of online education in China meant a proliferation of online teaching companies that we needed to support. I had made a few questionable technical decisions that came back to bite me in the shape of unexpected downtime. I developed severe anxieties that took me a lot of willpower to work through. The more people I felt responsible for, the more it pained me when something went wrong.

That's when I learned the true nature of entrepreneurial life. It is fun, but it is also painful at times. It is full of responsibilities, real or imagined, and it can bring great joy as well as significant pain. We never hired an employee throughout the lifetime of the business, and while we talked about it often, we never got to it. FeedbackPanda was run just by Danielle and me.

So when we started receiving the first acquisition offers, we began to seriously consider selling the business. We had never talked about that before, as we were quite happy to run the business as our full-time occupation. But more and more reasons to sell popped into our conversations, so that one day, when we got a particularly exciting offer, we decided to go for it.

We sold FeedbackPanda in mid-2019, just under two years after founding the company. It was an exciting and scary thing to do, and this book is one of the results of that journey. Having always been an avid reader and an admirer of the bootstrapped founder and indie hacker community, I write this in the hope that it will encourage founders and founders-to-be to start, run, and sell their own bootstrapped businesses.

I learned so much during the time from start to exit, from zero to sold. Now it's time to share the lessons and experiences of that journey.

WHAT IS BOOTSTRAPPING?

BEFORE WE DIVE into the details of the journey of a bootstrapped founder, we should take a look at the core topic of this entrepreneurial approach: **bootstrapping**.

The original meaning comes from the metaphor of pulling yourself up by your own bootstraps. That is a logical impossibility, of course. However, it is an excellent analogy to creating a business from nothing, without any outside funding or assistance. Bootstrapping is about accomplishing the unlikely using as few resources as possible.

Several names often get conflated with bootstrapping, mostly "self-funded," "customer-funded," and "indie-funded." Then, there is also the term "semi-bootstrapped."

Self-funded: A bootstrapped business starts with almost no money and slowly gathers steam. A self-funded business involves a significant investment of personal founder capital—and usually hits the ground running. Some founders use their savings, and some get loans or credit lines. A bootstrapped business is always self-funded, but not every self-funded business is bootstrapped.

Customer-funded: If you set up your business to be profitable from day one, and use the revenue you generate to pay for your services, you are customer-funded. This also extends to going into partnerships with customers to build specific features, where the customers take over the development cost, at least partially. A working bootstrapped business is eventually customer-funded, like any successful business, but not every customer-funded company is bootstrapped.

Indie-funded: If your business receives funding from independent, non-traditional sources like banks or venture capital funds, you can call it indie-funded. Crowd-investing and crowd-financing count toward this definition as well. The difference compared to traditional funding is the level of expectation regarding your growth and business goals. Indie funding sources understand that you may want to create a cash-flow-positive lifestyle business, and they are perfectly fine if you don't exhibit hockey stick-like growth.

Finally, a **semi-bootstrapped** business is a business that exhibits all the typical behaviors and properties of a bootstrapped company, but uses outside funding of any kind to accelerate parts of the business without subjecting itself to paradigm-shifting expectations of its growth trajectory. The business will still minimize its expenses, automate as much as possible, and build sustainable, long-term-focused processes. It just uses some money to fuel its marketing, development, or any other part of the business.

There is a debate about whether "bootstrapping" is the right word for what we do. Hiten Shah says it should be called "self-funded" from the start, and it feels like the whole debate could be solved with a Venn diagram.

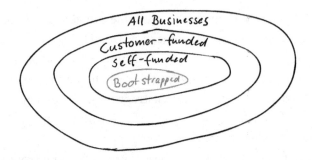

To me, bootstrapping is the act of creating a valuable, sustainable business with little to no funding. It's a founder mindset, a focus on making fiscally responsible business decisions and looking for sustainable long-term growth, and meaningful relationships with every single customer.

THE FOUR STAGES OF A BOOTSTRAPPED BUSINESS

EVERY SUCCESSFUL BOOTSTRAPPED business goes through four distinct phases: **Preparation**, **Survival**, **Stability**, and **Growth**, each separated by revenue and profit levels. Every stage introduces new problems and situations to resolve. I'll guide you through each phase in detail, describing what will happen to the business, the product, the founder, and the customers throughout the entrepreneurial journey.

In the **Preparation Stage**, the focus will be on finding an audience, their biggest problem, and a solution that solves that problem in a way to make people pay for it. You will find out how to price your product initially and start selling.

In the **Survival Stage**, the focus will be on finding a repeatable way to make money. You will learn how to work on the product, listen to your early customers, and start building out processes and automation to stay on top of your business.

In the **Stability Stage**, you have found your way to generating steady revenue. At that point, you will look into offering a stable, mature product, hiring people to help you run the business, and building long-lasting relationships with your customers.

In the **Growth Stage**, you will find yourself at a crossroads: should you keep running the company, or do you want to sell it? You will discover strategies and step-by-step guidelines that will allow you to do either, as you will learn how to remove yourself from the business.

Finally, you will learn about other options beyond boot-strapping, including venture capital, bootstrapper-friendly funding options, and traditional sources of capital.

THE PREPARATION STAGE

THE PREPARATION STAGE AND YOU

EVERY BUSINESS STARTS in your imagination. To some, it's an idea of solving a problem in a new way. To others, it's the dream of managing a company from a beach somewhere. Whatever the initial spark is, there is a long way between that first fragment of a plan to a sustainable business that's getting along fine.

First, you will turn your idea into a product you can sell. Then, you will create a business: a system that allows you to sell that product over and over again.

This stage ends when you begin selling your product to your audience. To get there, you will need to reach the following five goals:

1. Find your niche audience.
2. Find and validate their critical problem.
3. Invent and validate a solution to their problem.
4. Build a product to implement that solution.
5. Build a business that can repeatedly sell that product to your audience.

Your revenue will be at zero or even negative, as you have

pre-sales expenses. That means this may be the most expensive phase for a bootstrapped founder, as there is no way to generate earnings from a business that does not yet sell a product. However, operational expenses will be low as you will likely be able to coast along using the free tiers of the services required to build and deploy an initial prototype of your software product. Mostly, this phase will cost you time and focus.

FROM IDEA TO PRODUCT

FROM IDEA TO PRODUCT

TECH FOUNDERS—AND I count myself as one—focus on products because that is what we use to solve our problems. After all, when you run into a challenging task, what do you look for first? An in-depth scientific explanation for the epistemological essence of the task? Or a tool that will do the job for you seconds after you install it?

Most people, particularly entrepreneurs, will prefer the shiny product to the in-depth analysis. After all, we have a job to do.

That way of thinking often leads founders to create products that are solutions looking for a problem. It's no surprise that many of the products launched on ProductHunt fizzle out quickly after the launch: they address unvalidated problems for audiences that may or may not exist.

Successful businesses are built by solving critical problems for an audience that will pay for a solution to their issues. The Preparation Stage is when you make these foundational choices. Once in motion, a business has certain inertia that makes these decisions hard to change. Even though pivoting your business into new markets is sometimes the right choice, it's extra effort.

That's why it's a good idea to spend considerable time on getting it right in the first place.

Here's an important tip about conducting conversations with your prospects: record your prospects after asking them for permission. You will be far too busy making sure you get information from your customers to retain everything they said. Record the calls and wait a few days before you analyze the results. Right after a call, you may still be under the influence of primacy and confirmation biases, so let some time pass between the conversation and the analysis.

YOU PROBABLY HAVE IT BACKWARDS: STARTING A BOOTSTRAPPED BUSINESS

MANY BUSINESSES START with a product idea. They then try to find a market that's willing to buy that product. They fail because there were not enough customers. They fail because the product solved the wrong problem. They fail because the product solved the problem the wrong way. And sometimes, they fail even though the product solved the customers' problems.

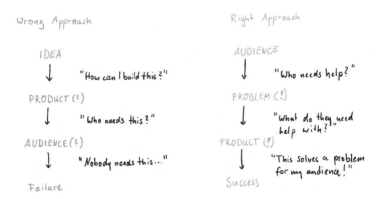

That happens because many founders build their businesses with a product-first approach. But audience research, problem analysis, and solution validation should happen before you think about a product. While this may seem counter-indicative in a world of polished products that we use every day, it is much more likely to build a great business on a validated market, filling a validated need for people who will be able to pay enough for you to sustain your business and your life.

Many successful bootstrapped businesses start with an audience, a specific niche. They find their customers' critical problems and provide valuable solutions that people gladly pay for. Their product is centered around continuously providing value to new and existing customers. Audience, problem, solution, and product can be looked at individually.

Audience → Problem (CRITICAL) → Solution → Product

WHO? → WHY? → HOW? → WHAT?

The questions you should be asking yourself are, in this order:

1. **Who am I helping?** You will discover how to find the perfect niche and make sure it can support your business in Step One: Your Audience.

2. **Why do they need help?** Learn how to find and validate their critical problem in Step Two: Their Problem.

3. **How can I help them with that?** Find a good solution and make sure it fits into your prospective customers' workflow in Step Three: Your Solution.

4. **What can I create to help them that way?** You'll learn how to create an easy-to-maintain and reliable product in Step Four: Your Product.

STEP ONE: YOUR AUDIENCE

BOOTSTRAPPING AN AUDIENCE

A BUSINESS WOULD BE nothing without customers. You can have the best product in the world, but you won't be able to build any meaningful business if there is no one to pay for what you offer.

So, where do you find those paying customers? The first step to building a business is answering that question, and for bootstrapped founders, there is one critical component: finding the perfect niche.

You'll see why niches are essential and what makes niche communities especially interesting: homogenous populations with tribe-like structures that can be leveraged by bootstrapped founders in unique ways.

We will take a look at what makes a fruitful market, and how to figure out if it will be a good one for your business.

For a bootstrapped business, the choice of your target audience has a few significant limitations: you will have to be careful to find a market that sits in the Goldilocks Zone between too small and too big, and, at best, it should grow in a certain way. You will discover how to find the numbers and figures to make informed choices about your audience.

After all, it all starts with the people you want to help. The more you know about them, the better.

THE POWER OF THE NICHE

IF YOU WERE to found a company that makes and sells beer today, you would probably start a craft brewery. You'd start a small operation, find the people who enjoy your product, and slowly expand your business.

You would not try to compete with Bud Light and Heineken for shelf space. You would prefer to provide a unique product to a small, specialized segment of the beer-drinking population. The craft beer enthusiasts would be your target audience.

You would start in a niche.

For your bootstrapped business, finding your niche is an integral part of the journey. In a niche, you will encounter less competition. Your customers will be very similar, and your marketing and sales activities can be turned into repeatable processes quite easily.

So, what makes a niche interesting for a bootstrapper? What is it about niche customers that you can leverage to create a sustainable business? How deep a niche do you need to find a good audience?

What's (in) a Niche?

When we speak of niches in business, we always talk about smaller segments of a larger population. We're looking for a specific subset of a more general group of people. The kind of specificity can vary wildly: sometimes we look for immutable things like age or gender niches. Other times the specifics we're interested in are fluid things like preferences or experience levels. Some niches can be large enough to contain millions of people, and others might just consist of a handful of individuals.

What unites all niches is that they are inclusive of some and exclusive of others. The members of the in-group will be reasonably similar, depending on the specificity of the niche. That's why niches work so well for bootstrapped businesses: if you can provide a tool that solves a niche problem very well, you can be sure that everyone in the niche will be interested in it.

Selling to a niche is very different from selling to the general public. If we go back to the example of the beer industry, you will see that Anheuser-Busch InBev, the makers of Bud Light, spend more than $1.5 billion every year. They do that because they need to be present in the mind of every single shopper when they think of getting a beer. For a small craft beer company, this kind of marketing expense is impossibly high, and it would be a waste. They would show their product to millions of people, but only a fraction of them would even consider drinking a non-mainstream beer. Niche businesses are better off spending much less money in much more directed ways. A craft beer company might put up flyers in a local pub that is serving lots of craft beers, or allocate a budget to exhibiting at beer festivals. A niche business will market to its niche and no one else.

Who's in a Niche?

So, what makes niche populations unique? The way I see it, they are mostly homogenous, often tribal, and allow for much better measurement and planning than huge non-specific audiences.

Niche Populations Are Homogenous

If you filter a large group of people by several specific properties, you will end up with an audience that shares those properties. As a result, these people will also share many other things that can make building products and selling them very convenient.

People in your niche will likely have the same problems. If they love fantasy football, they all need to keep track of their teams. If they enjoy fly-fishing, they all need to find information on where to fish and how the weather will impact their chances of a catch.

If you spend enough time investigating the problems of your niche, you will sooner or later surface their critical problems. These are the things that are common roadblocks for everyone in the niche. Solving that problem with a dedicated product will allow you to have a high chance of success with your bootstrapped business.

People in a niche will also share very similar goals and aspirations. People who love knitting want to make beautiful pieces of clothing. Craft beer fans want to find (and drink!) the best and most exciting beers in their area. Recruiters want to recruit as many well-fitting candidates as possible.

From a goal, you can usually infer a problem that is in the way of your customers' path to success. Solve that problem, and you can help everyone in the niche reach their goals.

People in your niche will also speak the same (metaphorical) language. While many niches are globally distributed, the people in them will all share a common understanding of what matters to them. Dungeons & Dragons fans will know what a D20 is, and woodworking aficionados will have no trouble understanding why you'd prefer Alternate Top Bevel over Flat Top Grind saw blades for a clean cut. In your marketing communication, you can assume that everyone in the niche has specific knowledge that you can build on. Not only does this allow you to be precise in your communication, but it will also show that you know what you're talking about; that you are one of them.

Niche Populations Are Tribal

That brings us to another fundamental property of niche populations: they are often organized tribally. Seth Godin wrote a book called *Tribes*, in which he describes a tribe as "a group of people connected to one another, connected to a leader, and connected to an idea." That sure sounds like a niche audience!

This interconnected group of people looking for leadership can be a godsend for your business. You can either leverage existing leaders in the community, who are usually called "influencers," or you can become a tribe leader yourself. There is room for a lot of leaders in most niche tribes. In such a position, you are regarded as an expert who also offers a product specifically designed for members of the tribe. This position makes selling significantly easier than hoping for random strangers to see your product and buy it on a store shelf.

People derive their identity from belonging to a tribe. If you can place your business in a way that makes your product a thing that "people in our tribe use," then you will have a guaranteed sales funnel for as long as your niche exists.

Niche Populations Are Measurable

In niches, you can find out the numbers more easily than in a more general population. If you're trying to find out how many potential customers you have, it will be much easier if you're a craft beer brewery that has advertisements running in 10 local pubs. Figuring out how many patrons they can reach will require a few evenings of counting people in those places. For Anheuser-Busch InBev, it's an entirely different story: for them, every human on earth who likes beer is a potential customer— but the chances of them buying are hard to calculate, and so is the effectiveness of a massive billboard campaign in hundreds of cities.

With large populations, measuring is a hit-or-miss activity, as everyone is competing for attention. Within a niche, you can expect much more engagement from your potential customers as soon as they are exposed to your content.

The better you define your niche market, the more confident you can be in your numbers. "People who like fantasy football" may be a vague definition that doesn't give you much to work with. "People who logged into one of the three most popular fantasy football websites over the last three months" will yield more actionable numbers. At best, you will get numbers that allow you to validate a viable audience for your bootstrapped business: not too small and not too big.

The Ins and Outs of a Niche

An interesting perspective on niches is that you can also look at what a niche *does not* contain. By defining things that you don't expect to see in your niche, you have access to exclusionary filtering as well.

Once you know what you don't have to care about in your niche, you have the means to deal with the inevitable noise that you'll find in every market, no matter how well-defined your audience is. There always will be misfits and contrarian voices. By knowing what you can ignore, your focus will be on the things that matter most to the most substantial part of your niche.

Opportunities of a Niche

With niche audiences being homogenous, tribal, and measurable, you have several opportunities to help your bootstrapped business succeed:

Low-Cost Marketing

Shared interests will allow you to speak to the needs of your niche audience directly. Creating content that has a lot of impact and will be read by a lot of people will be easier, as there is less competition for your audience's attention. More generic markets might be saturated with content, but inside a niche community, people will always be eager to learn more about their area of expertise.

Targeted advertising works very well for niches, too. As pay-per-click costs are lower for many niche terms, your ad campaigns will be much more cost-effective than if you were to target a more generic term. The more specifically you can define your audience, the more effective your campaign will be. This also extends to traditional media of communication. If your niche audience is fond of reading industry magazines, a print advertisement could put you in front of hundreds of thousands of readers who would be hard to reach using digital ads.

Partnerships in niches become a much more lucrative endeavor. Additional exposure and reach results in quick win-win situations, where both partners can significantly boost both their customer base and their reputation as an expert in the niche. Partnering up with other players in the niche allows you to reach customers at different stages of "niche proficiency," increasing the breadth of your sales funnel.

If you lead a tribe, it will eventually do the marketing for you. A large following will amplify your messages with a lot of reach, giving you credibility and encouraging newcomers to become customers so they can belong to the tribe.

At FeedbackPanda, Danielle started a tribe around her thought leadership in the field of online teaching. She became an advocate for the needs of these teachers, and they followed her actively on social media, engaging in conversations, spreading the word, and, best of all, even defending the company and the product against people who dismissed or publicly disliked it. That's the power of a tribe.

Word-of-mouth marketing is another effect of using tribal structures in a niche. If you give people the opportunities to share your content and messages with other tribe members, they will. The interconnected nature of tribes facilitates this rapid exchange of information, and if you leverage those channels, your product will sell itself. At FeedbackPanda, it took one well-placed social media comment to start an avalanche of word-of-mouth referrals that lasted for years.

Referral Marketing Systems

If you're in a niche with a healthy and active tribe, you will have success with customer referral systems. As Ryan Kulp explains, the effect of referrals will depend on the shareability of your product. Some products will make sharing easier, like network-effect-driven collaboration tools, where a new user will add value to the network for everyone involved. Other products won't be as easy to share, such as a tool that makes a recruiter find better leads—recruiters probably wouldn't want competitors to use this tool as well.

If your product is shareable, spend time on creating a referral system early in the life of your business. If it's not shareable, defer this kind of system until you have exhausted better, more effective marketing techniques.

Influencer Reach

Niche influencers are usually perceived as much more professional public personas than the more general kind of celebrity influencer. Most niche influencers are experts in their fields, and what they talk about positively gains credibility. Their following consists mostly of other members of the niche, making them an excellent candidate for spreading your message.

Luckily, these influencers are also much cheaper to partner with than the prominent super-influencers. Often, they are not even aware of their influence, or they don't necessarily see it as a monetizable activity. While I recommend you still offer them reasonable compensation, you can approach niche influencers as potential partners instead of just seeing them as a marketing channel.

Differentiation Is Easy

Lastly, it's easy to build a unique and differentiated product when the landscape of competitors and competitive alternatives is clear and uncluttered. Fewer competitors means more potential differentiation vectors: you can stand out much more by providing a service that is not yet offered in the niche.

Analyze your competitors for what they do well and what they don't when you do your market research. If you've done your problem validation right, you will see gaps in the market that are not yet served. Build your products around those gaps, and look into partnering with your competitors to expand each other's customer base.

Look out for non-competitor competitive alternatives: the things people use instead of using an actual product. This can be Post-It notes, an Excel spreadsheet that does not involve numbers, anything that is a general tool applied to a specific problem. These types of makeshift solutions are where you can find your critical problems—and that is where you can best serve your niche.

The only remaining question is, "How narrow do I need to make my niche?" In reality, this will depend on the size and quality of the initial group of people you niche down from. The more specific you get, the smaller your audience will be in scale. Like in machine learning, you run the risk of "overfitting" your niche; you might get too specific. There could be a few hundred "Star Trek fans that live in the New Orleans area and love to eat Quinoa," but that won't sustain a bootstrapped business.

In general, a good niche size will allow you room to grow to your Monthly Recurring Revenue goal and still leave space for a few competitors. To determine the size of your audience, you will need to do some research. Your target size should be small enough not to invite large competitors and big enough to sustain your business. If it's too generic, narrow the niche by being more specific in who you want to serve. If there are too few prospects, broaden the niche by loosening the requirements for someone to fit into the niche.

A good niche will allow you to build a product that solves one problem well. In the best case, this will be the critical problem of everyone in the niche, and your product will ideally solve it well enough for your customers to tell everyone they know, and allow your product to sell itself.

DECIDING ON A MARKET FOR YOUR BUSINESS

A BOOTSTRAPPED BUSINESS works best when it starts out in a niche. Most companies will do really well by just staying there. Some expand into other markets. But that initial audience is one of the most important things to carefully select when you start a business.

When we started FeedbackPanda, we had noticed a painful problem. A problem we experienced for ourselves. So we solved it for ourselves. We then saw that other teachers, just like Danielle, could benefit from our solution. They had the exact same problem. We knew our first version already solved the problem well. That's why we knew other teachers would pay for it.

But were there enough teachers? And would they be willing to pay? Did they have the same need?

In short, we needed to figure out if our combination of problem and solution had an addressable market. In my experience from FeedbackPanda and the startups I have worked at before, this can be determined by asking the following questions.

Is the Audience Large Enough?

Your audience will have to be big enough to sustain your business. It will likely also have to support competitors, as any successful business will attract competition.

Determining the size of our audience is a rather work-intensive task, but absolutely required before you decide to invest your time in starting a business in a market. It boils down to doing the research and asking subject matter experts in the field about the current size and the growth trajectory. If you think that you can make a good living with whatever business model you decide to use, the niche is right for you. If there are not enough people, widen the niche by adding adjacent groups to your audience and see if you can adjust the problem (and your solution) to serve those people, too.

Is the Audience Small Enough?

Contrary to popular belief, I think that for a bootstrapped company, in particular, some markets can be too big. Some audiences are too generic, some industries too vast for a great niche to exist. At least, in the beginning, you should have a clearly defined niche. As a bootstrapped entrepreneur, you will reach out to customers and be in direct contact. For that to work, you have to be able to find the right people. And, if there are millions of people in an industry, your chances of finding the right ones go down significantly. Finding the subject matter experts will be extremely difficult at that point.

If you find that your audience is too general, try adding constraints. If you're looking at teachers as your market, for example, make it teachers who teach math. Problems change, they become clearer, and solutions become more focused. Math teachers in K12 talk to other math teachers in K12, for example.

The smaller your audience, the more it has built-in network effects.

Can They Pay? Will They Pay?

Sometimes, you will be serving companies that have a budget for what you offer. Other times, you could help a currently underserved segment of a low-wage industry. The capacity and willingness to pay will be very different between those two.

While it is enticing to go for the big guys with the massive budgets, you will encounter a lot of competition there. The willingness to pay is there, but you will have to work hard to make them switch vendors or justify another expense. They will also be hard to retain, as they are capable of changing vendors quickly in such a crowded field.

Serving a currently underserved market comes with the opposite problem. There won't be much competition, and people are not used to paying for solutions. They often have scraped by using their own tools built on Excel or Google sheets. You will have to spend more time convincing people that your solution will provide substantial value before they grab their credit card. Once previously underserved customers commit to paying, they will be your customers for a long time. You can build a lot of goodwill from serving such a market, and it will create a lot of value for your company.

At FeedbackPanda, we have had the opportunity to serve such an underserved market. We still have customers from when we first launched the product, when word-of-mouth marketing was our only channel. These are the truly loyal customers who felt nothing but appreciation for being finally served. That allowed us to ask them to talk about us in their social communities, which they did to significant effect.

If you have found a painful problem, a niche audience that is both small and big enough for your business, and you have made sure your audience is willing to pay for your solution, you have found your niche. From here you can build out your product and marketing strategies for that market.

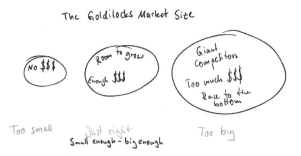

There are a few more things to consider that are great to have in a market, but are not important enough to be a good reason to not go into a market when they're missing.

If your market has adjacent product opportunities, that will give you a chance to think about future ancillary products you can sell. For our teacher market, where we focused on solving their productivity problems, one could imagine offering additional products that engaged the other issues that self-employed teachers might have, such as scheduling or tracking their invoices. To know that these issues are mostly unsolved as well allows you to think about where to expand the business when it becomes successful.

You should also think about how easy it will be to scale your business in that market. Most of the time, your market won't grow enough to keep your business growing as a side-effect. You will need to broaden your audience. Knowing that there are untapped groups and customer segments will make this a strategy you can keep in the back of your mind. For our business, it was knowing that while we were serving the teachers for several online English schools, there were still hundreds of other schools. They were both already in the market and popping up all over the place. We would then just add support for more of those teachers to increase our own growth rate.

Knowing if you need to focus more on sales or on marketing is very important. Some markets require you to reach out to buyers individually. For others, a good and well-targeted marketing strategy could mean you will never have to talk to a single customer before they subscribe or purchase. Being aware of how this will develop over time is essential in order to decide where to focus your attention.

What Are Good Markets for Bootstrapped SaaS?

If you see that significant forces are terraforming a market, creating an opportunity where there was none before, that is a good sign. Whenever a new kind of technology or process gets traction in a field that has not seen much change before, it will create little points of friction. Some of them will be critical. These will be the ones that warrant creating a SaaS business.

Any newly created niches are interesting for the boot-strapped SaaS founder. The problems there will be unique, exciting, and can usually be solved quite well if they are in a well-defined niche. Often, these niches are not yet regulated to death, so you will have the opportunity to experiment without having to follow strict guidelines or rules. You may often be the one setting those guidelines and laying the groundwork for future regulations.

Some markets, where a lot of small deciders with their own budgets make decisions, are very lucrative. These people can be convinced without needing to deploy corporate diplomacy. You can show them a product, and they will try it out, as they have no one telling them not to. Small businesses and freelancers are great audiences for a bootstrapped SaaS, as they have budgets. Small budgets, maybe, but if there is a painful problem, there will be money to fix it.

Underserved markets are a great place to start a company, as mentioned earlier. There will be no meaningful competition, customers will love the fact that someone is finally thinking of them, and you will get a lot of market share quickly if you find a market where scaling is not too complicated.

What Are Bad Markets for Bootstrapped SaaS?

Just as much as there are good markets to start out in, some markets will make it harder to run a bootstrapped business.

Enterprise markets are hard to sell into for a small company, although it's not impossible. Purchasing decisions take a long time, there are a lot of requirements even to be considered, and contracts tend to be custom and require a lot of work. Many enterprise customers won't buy from small companies out of fear they will vanish within a few years, and that fear is not unfounded. In fact, even for your own bootstrapped business, I would recommend against using services offered by companies smaller than yourself. You will be better off looking for a market that is comprised of small to medium-sized businesses and self-employed freelancers.

You can still sell to more prominent companies as long as their decision-makers are relatively far down the corporate hierarchy. If selling to a business involves any high-level management or even C-level approval, the market may not be for your bootstrapped company. At least not when you start out.

Monopoly markets with just a few big players will severely limit your options. You won't have many opportunities to experiment when every sales call is critical to your survival. And as a small business, your leverage is insignificant when your customers are much bigger than you are. Aim for equal size or smaller.

Markets where years of ruthless competition have created a

large number of bottom feeders are hazardous. In the beginning, you may be able to compete on price, but competitors with deeper pockets than you can sell at a loss for longer than any bootstrapped business. Also, customers in such a market are not the dedicated, enthusiastic, and joyful customers you want to serve.

When Markets Turn

Good markets turn to bad markets all of the time. There are sure signs when a good market is starting to turn bad, and there are indicators for when previously unsuitable markets are promising to become interesting.

Most companies are well aware of this and adapt to those changes. Often, entire divisions of businesses are dropped or sold off when a market that previously worked is turning into a loss center.

Markets that are becoming hostile to businesses usually are full of very similar competitors, fighting it out over price and marginal differences. This saturation makes it hard to enter a market, and even the businesses that are already in that market suffer.

Technological changes often destroy or abandon entire markets, as email did for companies selling fax machines. There still could be a niche for that technology, but focusing on legacy does not usually promise a bright future.

When markets shrink, that is often a sign of deterioration. Whenever the number of agents and purchasers in a market decreases, business growth stalls. People cut costs and unnecessary expenses get reduced. All businesses in that market will suffer.

Attempts at regulating a market after it has been unregulated or regulated only lightly spell out trouble for the companies in that market. We have seen this on a global scale with the GDPR and PSD2 regulations in Europe that drastically affected a few markets and made a lot of small companies exclude European customers out of fear of being fined millions. When rules appear, problems follow.

However, you will also find that markets that were once considered to be infertile ground sprout opportunities. This often happens in the wake of a technological or structural change. The internet made the online education market explode, and where before was very little technology in education, now there are many opportunities. New technologies create new processes. Both create new problems that did not exist before, and where no prior solutions exist.

Every market that grows in size significantly after a long period of stagnant growth is an exciting target. More people mean more customers, and with a noticeable increase in headcount, new and unique problems will arise.

Whatever market you choose for your business, make sure you select it with confidence and the numbers to back it up. The more you know about determining the size of SaaS markets, and the more you talk to subject matter experts and long-term residents, the more likely you are to make a sound decision. Making the correct choice is vital to the success of your business. Choose wisely.

DETERMINING THE SIZE OF A MARKET

When you're starting a bootstrapped SaaS business, you have to find a painful problem to solve. For that, you have to find an audience first. But how do you figure out if the audience is big enough to support your business today and five years from now?

There are three different approaches to determining this elusive number. Different methods will be needed depending on the kind of customers you want to serve. B2B, B2BC, and B2C markets each need different tools to figure out those numbers. You can find detailed step-by-step guides below, based on my own experience in startups working in all three fields.

No matter what kind of service you offer, you will never find exact numbers about the size of your audience. Most of the time, audience size is a moving target. Industries contract and expand, sometimes extremely fast, and any number is outdated within weeks. Even if anyone knew the exact figures, there would be little value in making them public. You would invite more competition if it looked juicy. If there is any number at all, treat it like a tentative figure.

To get to any significant audience size number, you will have to do a lot of research and collect a lot of information. You won't do this work in a day. It may take weeks or even months to sift through the data. Often, a subject matter expert will drop a number in a side remark of some obscure industry podcast. The more time you spend looking into many different places, the more precise your outcome will be.

If you have an enterprise-focused business, it is more likely that you will find public information you can trust. Consumer-focused companies have a harder time there, as information will be abundant but very hard to validate.

Even for enterprise markets, the numbers out there are likely to be skewed or inflated. It depends on the institution that releases them. Enterprise companies often are required to publish their financial records and reports, which include market sizes directly, or at least allow you to infer them in combination with market share ratios.

Some industry expert groups also release general industry reports, which often cost money. A good example of this is HolonIQ in the EdTech space.

These types of reports are well worth it, for two reasons. They commonly contain the exact information you need and much more that will allow you to make a very knowledgeable guess as to your chances in that market.

The second reason is the more important one: many entrepreneurs, particularly in the bootstrapped community, shy away from spending money as it goes against the spirit of being scrappy. You will have an immediate and often critical advantage over those founders who just guess. They usually guess wrong. When they do, they give up quite quickly. Spending a few hundred bucks in advance will save you thousands later, and you will get the condensed findings of subject matter experts in addition to the numbers you seek.

Finding meaningful numbers in a sea of unfiltered information is important. A good rule of thumb is to count the number of deciders and not just the number of buyers in a specific industry. These are sometimes the same people, but if you sell into enterprise industries, those roles will diverge. Targeting and selling to the people who decide is critical, so these are also the relevant people to be counted.

Reading up on the history and evolution of an industry before doing audience size research is highly recommended. This data will reveal the key players: you will learn about the tectonic forces of the industry that you may not be aware of, and you will absorb how change is accepted, welcome, and often resisted. That will actively inform not just your approach to determining the size of the audience, but also if it is an audience worth targeting.

Talk to people in the industry first. Ask them personally for their opinion about their industry, how big it is, and how big they think it could get. Find out who are trusted sources of information and on whose numbers you can rely. Do this part after having done some cursory research, and ask industry experts their opinion about the sources you have found. You will be surprised how many people who work in a particular industry every day completely dismiss many outwardly reputable sources.

Finding B2B Market Sizes

The easiest way to find out how big your B2B audience is would be by purchasing **industry reports** from reputable sources. In the EdTech market, for example, that would be companies like HolonIQ. They are often quite expensive, but the data they provide is a treasure trove of insight.

Industry magazines, both print versions and online editions, are a densely packed source of information. Not only do they contain expert opinions on the field, they also know very well how large their market is, as they are sold directly to members of that market. The easiest way to find out numbers here is to ask for the number of magazines they circulate. That can often be done by asking to publish advertisements in one of their next issues. Asking for the cost of an ad and the number of people who will see it will give you two critical insights: the audience number you're after and the amount of competition you will have to expect for your audience's attention.

More and more **industry-specific podcasts** are appearing all over the place. They often feature interviews with C-level executives from big companies, so they are packed with valuable information about the industry. Often, the people being interviewed will talk about the market they operate in, including market size and growth rates. The great thing about podcasts is that you can just reach out to the host, and you will likely get an answer. Ask them about what you are looking for and how you can find it, and they will give you pointers or even numbers they may have access to. Asking about advertising on podcasts could yield the same kinds of interesting numbers that asking about advertisements in industry magazines would.

Conferences are a staple in the enterprise world. Often, just looking at the vendor map of a conference will give you great insight as to the size of the companies, their position in the market, and the kinds of customers they serve. It will also allow you to find smaller companies that are in the same field but whom you may not have heard of yet. For any important industry conference, download or explore the conference vendor map.

Lastly, enterprise companies have extensive search engine marketing budgets. Figuring out the search terms they rank for will lead you to get some insight into how much competition is in that market. You will learn what companies have found out about the search terms their customers use, and how much you can expect to spend to be seen by those potential customers of yours.

Finding B2BC Market Sizes

In B2BC markets, where your customers are freelancers or small businesses, you will have less access to industry reports. Usually, there are not enough larger companies in those fields to make a living selling $500+ reports every year, so the industry reports that are available for B2B markets are likely very scarce for B2BC. The good thing is that most of the time, a B2BC market is somewhere in the **supply chain** of a larger B2B market, so you will still find information about the market as a part of a bigger industry in those **B2B reports**. However, they won't drill down deep enough for specific information to your B2BC market, so you will need to find other sources.

The big players in those markets often **publicly provide information about the size of their market to attract funding**. While those numbers are likely overblown for dramatic effect, they will give you an indication as to the order of magnitude you can expect.

One great thing about B2BC markets is that they are often community-based. Many freelancers hang out at the same **watercooler**, which often is either a social media site or a forum/community that is specific to their craft. Finding these communities is essential in determining market size. Social media groups are often a good indicator of size. If just a tiny niche of people from the market you're interested in already resides in a social media group of over 5,000 people, you can expect the actual market to be quite big. If you can barely find a group at all, your audience may be too small or somewhere else. Make sure to ask people who work in the industry to lead you to the place where they gather.

Find and talk to the **subject matter experts** in the market.

These people are often influencers, publicly communicating about the market and the developments within it. They have multiple mediums and markets, such as YouTube channels, Instagram pages, Twitter followings, and much more. Those are the people who you will find on industry podcasts and giving interviews on the industry blogs. Reach out to them. They will know exactly what is going on, how big their audience is, and what the market is doing.

The **hosts of podcasts** in B2BC industries are very good targets for your research, too. Not only do these hosts know a lot about the industry themselves, but they will also be able to connect you to the subject matter experts in their network. This is true for any market, but it's particularly useful in B2BC markets where there are so many more solo brands.

Finding B2C Market Sizes

Sales reports from companies in the field are a good start for determining B2C audience sizes. Most companies are private and thus don't publicly expose their financial data. However, you can find some information on how they're doing financially either by looking at the sales reports those companies provide themselves, or by investigating their tax reports with the authorities under which they operate. Those are often semi-public, and you can request them for a fee from the tax or commerce agencies in the country of founding.

It's worth looking into the companies of a market to understand the size of it. How many people are employed by those companies? How are they funded? Do they burn through cash, or do they have a reliable revenue stream? Getting answers to these questions will require asking the people who work for them. You can do that through **sales calls** or by reaching out to them directly with your questions. People often are willing to help people make progress in their field, as long as you're not direct competition. It never hurts to ask.

The competition in B2C markets is notoriously high, as those markets tend to be where everyone wants to end up. That makes gathering reliable information very hard. Often, **government institutions** will keep some statistical data and make it available either in their publications or upon request. The same goes for non-profits that exist in almost all markets. Reaching out and maybe providing them with some value or exposure could give you a lot of insight.

In summary, finding the size of your potential audience will require you to gather a lot of information from a lot of sources. Sifting through this information will take time, so plan accordingly. It's always worth it to be personal. Reach out to people who have some standing in the respective markets and communities. Be truthful about why you ask, and people will be helpful most of the time. Some won't be. There will always be skeptics, and some markets are full of them.

But if you're determined to find out if a market is a good fit and the right size for your business, you will get there eventually. Determination is vital here, as in most parts of starting a new business.

Remember that many founders give up at some point during this process. Stick with it, and you'll be ahead of the curve for sure.

STEP TWO: THEIR PROBLEM

IDENTIFYING A CRITICAL PROBLEM: WORKING ON THE RIGHT THING

ONCE YOU HAVE FOUND a suitable audience, you can start looking for problems. The great thing about niche markets is that the issues in them are specific and shared by the people in the niche. Solving a common problem will help a lot of people. You already have the right people. Now you just need the right problem.

The essential action in this step is to find the most critical problem your audience is experiencing. You are looking for painful problems, and you want to solve the most painful of them all. You also need to validate that this is an actual problem that people need to have addressed. Sometimes, we just want to complain, but we don't want to change our ways. You will need to find a problem so painful that we just have to deal with it.

Once you choose a problem to solve, you create a new business to market the solution to that problem. Your unique solution helps your audience deal with a pain they're feeling. Yet the company fails to take off, even though you have a good solution and excellent marketing material. People don't want to pay for it.

Why is that?

I believe that many bootstrapped businesses only do half the work. They solve a problem, but they don't address the most critical problem.

If you want to build a profitable business, you have to solve the most important problem your customer is facing, the one that, when solved, will change their life.

So what is the critical problem? What makes it critical?

How to recognize if you are focusing on **the critical problem** long before turning it into a business is paramount to a successful business. There are a few key properties any critical problem has, and if you find an issue that has these properties, you will have an excellent candidate for a successful, profitable business.

All businesses solve problems; that's why we start enterprises. But even though some businesses solve a problem well, they still fail. The community Failory has a "Startup Cemetery," where founders explain why they think their company didn't make it. The reasons expressed range from "Bad Business Model" to "Poor Product."

In most cases, someone built a business around something that people had asked them to create or because they thought it would be a good idea to invent that solution. That is not enough validation. Not even close.

Here are a few reasons why:

- You built a solution for customers who think they have that problem under control. You solved the wrong problem.
- You developed a solution that helps only at the margins. You solved the wrong problem.
- You built something, but your customers have bigger fish to fry. You solved the wrong problem.

You want to build a "need-to-have" instead of a "nice-to-have." You want to develop a painkiller instead of a vitamin. You want to be their aspirin.

How can this be done? By finding their most important problem: the one issue that is critical to their success.

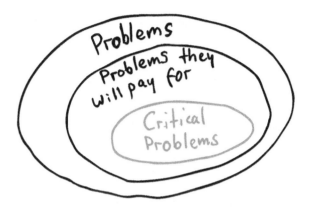

The Critical Problem

The most crucial problem a customer faces is on their minds most often. It's the most important because it's coming up frequently and is never easy to solve. It has the most impact on their lives, but it's not always the obvious choice. If you can help a customer with their most critical problem, they will benefit the most. No other tool will provide as much value as yours.

You could have a skewed perception of the problems within an industry. I have a friend who works in real estate due diligence. As an industry outsider, I always thought he spent most of his time in the building, checking for correct labels and fire exits. But it turns out that the thing that eats up his day is not the on-premises work, it's writing reports. If I wanted to build a business to help him and his colleagues, I would have gravitated to making the on-premises job easier. But what he needs is help with his reports.

You might loathe a particular approach, but other people might love it. At the beginning of my software development career, I hated writing documentation and writing reports. I would never have built a documentation-based product 10 years ago. I would have come up with many reasons why that just wouldn't work. But thankfully, I have broadened my mind since then. That's why I ended up building and selling FeedbackPanda, essentially a report-writing and documentation-maintaining product for online English teachers. Some people might love doing the things you dislike. Don't dismiss that.

Here is how you can tell if a problem is a critical problem.

A Critical Problem Is Painful

Problems can be a nuisance. They come up, and you either deal with them or ignore them. We can't ignore critical problems. They persistently make the lives of those who have them harder until they are resolved. They can't be just ignored, because they consistently reduce the quality of life.

For FeedbackPanda, this was true because teachers would spend more than two hours every day just writing student feedback. Those two hours spent writing feedback were two fewer hours available for their children, families, and other activities.

Find the critical problem where ignoring something causes a lower quality of life.

A Critical Problem Wastes Time or Money

Some issues are challenging but not wasteful. If you're a writer, you will sometimes spend a lot of time thinking about your ideas, but it's never pointless to intellectually refine your work. That's very different if you're writing a report that you're required to produce, particularly when you're sure that no one is ever going to read it. You must get that report done, but it feels like a waste of time and effort. A critical problem often feels like it is a waste of precious resources while being mandatory.

For FeedbackPanda, this was true because while the time spent on writing student feedback was unpaid, producing the feedback itself was mandatory. If teachers did not send in their feedback within 12 hours of teaching the students, they wouldn't even get paid for teaching. Often, the parents would not read the feedback.

Find the critical problem at the intersection of something mandatory and something wasteful.

A Critical Problem Is Not Optional

Some things can be ignored or delegated, but a critical problem can't be. If it's critical, people will have to deal with the problem every time it occurs. They can't just opt out of it. Solving the problem is essential to making any kind of progress in the work.

For FeedbackPanda, this was true because teachers had no choice. They had to provide feedback within a half-day, or they wouldn't get paid for the time they spent teaching. Every time they taught a student, feedback was mandatory.

Find the critical problem where people would love to opt out, but can't.

A Critical Problem Occurs Frequently and Repeatedly

The reason why critical problems are always on the minds of your customers is that the problems happen so often. Every day, every week, every month, the critical problems repeatedly occur. For your customers, it's always the most urgent thing at that time. The issue needs to be solved there and then, every single time. If it's not frequent, it is likely not a critical problem. If it occurs repeatedly and isn't easily solved, it is likely to be a critical problem.

For FeedbackPanda, this was true because teachers had to write a substantial amount of text for each 25-minute lesson they taught. Many of our customers taught 20 or more of those lessons per day. For them, this critical problem appeared 20 times per day, and they needed to write engaging messages every single time.

Find the critical problem where people need to do the same thing over and over again.

A Critical Problem Takes up Too Much Time

If a problem can be solved quickly, people either solve it the moment it appears or they set aside some time to do the work in a batch later, without feeling like it's a waste of time. If that is the case, the problem is not really critical. Only when you need to spend considerable time and effort each time you solve the problem will it be impossible to "just" deal with it. "Doing it later" also turns into a chore, as it may take hours or days to deal with a long queue of deferred problems. A critical problem will feel like an unwelcome chore: important, yet tiresome.

For FeedbackPanda, this was true because writing feedback for the parents of a student required a lot of mental effort: remembering the lesson contents, how the student dealt with the work, and what could be done to improve for the future, among other things. Anyone doing that after teaching for 10 hours non-stop would be mentally exhausted.

Find the critical problem where solving a problem takes a long time every time the problem occurs.

A Critical Problem Forces People to Solve It Using Their Own System

There is the joke that every SaaS is an Excel sheet transformed into business logic. The moment someone uses generic tools like word processors or spreadsheets to solve a problem, it's an indicator that the problem is valuable enough to build tools. Most problems don't have high complexity, and they can be solved on the spot. But a critical issue will be complicated enough to start developing a system. If your customers have a pile of Post-its or a chaotic assortment of Word and Excel files to solve a problem, you may have found a critical problem.

For FeedbackPanda, this was true because we found that most teachers who taught a certain amount of classes had invented their own systems. Some teachers used regular notepads to take notes during class; other teachers had already written feedback templates and put them into Word files. The most technically inclined had even created simple feedback-creation tools and forms. A community of teachers had started sharing their feedback templates in collaborative documents on the web. It was clear that people were aware that there was a solution to their problem.

Find the critical problem where people are solution-aware and have already created their own simple systems to solve the problem.

Bonus: A Critical Problem Is Something Companies Hire to Solve

In a tweet, Tyler Tringas (founder of Storemapper and Earnest Capital) mentions another way of finding critical problems: looking for which positions companies hire. If they pay a person thousands of dollars a month to do a job, it must surely be significant.

Looking at hiring is another perspective on the jobs-to-be-done framework, where the focus shifts from the product to what is important to your customers: not what *is*, but what *ought to be*.

So, look at where your customers want to be. Find the problems in their way. Clear the path. Build a product that will do this for thousands of people by solving their critical issues.

Critical Problems and Value

Because a critical problem is so prevalent and has measurable implications, your customers are very capable of calculating the value of a solution that solves it. They will be thrilled to pay as soon as paying for the solution is cheaper than continuing with the status quo.

They'll be willing to pay:

- if the solution **saves them time**
- if the solution **saves them money**
- if the solution **makes them money**

If it does all three at the same time, it will be a guaranteed hit. The more your solution provides along these dimensions, the more valuable it will be.

What Will Happen If the Problem Isn't Critical?

If you solve a problem that isn't critical for your customers, one or more of the following things might happen.

They Have No Interest in Paying

With non-critical problems, customers often find alternative ways of solving the problem because they want to save money. It's not worthwhile for them to look for and pay for a solution that they value less than alternative solutions. If spending the time to find and learn a free alternative solution seems like a better choice to your prospects, then your solution is likely solving the wrong problem, or it's addressing the right problem the wrong way.

They Don't Want to Pay Any Longer

Customers stop paying because they found a solution to a more critical problem, and they start paying for that, as it is much more valuable than your product. Your price could be too high (or sometimes too low, as it suggests a lower value).

Your Churn Is Uncontrollable

Customers cancel their subscriptions soon after subscribing. Disillusionment, lack of value, giving up, all indicators of a solution to the wrong problem. If this happens to you, reach out and ask what made them cancel and what you could have done to prevent that. While this is always anecdotal, it might show a more significant trend of where your solution is not fitting their critical problem.

Nobody Talks About the Product

If you provide a delightful solution to a critical problem, people will start talking about it. If even after many months of providing a service you still don't see any word of mouth, you will need to invest heavily in marketing. That will increase your acquisition costs significantly. If that happens and there still is no word of mouth happening, you will eventually run out of money.

Finding the Critical Problem

So, how can you learn about which is the most critical problem your customers have? It's quite straightforward: talk to them. Ask them what annoys them most. Find out where they want to be. Ask them what keeps them from being the best at what they are doing.

Expect the unexpected. Some problems may seem almost comically simple to solve, but that may be the preconceived notion of the technician in you talking. Meet your customers where they are. Some may never have thought of using Excel to track information that is not numerical. Others don't know how powerful a well-designed mobile application can be even in the hands of a traditional sector like cattle farming. Keep an open mind.

Focus on what you can help them accomplish. Ask what customers want and which state they want to be in when the work is done. Don't focus too much on the "how it's done." That is usually more based on tradition than on an optimized process. Try finding the intended outcomes and then figure out how to make them happen faster and easier.

Try going into these conversations without a preformulated idea. Go in empty and soak it all up. Spend your time listening more than talking. As Rob Fitzpatrick suggests in his book *The*

Mom Test, don't talk about your product. Have them talk about their problems.

Take your tech knowledge and try applying it to other fields. Think of the fact that most people are blind to developments outside their own industrial bubble. Incumbents often innovate very slowly, and some things that are tried and tested in one industry are entirely unheard of in another. Be ready to transfer your skills and knowledge, and expect people not to understand all of it immediately.

If you find something that will obviously make them significantly more money or save them a lot of time, then you have something to go on. Customers should *really* want to pay for it, almost have a burning desire to open their wallets. When they ask you if that is possible and you tell them it is, their mouth should drop to the floor.

If you see eyes widening and jaws dropping when you talk about solving their most critical problem, then you have the main ingredient for a great bootstrapped business that can thrive.

IDENTIFYING THE MOST CRITICAL PROBLEM IN A MARKET

WHEN YOU'RE LOOKING at a niche market, you will find many people have a large number of problems. However, people will only pay money for a tiny subset of those: the excruciating problems.

So, how can you find the most painful problems?

You will need to take a close look at the work that is being done in your niche. You'll need to talk to people, get them to tell you about the things that keep them from being where they want to be. In those conversations, you will want to listen more than you talk.

Painful problems have specific properties that you can look for: the types of underlying pains as well as the intensity and awareness of the problems themselves. These properties help to determine what questions to ask your prospects when you're trying to find the most painful problem in a market.

The Kinds of Pains to Look For

Every person experiences some level of the human condition at any given point of time in their lives: we have aspirations, goals, conflict, struggle, and hardship. We all have a place where we want to be and things that are in the way of getting there. That's where we feel pain. Your job while researching a niche is to find these pains and where they come from.

Pain can come in a million different shapes, but its underlying reasons can be grouped into three categories: *Time, Resources,* and *the Self.*

Time-Related Pains

Most productivity-related issues cause temporal pain: people feel like they're wasting time. These pains are caused by suboptimal processes and friction between tasks. If tedious work takes a lot of time, it keeps you from doing important and useful things instead. That leads to time mismanagement and relevant actions not being taken. By solving the time-related problem, productive tasks can be accomplished faster and sooner.

When people complain about inefficiencies, tedium, or pointless work, you're looking at a time-related problem.

Resource-Related Pains

People hate wasting money. Anything too expensive for the value it creates is a big problem for the person and the organization. Often, existing solutions are too costly, which will cause them to feel like a painful expense. Regulation imposed on an industry can make certain activities prohibitively expensive, both financially and from the amount of work that will need to be done. Resources are not just money: capital is only as useful as the people it's compensating. Human effort can easily be wasted, creating a resource drain. Solve these resource-related problems, and free resources can be allocated more efficiently.

If you hear people complaining about a waste of money,

prohibitive costs, compliance, or the wrong people working on the wrong things, you've found a resource-related problem.

Self-Related Pains

This group of problems is often overlooked. Everyone wants to be notable somewhere. This can mean holding a position in a company or being regarded as a supportive co-worker or friend. When people struggle with achieving these things, they feel self-related pains.

The four essential concepts to look out for here are *Reputation, Accomplishment, Advancement,* and *Empowerment*.

Reputation is a measurement of trustworthiness and expertise. People want to be regarded as a source of knowledge and reliance. Anything that creates uncertainty or doubt about someone's skill can be considered a self-related problem. You can help people be more reputable by transferring renown from a trusted source, through certification or credentials.

Accomplishment is a measurement of success and respect. People want to show to the world that they are good at what they are doing. Anything that suggests or risks setbacks or failures will be a self-related problem. You can help people accomplish more by reliably taking over their tedious work to allow them to be creative and practice their ingenuity.

Advancement is a measurement of progress and alignment. People don't want to stand still, and for life-long learners, advancing toward new opportunities is an integral part of their journey. Helping people advance could have exciting consequences: in some cases, assisting people in earning more money may elevate them out of the job they're currently doing. Many factors, including political ones, cause advancement problems. You can help by making sure that the quality of work and access to information are as good as they can be.

Empowerment is a measurement of meaning and liberation. It is a second-level version of advancement: helping other people succeed. People want to support other people, and helping them do that will result in a higher reputation, build a network of trust and mutual support. Restrictive permissions and inflexible processes usually cause problems of empowerment.

Different Levels of Problem Intensity You Will Encounter

Problems arrive on an intensity spectrum. Some are a bit annoying, and others are excruciatingly painful. An excellent course of action is to note your perceived intensity for every problem you encounter. To determine this intensity, I recommend applying the Eisenhower Matrix, which is usually used for feature prioritization.

The most **intense pain** is felt when the problem comes from a task that is both important and urgent. Such a task can't be deferred or delegated, which makes it a direct and noticeable pain. If you can solve this problem for your customers, this is the best kind of problem to have: it will occur often, needs to be dealt with, and it will be important every single time. Consequentially, your solution will be required all the time. Even a small improvement over the status quo will make a product worth some money.

The second-best problems to find are **tedious**. Those are not as urgent, but they are important. A solution to this type of problem will still have high customer retention as long as it makes the job significantly easier.

In third place, we find **pressing** tasks. Here, it becomes difficult for people to justify spending a meaningful amount of money on a solution. There could be valid reasons every now and then when time is particularly tight, but mostly, resources are better allocated to essential parts of the work. Your service will either need to be very affordable or do an extremely remarkable job of getting the pressing work done faster.

Finally, there are the **annoying** little issues. Services that solve non-important and non-urgent problems are likely to be regarded as a luxury, and their costs will be scrutinized at all times. Most people will just do the work when they find time for it, often delegating or indefinitely deferring it. Targeting such a problem will lead to high churn and high customer acquisition costs. Nobody pays you to find their remote when it falls down the back of the couch. They will just find it themselves.

You will want your product to be the main course instead of a side dish. You want your service to be the last subscription that gets canceled when budgets are shrinking.

Do They Know? The Problem with Problem Awareness

When you're conducting interviews with customers, you will hear them talk a lot about the problems that bother them. These are the known knowns. But your prospects will never be able to tell you about the issues they don't realize they have.

At FeedbackPanda, we ran into this situation right at the beginning. Some of our prospects were not aware that the time they were spending writing the same texts over and over again was a problem. They had gotten used to doing this over the years, and it had become a regular part of their routine. It took us a while to notice that these people would not be actively looking for a solution, because they thought they didn't have a reason to.

We fixed this by spreading awareness of the problem. Our early customers helped us a lot with that, speaking out on social media about how they felt this to be a problem and how happy they were that someone had solved it for them. Over time, this turned unaware teachers into enlightened customers.

The Prospect Awareness Scale by Eugene Schwartz from his seminal 1966 book *Breakthrough Advertising* provides an excellent introduction into customer awareness levels.

You start with the **Completely Unaware**. They don't know that they have a problem, they don't think of solving it, and they don't know that your product exists.

They turn into **Problem-Aware** once they notice that something is not working as it should. They still don't know how it could ever be solved.

Once they do, they are **Solution-Aware**. They know that somewhere out there, someone has a solution. They have heard that their colleagues use services to solve their problems, but they don't know which services.

Product-Aware prospects know which services exist in the market, and they are looking into which one is right for them.

Finally, the **Most Aware** know exactly what you're selling, they know it will solve their problem, and they're now just waiting for a good deal.

What does this mean for you, the entrepreneur, who is looking for a critical problem to solve?

It means that while the Problem-Aware will be a great source of potential problems, the Completely Unaware should not be overlooked. Many problems are known to the people in their industries, but the unknowns are just as important.

As a software entrepreneur, you will be transferring your skills and knowledge from one domain to another. This will be beneficial to the detection of these unknown unknowns. People who work in a specific field without ever looking outside it will develop occupational blindness. They don't find much opportunity to take an outside perspective, leaving significant detection gaps in the spectrum of problems they perceive.

How to Find the Unknown Unknowns

Where do people go out of their way not to do a certain job without describing it as a problem at the same time? Where do people "automate" their jobs with tools that, from your perspective, seem inadequate for the task? Where do they build makeshift solutions?

The moment you find people organizing data in Excel without making use of the numerical features of a spreadsheet, you are in the presence of problem avoidance.

You will find that Excel and Google sheets are widespread for these "custom solutions" that people build for themselves. If you see folders overflowing with Word documents, you're looking at something very similar. When the more technically inclined take their makeshift solutions to the cloud and cross-link a bunch of documents only to email links and files to their colleagues, you can be quite sure that there is a problem they themselves might not be aware of.

Remember: *users avoid, entrepreneurs solve.* Find the things that your prospects steer away from. Find the things that make them feel uncomfortable. Discomfort is a very clear indicator of a hidden problem.

Other Places to Look

You want to be the business that is in the right place at the right time. But what about all those who tried this before you?

What about those who were in the right place at the wrong time? What about businesses that found a critical problem and built a solution only to find that their audience was not ready for it? It's likely that someone, somewhere, had taken a shot, failed, and moved on.

The challenge is to find their traces. This is best done by flat out asking industry insiders about failed attempts at solving problems. Do they remember the names of products that turned out to be a flop? You could even get the name of people who have since moved into different industries. Keep pulling that thread, and you may find a subject matter expert with a lot of entrepreneurial insight into your chosen niche.

What about the businesses that were in the wrong place at the right time? Are there adjacent or comparable industries where a service has solved similar problems? What can you learn from their products and solutions? Reach out to those entrepreneurs as well, as they might have transferable knowledge that you can apply to your niche without encroaching on their territory.

Find the latest popular books released in your niche. Read reviews and summaries, or read the whole book if you have the time. You'll find concepts and ideas that might not yet have been implemented as a service. This is particularly true for academic papers and articles.

Follow the leaders. In social media, follow the thought leaders and influencers in your niche. See what they are saying, hear what they are complaining about, and read the conversations they're surfacing. Are they saying something controversial that gets a lot of pushback from the incumbents? That is an opportunity for progress that you can facilitate. You can also look into what is being said about competitors to find out what's lacking about existing solutions.

About Competition and Expertise

Don't mind competition. There is always a way to create a better product, and find a more fitting solution to a problem that people complain about. They would not complain about it if there were a perfect solution. Your job is to build just that.

Competition is a frame of reference, a reflection of the status quo. As an entrepreneur, that is only one of many inputs into your product decision.

Great products happen at the intersection of your skills and the opportunities of a niche market you care about. Make the most of your transferrable knowledge. People in the niche are often not even aware of things that are perfectly normal to you and other entrepreneurs. Basic tools for you may be godsends for others. Suspend your views of what is "normal" and "ubiquitous" when you engage in problem discovery. You will find things that have pained your prospects for years that could be solved within minutes.

What Questions to Ask a Prospect

Which questions would you want to ask your prospective customers to figure out their pains? Here are some suggestions to find problems, the underlying reason, and the roadblocks that will need to be pushed aside.

Efficiency

- What keeps you from being more efficient at work?
- Why can't you do more of what you do?
- Which tasks feel like they are a drag?

Effectiveness

- What limits you from doing your job the right way?
- Which tasks are the most pointless?

- What annoys you about working with competitive products? What is your experience like with each of them?

Financials

- Where are you spending too much on tools?
- Where are you spending too much on consulting?
- What is your budget for software tools?
- What is your budget for outsourcing work?

Reputation

- What parts of your skill set do you need to work on?
- Which parts of your job do you hesitate to start?
- How do you show your colleagues that you're an expert?

Empowerment

- How can you help other people succeed?
- Do you share success?
- Is lifting up people something you are expected to do?

Accomplishment

- How do you celebrate your victories?
- How much do others see of your work?
- What's in the way of your next big success?

Advancement

- What would it need for you to climb the career ladder one more step?
- Where do you want to be professionally?
- How can you reach financial security and stability?
- Where do you see yourself growing toward?
- What challenges did you have in your professional career so far?
- What challenges do you have in your professional career at this point?

Avoidance Detection

- What part of your job do you loathe?
- What tasks do you delegate the most?
- What tasks should not be part of your work?
- Is there anything that seems utterly needless in your day-to-day work?
- If you wanted to shock the whole industry, what would you change about it?

Problem Awareness

- Which is your most pressing problem?
- Which is your most painful problem?
- Which is your most tedious problem?

Other Places

- What products were introduced to the market that ultimately failed?
- Was there ever someone who wanted to solve problems for you? What happened to them?

For any question, listen intently to their answer, then probe for and write down the problem, the intensity, the underlying reason for the problem, and their awareness of both problem and solution. Make a list for every single prospect you call, and merge all of those lists, counting problem occurrence for every problem that was mentioned multiple times.

When you're revisiting this final list after the conversations, rank your notes by descending intensity. The most critical problem will be on the top of that list. It will likely have been mentioned a few times, too.

You will still need to validate the problem with your prospects, which I suggest you do in a follow-up call to a random subset of them. This allows you to verify that the problem is real, they are or have become aware of it, and they are interested in solutions.

Assuming that you have validated your audience and made sure that your niche can support your business, you have now found one or many critical problems that are very likely to allow you to build a sustainable bootstrapped business.

Pick the problem that you feel most passionate about.

Now you can begin working on your solution to that problem.

PROBLEM VALIDATION: TALKING TO THE RIGHT PEOPLE

"Talk to your customers," they say, "because that's the only way to build something people want."

The collective wisdom of the bootstrapper scene is not wrong. But talking to your customers is only half the truth. It's just as important to speak to the right kinds of customers as it is to ignore the rest. We had a number of these conversations at FeedbackPanda, both for validating problems that would impact our main product and our integrations.

Your goal in every problem exploration and validation conversation is to find your prospective customer's problems and figure out which ones are critical. But what is their goal? What motivates them to have this conversation with you?

They may want to be supportive, leave a good impression, show their expertise, or just try to get a better price. People will be selfish in many, often unexpected ways.

Make sure you are talking to someone who is aligned with your goals. If your customer's goal is not conducive to finding their critical problems, you risk getting further away from problem validation while they get what they want. You can only sustain your business if your goals are aligned with theirs.

How can you learn more about their underlying goals and aspirations? You won't be able to detect this before you talk to them. That only leaves the actual conversation: you will have to observe your problem validation conversation with them, discover if they are a good or bad fit, and only act on the interactions that show signs of goal alignment while discarding the others.

The Best-Case Conversation

The best case is an in-person conversation with an industry expert who has skin in the game and is aligned with your goals.

You want an in-person conversation. Calls are acceptable, too, but face-to-face interaction allows for more presence and will enable you to detect emotional distress and confusion better. The important part is that you can reliably and immediately steer the conversation toward problem validation, should it be derailed. For this reason real-time video communication is preferable to text-based or asynchronous approaches.

Keep in mind that it's a conversation, not an interview. This kind of research is not about getting measurable answers to pre-fabricated questions. It's about extracting and discovering problems. It will be a different conversation every time.

Your prospective customer should be an expert in their industry. They don't need to be a leader or influencer, but they should know a lot about the industry. There is an argument to make for interviewing the whole spectrum of skill levels, as your product might be useful to any stage of expertise. However, the likelihood of surfacing interesting problems is higher if you interview an expert: after all, they have gone through many of these stages before ending up where they are now.

Having skin in the game means having something to gain from using better tools and having something to lose if you don't. You want a prospect that needs to be a winner in their industry. If they don't care about their work, they won't care about their problems either, thus being a sub-par candidate for your problem validation efforts.

How to Prepare for a Problem Validation Conversation

To prevent misleading communication that may confuse your customers, you will have to focus on how humans communicate. You will need to introduce ideas indirectly by asking about the validity of the underlying problems. Better yet, don't introduce your ideas at all, but guide your customer toward exploring the problem space surrounding those ideas themselves. If you seed your ideas, you will taint the explorative nature of the conversation. It's like giving away the ending of a book too soon. All of a sudden, the discussion will be steered toward your idea instead of exploring problems.

Don't talk, just listen. Ask a lot of questions, but don't go into explanations. In a problem validation conversation, the customer is the expert. That holds true even if you know you are more knowledgeable about their industry than they are. In the future, you will need to convince them and their peers to buy your product. Your expertise will make no difference if your prospective customers don't think your product solves any of their critical problems.

Prospective Customers

It's usually hard to find and reach out to prospective customers. Often, you will need to employ cold outreach strategies. I found that if you have to do cold outreach, you can still do it through a luke-warm channel. If you are already close to your prospects by hanging out at their water cooler, their social media groups, or communities, place a message that you will be reaching out to respected members of the community to do some research. That sort of primer has two effects: first, some people might reach out to you and ask to be interviewed. Second, people will have a point of reference when you send them an email, having previously read about it within the trust context of their community.

After that, call. Use video chat if you can, even if it's just you on the screen. Make time to build a connection with your prospect. If they don't have time for you, ask them to connect you with someone who does.

You can also find people in two other gathering places: industry conferences, where conversations are usually quite formal; or meetups, where informal chats are possible, and you will find a less censored version of people's perspective on their industry. Both these events allow you to have face-to-face conversations with industry experts, and introductions can be made on-the-fly, without having to go through email or phone calls.

At FeedbackPanda, we combined these. Danielle organized a teacher meetup on the same day a teacher conference happened in Chicago, and she invited our customers to come after their conference day was over. Free drinks and FeedbackPanda swag were waiting for them. The result was that she met many of our customers, many of them well-connected in the tribe of teachers that were our audience. Those connections led to many warm introductions down the line.

Avoid People Who Are Trying to Please You

Compliments are a problem. They don't help you. If compliments happen, ignore them. If the customer continues to compliment everything you do, the data will not help you.

You can salvage these types of conversations. Dive deep into problems and their implications. Completely ignore any of their opinions about your product, your ideas, or your plans. Focus exclusively on their day-to-day operations, and redirect all talk of your product toward their experiences.

Whenever I had a conversation with a customer that was overly passionate about telling me that everything we did was perfect, I would be grateful without encouraging further compliments. A "Thanks, I'll let the team know" often satisfied their desire to show gratitude, and it would help to steer the conversation toward a more neutral place.

Avoid People Who Have No Skin in the Game

If your prospects don't have access to the budget or have no impact on the decisions made in a business, you will not get the full picture. They may surface new problems, but if you can't learn about the perceived value of a solution for those problems, you could build a product that is not generating enough overall value for people to purchase it.

Ideal candidates are enthusiastic about where things are going. They want to participate in the change that makes their industry better.

If they don't seem to care about their problems or are apathetic, you will see a distorted perspective on their jobs. Imagine a worker who knows that they'll quit a month from now. Will their viewpoint on which problems to solve for them right now be aligned with creating a product that solves long-term issues for their business? Wouldn't you rather talk to someone who plans on having a career in that industry for years to come?

If you run into such a prospect, ask for introductions. Ask them to connect you with a peer or superior that could help you explore and validate problems in the industry better and with more in-depth insight.

We didn't have a lot of those conversations, but the few that we had were over reasonably soon. Don't be afraid to stop the conversation, thank them, and move on. If they don't care, they'll be glad to be left alone.

Avoid People Who Only Tell You Their Ideas

You are validating a problem, not your customer's assumption. If they are barraging you with their ideas, you will be limited to the outcomes of their perception, not the reality of their problems.

Customers have a hard time understanding what they truly value, so their solutions are limited to what they know. Experts can be blinded by years of routine, overvaluing the status quo, and undervaluing even paradigm-shifting improvements.

But you can get something out of these ideas. Ask your prospect why they thought of them. Have them tell you the steps that led to the idea, note the assumptions, and ignore the idea itself. Within those assumptions, you will find hints of problems, and those can be useful for your exploration of the problem space.

I've learned to deal with the idea-dispensing kind of customer through the day-to-day conversations I had doing customer service. That gave me lots of opportunities to redirect the flow of the discussion toward the underlying problems while acknowledging their idea with a "We have added this to our list of ideas," and "We'll discuss it during our next feature design meeting." Statements like this will let your customers understand that you won't be creating this feature anytime soon, but you are aware of it having been suggested and are now vetting it. This perception can be used to then immediately dive into the reasons for them recommending it, as your customers will feel involved in the vetting process at that point.

Avoid People Who Love Complaining

In some cases, you will run into a customer that will find fault with every single imaginable thing. They will complain about their work, their boss, their colleagues, the impact all of this has on their lives, and even about the tools that were made so that they could have an easier time.

While within those conversations, you can find good problems to work on, they will be buried under an avalanche of nuisances and annoyances. Digging through this heap of irrelevance may not be worth your time.

Try salvaging these conversations by severely limiting the scope of your questions and their answers. Ask them to name the most important thing, the job that takes them the longest. Prime them to look for the extremes.

If you had a conversation that, in retrospect, seems biased, do not act on it. Write down what led you to suspect bias, and use this in future discussions to end them once you detect it again. It will feel like a waste of your time, but dismissing information is a necessary part of validating problems.

Important Things to Consider

Avoid quantitative methods like surveys. They will not allow you to dive into underlying reasons, and your questions will limit the scope of the replies you can get without allowing you to steer the conversation.

Finally, read up and try to be aware of cognitive biases in your conversations, both in what you are saying and how your prospective customer responds. If possible, record the conversation and do your analysis a few days later, when you can have a fresh look at it. You're building a long-term business, so a few days are a fair price to pay for having a neutral perspective on the essential step of problem validation.

STEP THREE: YOUR SOLUTION

A SOLUTION ISN'T A PRODUCT... YET

WITH A WORTHWHILE AUDIENCE and a validated problem, you will now need to find a solution. A solution is not the same as a product—yet. A solution is a more general answer to the question "How could this be done better?" A product answers the question "What do I use to deal with it?" The nuance here is in being specific enough to solve the problem without locking yourself into a corner by building the first possible solution that comes to mind.

For example, let's say you have chosen rural hairdressers as your niche audience and have validated that their critical problem is dealing with winter cancellations because their customers get stuck on snowy roads. Something will come to your mind as a great solution. You may think of helping them manage their booking, so it takes into account local weather data and routing information. You may think of letting the customer quickly inform the hairdresser when this happens so they can reschedule. You may think of automatically rescheduling appointments when snowy days are expected. All of these solutions could probably make a meaningful impact on the lives of your customers. None of these solutions are products yet. They could become apps, services, processes, web applications, or just new ways to operate a business. You need to validate the solutions you find to choose the one that has maximum impact.

SOLUTION VALIDATION DOESN'T HAPPEN IN A VACUUM: TALKING TO YOUR FUTURE CUSTOMERS

ENTREPRENEURS ARE good at coming up with ideas. We envision solutions to the problems that trouble the audience we have chosen to help. We think deeply about a problem, mentally shape a product, and see how much it would benefit the quality of life. Then we get to work and build the prototype, eager to release it as soon as possible.

But just like the problems we work on, we need to validate the solutions we create. Working on an issue that isn't critical for customers is risky, as it could result in a product no one needs. Working on a solution that doesn't work for customers has the same consequence. That's why solution validation is an essential step before we dive into creating the product.

Solution validation is best done in direct communication with your prospective customers, just like when you validated that the problem you were going to work on was a critical one for your niche audience. Call up your prospects again if you can, or find new potential customers, have a chat, and ask them a few questions.

The main question you want to answer through these calls

is, "Will this solution solve the problem as expected, and won't it create more problems along the way?"

These calls will be different from the product validation calls you did at an earlier point in the Preparation Stage. This time, you will have to talk about your solution. As an introduction, explain what it would do, what steps your customer would have to take, and how you envision it to be part of their work. You will need your customer to understand how your service would be used in order to set them up for the questions you'll ask to validate your solution.

In asking these questions, you'll be making a risk assessment. Usually, when you look at risks that could come from using a particular service, you'd look at the severity of impact, the likelihood of occurrence, and the probability of detection of each potential risk. You'd then list each of the risks, ranking them by some sort of risk class classification. While this is often overkill for single-purpose services, it helps to make sure you build a reliable, side-effect-free product.

To be able to find these risks, you will have to ask a few leading questions and pay close attention to what your prospects have to say. There are two significant perspectives I suggest taking here: workflow impact and jobs-to-be-done.

Workflow Impact

Your service will never be used in isolation. It will always be embedded in some sort of workflow, one tool among many to solve a particular problem that occurs as a result of an action and that, when solved, will allow for follow-up actions to be taken also.

Workflows can differ wildly between your customers, but there is likely some common ground. Your job is to find out what that shared experience is and how your solution fits for the highest number of customers.

A good question here is, "At what stage of your workflow will you be using this solution?"

Answers to this question serve two purposes. They will validate your assumptions about where you expected your product to be used. More importantly, they will also uncover the stages of your prospect's workflow in which you didn't expect your service to be used. If you find a significant number of prospects mentioning a stage you missed when envisioning your solution, you can immediately get back to the drawing board and compensate for the oversight.

An example of this phenomenon occurred when we validated a solution for a FeedbackPanda integration into a teaching portal software that our customers used to teach. We reached out to a handful of customers expecting our desktop-only integration to solve the job of creating student feedback right where they would teach, only to find that many of them did their feedback later in the day from their phones or tablets. If we hadn't asked at which stage of the workflow they would need our solution, we would have served them insufficiently. As a result, we built a mobile application as well as a desktop-based integration.

It may also be the case that your service will be used at multiple stages of your prospect's workflow, and it could be used differently at each of these stages. Knowing this will allow you to either focus on one of those stages exclusively or to make your service detect the stage at which it's used and present a dedicated interface.

At FeedbackPanda, the needs of a teacher varied significantly depending on if they were initially creating a piece of feedback or if they were editing an existing student report later throughout their day. For new feedback, the focus was on the lesson content and prior feedback that had been written for the student. For existing feedback, the focus was on meta-information like ratings, parent responses, and overall statistics. The display component for student feedback detected this difference of intent and offered different user interface components depending on the stage of our customers' workflow.

Looking into the stages of the workflow allows you to develop a better and more in-depth understanding of how your customers handle their day-to-day activities. It will show you opportunities for features and integrations that you may miss if you only focus on the specifics of your product. Of course, you should still build a product that does one thing well. But it won't hurt you if your service plays along nicely with the tools that are already used by your audience.

Jobs-to-Be-Done

This brings us to the other perspective you should take: how does your solution impact the jobs-to-be-done?

The concept of JTBD is a helpful framework to look at what ultimately drives people to do work: not what is, but what ought to be. People are result-driven, and they use technological solutions, not for their intrinsic quality but to get a job done.

It also means that for every problem that your customers are aware of, there may already be a solution in place to get that particular job done. That solution might be crude, and it can take a surprisingly high number of shapes.

Just imagine a scenario like this: there's a computer in a data center that needs to be rebooted once a day. How many different ways could this job be done?

1. A developer could write a script to restart the computer after 24 hours of running.
2. The intern could walk over to the computer every day after work and press the restart button.
3. Some remote management software could log into

the computer every day and reboot it using simulated mouse movements and key commands.

4. The CEO of the company could make it a ritual to do this job every day, showing that they still work on the small stuff.

5. A system administrator role could be created to take care of this job and many other similar infrastructure-related activities.

Do some of these solutions sound bizarre? Definitely. But you can bet that all of them are being actively employed somewhere to solve a problem as simple as rebooting a computer.

This list also shows that the cost of solving a problem can vary wildly. Automating the job may cost a couple of minutes of your developer's time, but creating the new role of the system administrator to deal with these kinds of problems suddenly impacts the bottom line significantly.

That's why it's crucial to find out what's in place to solve the problem right now. You need to know what or who you are replacing. Every existing solution has a cost attached. You will need to figure this out for your own pricing.

The example with the CEO is supposed to illustrate that there are three kinds of costs. So, the question you need to ask is, "How much does the existing solution cost in terms of time, money, or damage to 'the self'?"

It's excellent if using your solution can save a business some money. But if it alienates a CEO from their self-perceived connection with the company, you will have a hard time selling it to them. Understanding the emotional impact of changing from an existing solution is an integral part of the solution validation process.

Another vital question to ask is, "Could this solution cause friction in unexpected areas?"

The point of this question is to find hidden dependencies.

Imagine you're selling a CRM to small logistics businesses like door-to-door delivery companies. You're trying to replace the chaotic piles of Excel sheets and Word documents that they have been using to keep track of their customers in the past. Your solution will take care of this, but you're carefully validating it, so you ask about where else they are using Excel sheets. It turns out that a majority of your customers have an Excel plugin to deal with their fleet management and driver tracking. If your solution does not take into account this integration, it will add more friction to their process instead of removing it.

If you don't ask how far the current solution to the job-to-be-done extends into the operation of their business, you will miss critical friction points that need to be addressed by a solution that is worth switching to.

Sometimes, this requires a lot of digging. The person you're talking to may not be aware of how their colleagues use the current solution, and how far it may have crept into other processes. You will want to talk to multiple people working with the current system to increase your chances of spotting those risky friction potentials.

How to Talk About Risk

From your prospective customer's perspective, using your service should remove risk, deal with the jobs-to-be-done more efficiently, and make the overall workflow smoother.

To be able to assess that, you have to spell out the risks clearly when you're doing your solution validation. Remember that this is not a sales call; you're not trying to trick them into ignoring risks to their business. You're validating your proposed solution so that you can confidently sell it to your prospects later. Here and now, you are figuring out how to minimize risk and maximize opportunity.

So, spell it out. Engage your prospects in a lively discussion about their fears of changing their system. Ask them for previous painful experiences they had with switching to new solutions, and what could have made those transitions better.

Think about the kinds of guarantees you can give your users with your solution. Can you make it reliable enough to offer Service Level Agreements? Do your customers expect those? Ask them about what kinds of guarantees the products they already use offer, and how often they have to make use of those. Depending on the niche, you will find that some of those guarantees are required by the regulatory environment, while in others, they are merely peace-of-mind up-sells done by crafty salespeople.

Throughout your solution validation conversations, you want to project a clear interest in solving your customer's problems without causing new ones. If you communicate this clearly in each call, you will create goal alignment between you and your prospect: you both want a great solution that makes things easier for the customer.

ASKING THE RIGHT QUESTIONS: FOCUS ON PROBLEMS NOT SOLUTIONS

WHEN YOU TALK to your customers or prospects, you will find that there are questions that always produce meaningful results: where they are now? Where do they want to be? What stands in the way of getting there?

Essentially, this is applying the jobs-to-be-done framework to your communication strategy, trying to find their realistic and aspirational states, and then building a solution that allows them to go from one state to the other.

When we're talking about jobs, don't limit yourself to activities or tasks. Jobs are final states, some form of accomplished goal. They can be solved with small tools or gigantic systems. In the end, every job-to-be-done is a chance to evolve a process. It's an aspiration to create something that has a lasting benefit for your customer's business. A job is someone's struggle to make their life better.

Look at it from your own business owner's point of view: you don't want to solve petty problems day-in and day-out, you want to build a vehicle of growth and prosperity. You're focused on the long-term perspective, and your prospective customers do the exact same thing. Their jobs-to-be-done are equally focused on long-term accomplishments: the things that ought to be.

Focusing on your customers' problems at the same time as envisioning the optimal state of being will give you insight into the priority of the issues and what the final product has to allow your customers to use.

That is why you should avoid these kinds of questions:

- **Avoid asking about features.** Your prospects will be primed by the tools they know, and they will suggest variations of things that have failed to help them in the past. Why repeat what doesn't work?
- **Avoid asking about things that annoy them.** You will drown out the bird's-eye perspective if your prospects have to dive into the vast ocean of daily annoyances. You're after the big problems of their whole industry. Don't get distracted by tedious minutiae.
- **Avoid asking about their strategies and tactics too much.** While there is something to be learned from how your customer approaches solving their problems, they are results of highly path-dependent choices made in the past. You don't want to know what was. You care about what is and what ought to be.

So, what should you ask about?

- **Ask about where progress is hindered.** Progress is a clear indicator of jobs-to-be-done. After all, you have to move from what is to what ought to be in some way. Progress is that transition. Ask people where they perceive it.

- **Ask about tension and friction during value creation.** Where are things harder to accomplish than they ought to be? That is why your customers want to use your product.
- Once you have found hindered progress, tension, or friction, discover the underlying needs and desired outcomes of the processes involved. **Ask about the context of the job-to-be-done**: who is involved, who holds the stakes, and who is ultimately responsible for the job-to-be-done?

Ask these questions, have these conversations. Find your customers' jobs-to-be-done, and then envision solutions to the problems that cause those jobs to be left undone.

The winning solution, and finally your product, is a result of those conversations, not apart from them. Treat conversations at this stage as a competition of ideas. In fact, "solution validation" may not be the best way of looking at it after all. It's about finding the most impactful, most value-producing solution with the least amount of friction and the highest possible chance of adoption into your customers' existing workflow.

STEP FOUR: YOUR PRODUCT

IT'S TIME TO GET YOUR HANDS DIRTY

FINALLY, and only after looking into the audience, problem, and solution, can you arrive at the product. This is the part that the technical expert in every entrepreneur finds most exciting: turning the idea into a real thing—manifesting the potential into a tangible product. Only by having spent a lot of time and energy on shaping the idea through the previous stages can you be sure that when you dive into building the product, you can create a sustainable bootstrapped business by selling it to customers who will pay for it.

In the startup world, everyone is talking about the MVP, the Minimum Viable Product. There is an ongoing battle over what that means.

To some, it's the first, very embarrassing version of the product that works. It's a prototype, the first version of many, a bundle of core features built with rudimentary aesthetics to quickly get the product out there. Their MVP will lack a lot of parts, and many things will still have to be done by hand.

To others, it's something they can be proud of: a polished system, well-designed, and with a heavily tested user interface.

Their MVP has to do almost everything the final product will be doing.

No matter where you stand on these issues, there are a few general guidelines that will make sure you can create a product that stands a chance:

1. Your product will never be finished—treat it as an ongoing concern at all times.
2. Allow for quick and safe releases, release early, and release often.
3. The less exciting your tech choices, the better.
4. The fewer things you have to build yourself, the better.

With an MVP, you want to test the waters, and you will want to be sure that you can make money on the most basic version of your product. What "basic" means will be up to you, but there is a saying attributed to Reid Hoffman, founder of LinkedIn: "If you're not embarrassed by the first version of your product, you have launched too late."

THE MYTH OF THE FINISHED PRODUCT

BEFORE THE INTERNET made transferring large amounts of data cheap and easy, software used to be distributed on CDs or DVDs. For any given application, there was the "Golden Master," a final version of the software, ready to be copied millions of times.

Those days are over. Every day, millions of software updates get dispatched. For many services in the bootstrapped world, customers will never notice: they'll just refresh their browser pages, and the latest version of the application will just appear.

With updating being so easy, no product is ever finished. Even when you release what you think is a "feature-complete" version of your product, it will only be "done" for a while.

There is one main reason for all software being only temporary: the changing circumstances of your customers. It can manifest in many ways, for many reasons: 1) as entrepreneurial dissatisfaction with the status quo; 2) a reaction to movements in the industry, the competitive landscape, or the regulatory environment; or 3) a reaction to changes in needs and your understanding of your customers.

Being able to update your product quickly can still be optimally leveraged for your bootstrapped business, but it's important to also know when not to change things.

Entrepreneurial Dissatisfaction

Every product is the result of a measurement made at one point in time: you validated your audience, their problem, and your solution. You decided on the scope of your product from that information. But that data isn't static. It wasn't even complete when you went through all of those validations.

In short, your analysis will always be imperfect, because you don't have the complete insight: there is no perfect vision in the ever-changing world of entrepreneurship. Your interpretation of what is needed to solve your customers' critical problem always will be incomplete, or a premise may have changed over time.

What matters is what you do about it. Your vision of the product is the touchstone of what should be in your product and what shouldn't. If your vision changes, so should your product.

It's a good idea to reflect on your assumptions, your analysis, and its accuracy every now and then. I recommend doing this consciously at least once a quarter, as a form of Continuous Validation of the business, the product, and alignment with your vision.

We did this in a very informal way at FeedbackPanda. Every few months, Danielle and I would sit down and talk about the feature suggestions and ideas we had come up with or received, and checked if anything among them was interesting for making the product better. We dismissed much more than we considered, and it kept the product current without being bloated. We even removed features at times.

Your product will never be finished because your audience

and their problems are moving targets that you learn to see more clearly the longer you work at it.

Changing Regulatory Environments

When the General Data Protection Regulation (GDPR) passed into law in May 2018 in Europe, companies all over the world frantically added cookie consent banners to their websites. They started implementing data protection features into their products, because all of a sudden, there was a chance they'd be fined heavily if they didn't change their products.

We had been careful not to collect any potentially dangerous information with FeedbackPanda even before GDPR was announced, as I felt we should avoid having payment information or customer address information stored in our database. I trusted that services like Stripe or Auth0 were more capable of securing this kind of information than I could ever be. As a result, we didn't have to do much, other than adding a pesky cookie consent banner to our marketing website.

In some industries, there are already extensive protocols to follow: you need to be PCI compliant when you work in payments, or you need documentation for HIPAA compliance, for example.

Some markets are relatively unregulated when you start, but are targeted by lawmakers eventually. We witnessed this in the Chinese EdTech landscape. Our mostly North-American customers were contracting for Chinese Kid English companies. When Chinese authorities decided that Chinese children could not receive after-school tutoring after 8pm and restricted the amount of information the schools were allowed to share about the students, the Chinese Kid English companies had to change their product and business models significantly. Some companies even closed because the regulation made it impossible for them to operate at a profit.

Your product can never be finished because the legal requirements and limitations of an industry are always changing.

Changing Technology Landscape

There are domino effects that can impact your business in surprising ways. Here is another FeedbackPanda example that illustrates the dependencies and complicated interconnected parts of the software world.

The Chinese Kid English companies our customers worked for were using web-based teaching platforms to facilitate video-based face-to-face teaching. Our product FeedbackPanda integrated into these platforms using a browser extension.

Everything was getting along fine—until it didn't.

In 2017, Adobe decided to end-of-life Flash, its popular multimedia software and browser plugin. The maturity of web technologies like HTML5 and WebAssembly made it less and less appealing to support an outdated plugin, so they decided to stop supporting Flash by the end of 2020.

Consequentially, browser vendors had to react. The security implications of this decision reached far and wide. Before the end of 2020, all major browsers would have to phase out their Flash support, as integrating software that is not receiving security updates is a great risk for browsers, which are used by millions of people every single day.

So, the team at Chromium, the technology behind Google Chrome, set a roadmap to phase out Flash support over several years. One particular step along the way was disabling the flash plugin by default by July 2019. After that point, the user of Chrome would have to reactivate Flash every single time they started the browser.

When this change was a few months away, the developer community started talking about it. Within the development teams of the Chinese Kid English companies, it must have made the rounds as well, as all of a sudden, these companies understood the complexity of their tech choices: the system they used for video calls was built on Flash. And, if they didn't change anything soon, their teachers could not teach reliably any longer, and would not be able to teach at all by the end of 2020 when their browser would automatically update and disable Flash support.

One choice was to switch to a different video call technology provider, finding one that used HTML5 video, something that would continue to be supported.

But they did something else. The schools chose to stick with their video provider. The problem now was the nature of evergreen browsers, automatically updating eventually. Instead the schools went for something that we didn't expect: they froze their teachers' browsers in time by having them teach through an Electron-based application. Using Electron is like shipping a web application packaged with a browser to run it. And with a package, they could stay in control of the update process, effectively freezing their teachers' Chrome version in a pre-2020 state forever.

Problem solved for the Chinese Kid English companies. They now had to release updates both to their website and the teaching application that would load their site in that old browser version, but the Flash issue would have no impact.

For FeedbackPanda, it was the opposite. By moving away from a browser-based teaching portal to the Electron-app-based solution, our browser integration would not work anymore. Within this Electron wrapper, browser extensions could not be installed, which was a limitation the schools chose to accept for not having to spend millions changing their video call provider.

For us, it meant that a major integration into the workflow of our customers was at risk. The schools were actively encouraging their teachers to teach through the app, and without having ever planned to do so, I started researching ways of integrating browser extensions into standalone Electron applications.

I finally found a solution that would allow our customers to integrate the same way they already knew from their browsers into their new teaching apps. This integration involved another standalone Electron-based app that our customers would have to install and use. Hence, it wasn't as easy as installing an extension in a browser, but it still was much better to have a few extra steps than not to use our service at all.

This kind of change could happen on a schedule as it did with Flash. It could also occur from one day to another, as it usually does when Google releases an update to its search engine algorithms and puts an entire niche out of business.

Your product can never be finished because it's embedded in a world of changing technologies.

Changing Customer Workflows

When industries adopt new and improved practices, workflows change. There are four kinds of changes in a sector that can trigger this, which can be differentiated along the two axes of "Are the core activities threatened?" and "Are the core assets threatened?"

First, you have the one with the lowest chance of making you change your product: progressive change. Core activities and technologies stay mostly the same over time; only minimal change happens. Think of airlines, an industry that has changed very little over the last decades. If you have a product that integrates with the systems of this industry, it will not need to be changed much over time.

Second, there is creative change. In the movie industry, technology gets improved because there is a desire to become better and create things that are new and exciting. New technology can change whole areas of the industry very quickly, and that adoption comes with a change of how things are getting done. Assets are being developed and improved, leaving the activities mostly the same.

When only core activities are threatened, we call it intermediating change. Here, the fragility of interpersonal relationships leads to changes in how things are done: look at how car dealerships used to work and how much has been changed by technology and ubiquitous information. The power dynamics of a sales relationship have flipped, and so have the processes in the industry.

The most dangerous kind of change is radical change. Here, both activities and assets are threatened, and everything can change. Have ever seen a rotary phone, and wondered what happened to the businesses that produced those? Remember travel agencies? When people book vacations today, they rarely use a phone much less leave the house. Travel agents have to approach marketing and sales much differently today. If you have a product that helps travel agents make sales or coordinate travel plans, you will have to react to seismic shifts in your industry and provide solutions to the problems of today.

Your product is never finished because changes in the industry you serve will change the workflows of your customers, forcing you to adapt your product.

Changes in the Economic Impact of a Feature

There is also the possibility that a change to your business or product has significant side-effects that will turn something that worked well before into something harmful for your business.

The example of Baremetrics introducing a freemium plan illustrates this clearly. They made available much of the functionality of the paid subscription levels to free accounts in the hope of finding more leads and have users see the value proposition more clearly. Soon after launching the free plan, the free users started to outnumber paid users and the amount of data that Baremetrics had to process started causing performance and database issues. Customer support was doubly affected: there were all these new freemium customers to support, and the paying members needed help solving the problems caused by the performance issues.

Their churn went up, their revenue didn't hit the expected goals, and they called it a failed experiment. But for both the freemium attempt and for turning it off eventually, they had to change their product. Ignoring the changes they had to make as they ran into scaling issues, this is product work that was not in the initial vision, but needed to be grafted on at a later stage.

If a feature of your product turns from lead magnet into a churn multiplier, you need to remove it. If a feature you previously considered to be a bad idea turns into a potential revenue increaser, you need to add it.

Your product will never be finished because the economic impact of certain features is dependent on the choices you make after or before implementing them.

Bugs: Correcting the Dysfunctions You Never Meant to Create

No piece of software will be error-free, because it is built by fallible beings, operated by fallible beings on complex machines, and consumed by fallible beings haphazardly operating even more sophisticated machinery. There will be glitches, and there will be errors.

While it's every developer's ambition to squash these things before they hit the production systems, some will sneak through, and you will have customers reach out and report them, often in a very agitated state.

I've learned to use this as a brand-building exercise. When people reported bugs in the FeedbackPanda interface, I would calmly thank them for the report, tell them that I was right on it, fix the bug right then, and immediately tell them that it was fixed right after deploying the new version of our service. At times, this took less than 30 minutes from the customer service chat until the fixed version was deployed.

This reliably resulted in amazement and, in some cases, even converted the customer from a mere user to one of our loudest evangelists. Being heard is one thing. Being listened to and finding that something is made better as a result is another. If you can give your customers this feeling, they will feel valued, understood, and will become loyal. Many of those customers would rush to our aid whenever we had technical trouble, telling people on social media about their experience and that they knew we would do everything in our power to restore the service. This gave us precious time to fix the problems instead of talking to customers in a variety of social media groups.

With every bug you fix, your product becomes better—as long as you don't introduce new bugs by fixing the old ones.

Three Ways to Think About Features

I see three distinct approaches to features: you can add them, you can change them, and you can remove them. But one of these is often overlooked.

Most founders love to add new features, as they often equate features with the potential of generating value. Whenever new customer needs get discovered, you add a feature. When you want to start value-nurturing your customers, showing them how much they benefit from your product, you add a feature that does that. When you want to turn your product into a network-effect engine, you add a sharing feature.

Founders are also happy to change and adjust features when needed. When customer needs change, you change your features. When your business is moving up-market or down-market, you adjust your functionality.

Only a few entrepreneurs are happy to remove features from their products. Even when customers don't need a particular activity anymore, the feature is left untouched. Even when a feature was built to solve a need that turns out not to exist, it stays in the product. Even when a feature is clearly damaging in terms of economic impact, we don't remove it immediately.

Why is that? What makes us so hesitant to remove what we can see isn't working? It's the thing that makes an entrepreneur great: boundless optimism. Here, it's just applied the wrong way and mixed with an unhealthy dose of the sunk-cost fallacy. That fallacy states that we perceive something as more valuable than it is when we have spent considerable resources in creating or attaining it. We would rather "see it through until the end" than counting our losses and getting rid of it.

If you have a feature that no customer uses, remove it. I did that with a very specific button in our interface that we had put into the product as a means for our first few users to migrate their data, before we had integrations into their online class-rooms. The button in question would allow them to assign a unique ID to a record that we couldn't detect before the integration, but the ID would be automatically assigned and used when the teacher had the browser extension installed. After a few weeks, all teachers were effectively migrated. Still, it took me months to remove that button.

And when I removed it, a single user immediately complained about it being gone. In an utterly unexpected way, they had started using our product with their own self-designated IDs for their records, which had no impact on our system, but was a means for them to add more information to their data. When we removed the option to change that information, they started complaining.

It gave us a good insight into how some people could be using our product in unexpected ways. Removing features will do this; it will unearth the hidden outliers, the users deviating from the conventional path. If you have a feature that is damaging to the value of your business, remove it.

At some point, I envisioned that we should be able to show each teacher extremely detailed statistical information about their data, right on everyone's dashboard. But with thousands of teachers having thousands of records, the calculations involved were very resource-intensive, not unlike the Baremetrics example mentioned before. I had to cut back on displaying this information on the dashboard and moved it into a separate component that would only load and calculate data when a user requested it deliberately. Crisis averted.

Finally, if you're building a network-effect-based product and you find that a feature discourages your users from participating in the network, remove it. This friction can severely impede the growth potential of your product. Remove all obstacles and extra steps that keep your customers from engaging in network-building activities.

While you will likely be adding and changing features more than removing them in the early stages of your business, prepare that eventually, you will need to remove features. Avoid becoming too attached. You may be reluctant to remove something you spent a lot of time on. However, you'd rather have a slim and focused product than a behemoth that does a thousand things, but none of them well.

The Kind of "Finished" You Never Want to See

The only time when your software is actually finished is when it has precisely zero users and no changes to respond to: when your business has failed. That will be the day when you can stop looking at your market and your customers' needs. Any other day is an opportunity to improve your product.

Your product will never be finished. It will need to adapt to things within and without your control. Leverage the fact that it is easier than ever to deploy a new version of your product quickly and give your customers the best experience you can provide.

THE DO'S AND DON'TS OF THE MINIMUM VIABLE PRODUCT

LEONARDO DA VINCI SAID, "Art is never finished, only abandoned." This is definitely true for software as well. The only antidote to abandonment is to put your work in front of other people, even when it's not perfect yet.

The startup industry uses the term MVP (Minimum Viable Product) to express this in-between state of being both a wonky prototype and a good-enough product for public consumption.

If software can never be truly finished, any stage of it is your best guess at what it should be at the time it's created. As the MVP is the first version of your product that your audience will be exposed to, it is crucial to get it "right enough" while being okay with it not being "perfectly right" at the same time.

The MVP is your first real contact with your customers. It has two main functions: to allow your early adopters to gauge the value of your service, and to enable you to charge them money to gauge their sincerity. The MVP is the first handshake between you and your customers. To have your MVP leave a great first impression, you will need to scope it sufficiently and time it well.

Scoping Your MVP

There are two boxes to tick when it comes to your MVP: it has to be the **minimum** of what is needed to make your product **viable**.

What's a minimal product? It's the core functionality only, a simple tool without any fancy additions.

What's a viable product? It's the essence of the solution to your audience's problem, a tool that does exactly what it promises to do, and nothing more.

Both "minimal" and "viable" limit the scope of your product, from different directions. You can always make your product more viable, but you can't make it any more minimal without losing your customer.

A minimum viable product should contain a few structural components to make it usable by your audience: your users should be able to sign up and log in, solve their problem, and be able to pay for your product. Anything else is cruft, at least for your MVP.

Depending on the technical skill of your audience, you can get by with a rudimentary interface. If you build a tool for developers, an API and some documentation could be enough. For customers who need a bit more than that, you will have to provide a well-designed interface.

Luckily, creating a well-designed interface is easy for an MVP: if you only solve one core problem, there won't be much potential for confusion. Every interface component you put into your MVP should lead your customer to your core functionality. If you find yourself having trouble with your interface and user journey, you may have too much non-critical functionality in your MVP.

Your MVP should be a "Mafia Offer," something your customers can't refuse because it's too good to pass up. You can accomplish that by focusing on achieving the "minimum viable" part of your MVP. Solve one critical problem really well. Don't do anything else. If there is nothing to distract your customers from seeing the value of the product, you have succeeded.

Beware of reacting immediately to early customer feedback. Your MVP is particularly prone to the core problem of software engineering: requirement volatility. Your prospective customers will expect different things from their tools over time. Worse yet, they may not know what they need, or they may have internalized their work too much to adequately express what their requirements are. Some customers will tell you what they think you need to hear instead of telling you what they know.

All software is an imperfect approximation of a solution to a less-than-well-defined set of requirements. Your MVP will be, too, and that is fine. It just has to prove that your core functionality solves your audience's critical problem well enough.

One last thing about the scope of your MVP: beware of platform overextension. Don't try and build the very first version of your product for all possible platforms it may be used on and for. If you build an app, find the audience that needs your product most, and build for their platform alone. Your app MVP doesn't need to be available for iOS, Android, BlackBerry, and Windows Phone at the same time. One of these platforms will fit your product best. Build for that one.

For FeedbackPanda, we tried to find the most important platform and build for that. Since the product was a web-based SaaS for online English teachers, that meant something slightly different for us: choosing the right online school to integrate with. We integrated with the most significant player in the market first, tested, and went for the rest much later. The system we chose before all others was the one we knew most about, and that helped us to focus on building the core functionality without getting lost in the details.

Timing Your MVP

It's incredibly hard to time when your MVP is done. Here's the problem: you're much too invested. You have the grand vision of what your product could be. And here you are, looking at a version that is slimmed down to the extent of being unrecognizable. It will always feel like it's not good enough yet.

Here is how you can reframe this perspective: all your customers want is to have one less problem in their lives. They are sitting in front of a bowl of soup with a fork. You have a tiny spoon to offer, but you think you could make a much larger spoon. Your customers will be perfectly happy with the small spoon, because no matter what it can do for them in the future, it will already help them with their bowl of soup, right here and now.

The happy path for any customer is to ship the MVP as soon as humanly possible. You need your customers to interact with your product at the earliest possible moment. Only then can you find out what works and what doesn't. You need the MVP to become part of their daily workflow. That will surface interaction conflicts and feature inconsistencies better than any reflection ever could.

Understand that your first users will be early adopters and innovators. They understand that new products are not "done" and that using an imperfect product will still be better. Early adopters are aware of their impact on the trajectory of a product, and they will play with something that doesn't work perfectly much longer than a mainstream customer ever would.

Ship early, and release to early adopters. If you can get them to use your MVP and actually commit to it by paying you a non-trivial amount of money, you will have a real shot at building a sustainable business.

Features a Successful MVP Should Have (Eventually)

If you want it to measure customer commitment, add a rudimentary payment system from the beginning. Give liberal amounts of free trial time, but set an end to it. An indefinite trial period could keep people around, but it won't allow you to determine if your product produces enough value to warrant paying for it.

If your first customers only stay with the product because it's free, you do not know the viability of your future business. If you offer a subscription and people start signing up, you know you're onto something. If they don't, then you have something you can ask them about.

Security and privacy should be present in your MVP from the beginning: don't ingest personally identifiable information more than you need to. Use Identity-as-a-Service solutions like Auth0 from the start, and don't implement your own payment system either. Services like Stripe will handle capturing payment and billing information in a PCI-compliant way for you. In general, don't keep secrets in your database. This burdens you with being very up-to-date with security standards and software updates, which are not core parts of your business. It also makes your small business a lucrative target for hacking, and this puts you personally at risk. Avoid the whole thing by having experts do this for you.

We found one thing to be incredibly useful in the MVP and all later versions of our product: client-side monitoring. By getting notifications for errors immediately after they happened in the browsers or apps of our customers, we could see the stack trace and additional information before the customer even noticed the error. On quite a few occasions, I had already composed a customer service response while the affected customer was still typing their initial message. Reaching out to a customer before they have even thought about talking to customer service is one of the most effective ways of delighting a customer in a situation that is typically negative.

It's also important to provide a way for the customer to reach you. Give them an easy-to-use contact form, a real-time chat solution like Intercom or UserList—just make sure they have some way to reach out to you when necessary. You're interested in their feedback as soon as they have something to tell you. Make that easy for them to accomplish.

None of these features have to be part of your MVP from day one, but they should eventually become part of it in some form or another. You can do a lot of the work manually for a while, working with basic tools such as spreadsheets, email, and even phone. But eventually, you will want to funnel all the activities through your (soon-to-be-)automated systems.

MVP "Cheats"

It is extremely helpful to build a product that solves your own problem. You will know when your MVP is minimally viable since it will solve your problem enough at some point. From there, it will be good enough for others as well. This practice is called "dogfooding," named after a television ad from the 1970s, where the owner of a dog food brand claimed that he fed his dog food to his own dogs. In the IT world, this process has been made famous by Amazon, where Jeff Bezos forced all his development teams to build internal APIs that would eventually be made available to external developers, too. That way, all external services would have gone through a long time of internal use, ironing out the bugs and making the interfaces usable.

Another way of thinking about your MVP is to make it a Minimum Loveable Product. What is the first version of your product that an early adopter may take a screenshot of and share with their network? What features do you need for a user to have their jaw drop to the floor? What configuration will make it crystal-clear how much time or money they can save by using your product? Getting your MVP to the point where your customers have no choice but to talk about it is what the MLP is all about.

A Few MVP Examples

One of the finest examples of a successful MVP is EndCrawl, a SaaS in the movie industry, providing end-of-movie credits. John Eremic, the founder of EndCrawl, worked in movie post-production for almost a decade, and he found that every production company had trouble with their movie credits. He wanted to build a service to make this much more manageable.

The EndCrawl MVP was a Perl script that John had built at his breakfast table on a Saturday morning. It ingested a pre-formatted Google sheet that the movie company would edit with their information. Every time they needed a rendered version of the credits, they would just send an email to EndCrawl, and within 15 minutes, they would receive a link to the finished rendering—a process that had usually taken between six and 24 hours previously.

This is what an initial MVP looks like. It is minimal. It's just a Google sheet and an email. It's viable. It solves the customer's problem. It's loveable. It solves the problem surprisingly quickly. With EndCrawl, the full SaaS UI came later. It wasn't required to validate the product: production companies were happy to pay $500 to interact with an API through email. And that's all your MVP is required to do.

Joel Gascoigne of Buffer took the two-page MVP route. Buffer created a landing page which explained what their tweet-scheduling tool would allow a user to do, and would show an email signup page if someone clicked the "Call-to-Action" button:

This validation strategy was enough for Joel to see that there was some interest in a tweet-scheduling product, and he wanted to learn even more about his customers before building out the functional MVP. He added a page in between the landing and the email capture, and asked prospects to pick a price level they would be interested in paying, together with a free option. This resulted in some interest in paid plans, which was an indicator that tweet-scheduling was something people would pay for. That was good enough to build out the first version of Buffer, a product that was the foundation of an incredible bootstrapped business.

If It Fails, Don't Throw It Away

Like everything in the beginning stages of your bootstrapped business, the MVP is mostly a tool for validation. Expect that some of your customers will not like your MVP for some reason, and your job is to find out why. An MVP with acceptance problems has not yet failed; it's just incomplete. Understanding where the customers have trouble making use of your product is required to make it more accessible.

Sometimes, however, you may have created the right product for the wrong customer. In this case, start over, but don't throw away what you have created. Your future business or someone else may be able to salvage your MVP and turn it into a flourishing business for another audience.

In general, you will have a choice: you can adjust your MVP to solve the problem better, solve a different problem for your audience, or look for another audience. I recommend trying to salvage your MVP before scrapping it altogether. However, at some point, you may want to call it a day and look for greener pastures.

I have done this many times before with products or ideas that didn't survive the first contact with the audience they were intended for. It hurt every time, but whenever it happened, I understood that I had just learned a valuable lesson about what I thought reality would be like and what it actually turned out to be. Every time you have to correct your perception of reality, you're inching a bit closer to your customers' truth. And that is where you will be able to serve them eventually.

If your MVP causes your customers to pay for your product, great. You have validated that you're on the right track. You can now focus on turning it into a business.

If it doesn't result in paying customers at all, even after a few iterations, great. You have validated that you were on the wrong track, and you won't be pursuing that direction any longer. You just saved yourself from trying to build a business that won't resonate with customers.

Validating that you are on the right path is why you build an MVP. Either success or failure of the MVP will allow you to become a better entrepreneur.

HOW TO RELEASE AS A BOOTSTRAPPER: OFTEN, EARLY, AND SAFELY

LIKE LEONARDO DA VINCI, we say, "Software is never finished, only abandoned." While this is true, it doesn't tell us anything helpful. So, we can rephrase this into something we can act on: "Software is never finished, only released."

In most cases, technical founders will be able to do Cowboy Coding, which means that they have full control over the development and deployment process. It also means that reliable systems are not sufficiently established, as things are "done the way they are done," particularly in the beginning phases of a startup.

If you want to set up your release process in a future-proof way from the beginning, here is what is most important about releasing your product in a bootstrapped business: release often, release early, and release safely.

That way, your engineering and release culture will allow you to be nimble, react to customer feedback quickly, and build a stable infrastructure for the essential asset of your business: your product.

Release often & early

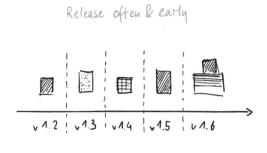

Release rarely & late

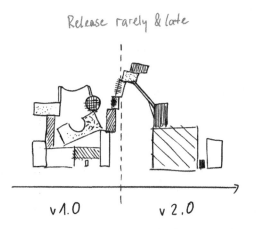

Release Often

When I worked for a VC-backed startup at the beginning of my engineering career, we would release expansive feature sets, sometimes months apart at a time. As a result, I would work on many different small features. There was a lot of extra work whenever one developer's code conflicted with another developer's, and the days following release day were full of customers reaching out about problems—all at once.

You can prevent this by releasing more often. At Feedback-Panda, I released almost daily, and at least once a week. Whenever a feature was done enough, it would be released. I didn't wait for a release day; I just made sure I wouldn't release while most of our customers were using the product, which was a three-hour window I would usually avoid for anything that was not a bug fix.

Releasing often prevents horizontal overengineering. You won't work on too many features at the same time. In the best case, every release is precisely one feature, with all of your focus going into getting it right the first time. By releasing at least once a week, you will force yourself to concentrate on a minimal number of things. This focus on single features allows you to build many small things over time, one after the other, and immediately validate if they are useful or not. If you bundle them up into one big release every few months, your validation data will lose a lot of accuracy and granularity.

Releasing often allows for feature implementation feedback. You can learn very quickly how well the released feature solves the problem it's supposed to solve. Since you've delivered a single feature, you will be able to attribute any unexpected side-effects to your release. Many client-side error-monitoring tools can assign a suspect release to every new error, making an educated guess as to which deployment may be responsible for a newly encountered error.

Releasing often allows your product to evolve progressively. No change will ever make a customer think that "everything has changed." Customers get used to your release cadence, and they will have a much easier time integrating small changes into their workflows.

Don't forget to keep your documentation and Standard Operating Procedures up-to-date. For engineers, it's a lot of fun to build, and a great joy to see customers use newly released features. The part where you take new screenshots for your knowledge base and write new step-by-step guides for your Operations Manual may not be as exciting. But those steps, when taken routinely, will make sure your business runs on as much automation and documentation as possible, which will make it more sellable in the future.

Release Early

When I released a feature of FeedbackPanda that would allow our teachers to share their feedback templates with each other, I released a crude version that took me two days to build. It worked only for one of the schools we supported, it had a very basic interface, and all our customers could do was find a shared template and import it into their database. This feature eventually turned into what we called the FeedbackPandaCloud.

After we released the feature, our most adventurous customers started using it, and they reached out with both positive and negative feedback. They explained at which points in their workflow they found this feature to be an improvement and where it confused them. A day later, I had addressed many of those initial concerns.

The next iteration of the feature happened a good week later. In the meantime, I deployed several bug fixes and small improvements to other, more integral parts of the product, some of which were related to the interface components used in the sharing feature.

Releasing early prevents vertical overengineering. You won't work on one feature for too long. After you release a feature, you're free to work on something else. Not focusing on one feature for too long prevents going down endless rabbit holes, which is a big concern for many solo founders.

It will also make your features very succinct. By releasing when features are just a few days old, you will effectively be releasing MVP versions of individual features. You won't have months to fiddle with irrelevant details if your feature needs to be good enough in three days.

Releasing early allows for feature integration feedback.
Your customers can tell you very quickly how well the feature
fits into their existing workflow. This is great because every
feature you release will need to be tweaked in some way, eventually. Since you want to provide the maximum amount of value
to all of your customers as fast as possible, getting valuable
feedback early in the lifetime of a feature is a significant
advantage.

If you work for months on a feature only to find out that
you misunderstood the nature of your customers' problem, that
is a month wasted. If you can find that out after working on the
feature for just four days, you saved yourself three weeks. That's
why releasing early is important: it frees up time for other,
equally or more critical opportunities of creating value for your
customers.

**Releasing early allows for features to evolve progres-
sively.** You will make small changes to your features over time,
responding to real-world usage and customer requirements. No
battle plan survives contact with the enemy, and as expert as
you may be as a founder, the expert in what your customers
need will always be your customers themselves.

Iterating your features is a good practice because you will
need to make changes anyway, either from customer feedback
you receive or when you learn something new about the workflow of your customers. The chance that you can release a
feature once and never touch it is slim, and the changing nature
of both your business and the needs of your customers will
make you revisit your product often.

If a feature is lacking a critical component, you will learn
about this very quickly. In the case of our FeedbackPandaCloud,
people requested a way to edit templates before importing them
into their own database. Since I had started building the feature
with a skeleton functionality, I could easily add new features
later.

It's not just customer requirements that make this progressive approach attractive. In some cases, your features don't need to be full-fledged because it doesn't yet make sense for your business. When I integrated a subscription payment system into FeedbackPanda, all I needed for the first couple of weeks was a way for people to subscribe. The first public version of our service had a subscribe button only. There was no option to cancel or upgrade a subscription. Customers had to reach out through our customer service channels. Only after a few dozen customers had expressed the need for specific functionality would I implement it and release it. Bit by bit, plan upgrade and downgrade, cancellation, and invoice-related functions appeared in our product; I only ever implemented these features when it started taking too long to solve these tasks manually.

Release Safely

When I released a feature that was supposed to show every customer a few statistics about their usage of our product, I didn't think that this would impact our service much. After all, what were a few additional requests to the database? All of a sudden, my monitoring tools started bombarding me with notifications; my phone rang from the robocalls that I had set up when our system became unresponsive.

What had happened? It turned out that while I tested my statistic-collection logic on my local computer on a test account with a few dozen items in the database, the performance requirements of the database queries increased exponentially with the amount of data in a customer's database. All of a sudden, hundreds of teachers with tens of thousands of items in their databases were refreshing their websites, triggering an unstoppable avalanche of requests to our database, which promptly locked up and didn't respond to requests anymore.

Our service went down, and when it returned, the renewed onslaught of database queries caused it to break down again.

I immediately understood what was causing these performance issues. And, I had to get the service back up and try to keep the downtime as short as possible.

This downtime lasted for not even two minutes, because I had foreseen that something like this could happen, and had designed our release infrastructure to allow for instant rollbacks. With one command, the previous version of our software that didn't contain the statistics feature was switched back on, all traffic was routed to that instance, and within a few seconds, the database had enough breathing room to start working correctly again.

Never release something you can't roll back. You can't know for sure that your code is entirely error-free. In particular, when unexpected user behavior turns a benign feature into a resource-blocking monster, you will need to get back to the last version of your service that worked. The more automated this process, the better.

Three main things are important to create a system capable of automated rollbacks: artifacts, versioning, and bidirectional migrations.

Package your releases into easy-to-deploy artifacts. An artifact is a bundle, a package that can be easily copied and run on a server, either as some sort of executable or as a container that systems such as orchestration tools like Kubernetes can manage. The idea is that everything is well-specified, and you don't need to move around files or assets. Usually, this involves a build process, where your whole application gets compiled, optimized, and packed up so that a final artifact can be created.

Artifacts are usually idempotent with the sources that created them: compiling your artifact from the same code twice will result in the exact same artifact. This means that if you want to roll back your service to the prior version, you don't need to do any compilation again, you can just reactivate the previous artifact.

Version your release artifacts. You can reliably roll back to a version that worked if it has an easily discerned version number. If you just released v1.2.5 of your service and it breaks all of a sudden, you know that activating v1.2.4 will get your system back to stability. Versioning is a peace-of-mind activity, and many orchestration systems require it to distinguish artifacts.

Synchronize your database using bidirectional migrations. Imagine you have to make changes to your database with a release. You need to change the name of an important field in your user table that is related to your authentication flow. Your release goes through, changes the name of the field, and minutes later, you need to roll back the service to a prior version. If you don't have a way to revert the change you just did in your database, likely your service won't start. You'll have to frantically correct the change manually. Under stress, this can lead to errors from which you may not be able to recover.

Having migration logic in place that can go both ways makes it possible to release database-related changes very safely. Many web development frameworks like Ruby on Rails and Elixir/Phoenix have this feature built-in, but you need to know how to use it. Making bidirectional migrations a part of your release flow from the start will save you from a lot of potential trouble further down the road.

Automate the process. You will benefit immensely from removing manual steps from the release process. Continuous Integration, the concept of automating build and tests, makes releasing extremely easy and manageable. This level of automation makes your business more sellable as well: if a developer you hire (or the one that replaces you after you sold the company) can release a new version of the software at the push of a button, this will net you a premium when your business gets acquired.

An automated process removes the one component that could mess up more than anything else: you. If you are required to execute steps manually, you could forget important parts, and risk bringing down your service with a botched release. An automated build system allows you to have checkpoints, stopping any dysfunctional artifact from ever reaching your production system. It's one less thing to think about.

Release when it's a good time. Don't release at the time of day when most of your customers are using the product at the same time. Often, there are a few times a day when your traffic is lowest, and those are excellent release time windows. "Don't release on Fridays" is a famous saying in the industry, as any corrective work will bleed into your weekend. Make sure you have the time to potentially roll back or hotfix your release.

Consider slow rollouts and feature flags. This may be an advanced approach to releasing, as you will likely not need this for the first few versions of your product. But it makes sense to at least consider building feature toggles into your product: a way for you to activate and deactivate access to certain features for your customers. Feature toggles will allow you to tie functionality to subscription levels eventually, and it will also give you a way to deal with emergency performance issues. I would have loved just to turn off the statistics feature that caused my database to break down instead of having to roll back the release. Slowly rolling out the new version to our customers instead of just releasing it to all of them at once would also have given me a much less stressful time figuring out the performance issues. I started implementing these things shortly after having experienced the statistics fiasco.

Releasing and TMI: How Much Do You Make Public?

Your customers can find out you released something through two means: they stumble upon it in your product, or you communicate the change to them in some way.

For many small changes, you won't need to inform your users. If you were to tell them every single day that you moved a button a few pixels to the right or added an image to a block of text, they would soon feel overwhelmed. Save your announcements for the significant, impactful features that you want your customers to know about. Blog posts and newsletters are great places to communicate those.

While product update information has a "push" character, as you inform your customer directly, you also have the option of a "pull" source of release update information: offer a changelog. Changelogs can be shown to customers in the shape of a notification button, which they can click to see what has been changed recently. For technical audiences, this makes a lot of sense. For others, it only works when it is informative and helpful. Many customers only care about things that will indeed affect them. Don't spam them with the minutiae of your product development. In the end, customers don't have the attention span to read up on all of your many changes: they use your product to solve their critical problems. A good approach to releasing allows for that, and it will make sure they continue to be able to use your solution to have one less obstacle in their day.

How to Get to a Simple But Effective Release Management System

Your requirements for release management will vary wildly on the fidelity of your software. For example, if you run a SaaS with a web app, a mobile app, and some substantial background computing, you will likely need to release the backend and the frontend code and artifacts separately, involving a lot of automation very early in your product's life. If you run a web-based SaaS without any extra fluff, you will likely be able to set up a simple release pipeline and be okay with it for a long time.

As long as your setup allows you to release early and often, you're fine. The moment you notice yourself doing something that can be automated, integrate it into your release management system.

When I started developing FeedbackPanda, I ran the prototype locally on my development machine until it had all the necessary functionality. Very quickly, I containerized the application using Docker. That allowed me to fix the versions of all included libraries and runtimes, making builds more testable and reproducible.

In the beginning, I had all the configuration hard-coded into the application. There was only my local database, and all the API keys for the service were unchangeable once the build was running. This was fine for development but was keeping me from deploying the software to the public. Making this configuration part more flexible took some time, and it also meant that certain adjustments were needed to the code to be able to inject secrets (like the database username and password) into the application from outside of the container.

The extra effort paid off, as a Docker container can be run on any cloud provider that supports the industry-standard runtime *containerd*, which any major company does. That gave me a lot of options when it came to picking a hosting provider.

I would still build the Docker images locally on my development machine, and upload them to a container registry. This was fine until I was working from a place with very low bandwidth and shaky connectivity. At that point, uploading a Docker image could take more than an hour, which is an eternity if you want to deploy a hotfix for a bug that just appeared in production. Very quickly, I automated away the build step into a cloud build service, which made it both faster and less dependent on me being connected to a high-bandwidth line to deploy.

Build the release automation that enables you to release whatever you need, whenever you want, always allowing you to revert to the last working version.

THE BORING TRUTH OF SUCCESSFUL PRODUCTS THAT SURVIVE

MOST PRODUCTS that you will see staying on the market have something in common: they do one thing very well—and not much else. Weber sells grills that are fantastic at grilling. The furthest they have strayed into new territory so far has been adding an app-readable thermometer. Still, that gimmick and anything else about their products is focused on making using their grills a great barbecuing experience. That's what it is about: having a barbecue that grills.

In the SaaS space, Stripe is a great example. They provide a clean, well-designed, programmer-friendly service that allows you to charge your customers. While Stripe, as a company, offer a few adjacent services, their focus is always on making getting paid by your customers as comfortable and low-friction as possible. That also means that they won't offer fancy, complicated products that integrate into your CRM or Marketing tools. For that, they started a third-party marketplace. Only when it benefits all of their customers will they add new features to their core product. Simple beats complicated.

How can you stay simple?

Simplicity is achieved by reducing complexity or not introducing it in the first place.

Focus on Doing One Thing Very Well

Every profession has its specialized tools. Doctors operate using specific scalpels and clamps, plumbers have their pliers and wrenches, and it's no surprise that the best kind of cutting tool you can buy for cooking is called a chef's knife.

The best results in your work come from using the best tools at your disposal. Every professional tool excels at one particular job. As a bootstrapped founder, you want your product to do the same.

Being laser-focused on creating a product that solves one problem very well is not just a good idea, it's a requirement for founders without giant heaps of money. The fact that you only have limited resources available means that you need to be very picky about how to spend them. Your money and your time should be put to creating as much value as possible. If you're working on a professional tool that solves one particular problem and nothing else, you will always know what to work on.

I'm aware that this is easier said than done. Founders naturally think expansively: they see something great and imagine it to be even greater. Software is particularly alluring, as it's so easy to add things. When you look at your product and your business, think of a chef's knife instead of a Swiss Army knife. You don't see famous chefs slicing their vegetables with a Swiss Army knife.

The customers who buy your product also purchase many other products. Your chances of building a successful business are higher if you create something that no one else can make instead of trying to develop a product that does everything.

This is not to say that all-round tools like the Swiss Army

knife aren't useful. But to make a product that does a lot of things really well, you need a lot of resources and expertise. The chances are that if you are a solo founder or in a small team, tackling one specific challenge can be accomplished more realistically.

Keep Your Software and Processes Simple

Simplicity can only be accomplished if every part of your operation is as simple as possible: your product, your software, your infrastructure, and even how you go about your daily business. Many of the ways to make your software product simpler can also be applied to your business processes.

Optimize for Hot Paths

In your software, some modules or functions will be executed more often than others. If your product is an image-thumbnail-generating cloud service, the part that resizes user-uploaded files into different ready-to-be-delivered images will run all day long. If you can speed up this single process by 5%, your entire service will be 5% more efficient.

When you want to start simplifying your software, look for these hot paths. It's the low-hanging fruit for optimization. The same is valid for processes you regularly have to do. At FeedbackPanda, we used to reach out to our customers manually whenever a charge to their credit card would fail. We would have to do this every day, at first for 10 minutes. A few weeks later, this task would take almost an hour. That's when we noticed that it was ripe for optimization. I built an automation process that would automatically inform customers about the problem and how to fix it. Only a few customers would have any additional questions, and we cut down the time for this task to effectively zero.

Do this with hot paths all over your business: tedious manual processes, resource-intense tasks, and software components. If you optimize the hot paths often enough, you'll end up with a very streamlined business.

Ignore Calls for Features

Customers will ask for things. Some of these things will make a lot of sense. But you're still better off not turning those things into features just yet. Every customer sees their own problems and envisions a solution tailored to their needs. Often, this solution conflicts with the perceived solution of another customer, who is fine with the way things are or would stand to be confused by any addition.

Everything you add to your product is a source of potential confusion and friction. Until you can make sure that the vast majority of your customers benefit from a feature, don't add it.

Consider it, sure. Build a draft prototype if you must, and see how a feature would impact your product. But beware of releasing it too soon. Once customers start integrating something into their workflows, it will be tough to remove, even when it clearly makes things worse.

Beware of edge cases and creating features to solve them. There will always be new edge cases cropping up, and adding one more feature may solve the problem there and then, but it will also create bloat that is very difficult to remove over the long term.

Toward your customers, don't defend or justify your actions. Tell them that you've noted their request, and you will work on making sure you solve their problem. Be appreciative that they brought something to light, even if you don't think it warrants a feature. A customer that reports issues when they happen is better than one that just cancels their subscription silently.

Changes Should Affect as Many Customers as Possible

Whenever you consider making a change to your product, have it improve the lives of all users at the same time. If you solve 10 different problems and speed up one of them by 100%, you will still leave most of your customers receiving zero benefits from that. If you do one thing only and speed up your product by 10%, all of your users will benefit from that immediately.

A small improvement for all of your customers has the same impact as a significant improvement for a few, and it will compound over time. Every customer will benefit from that change. Focusing on simplicity allows you to optimize your product and stay adaptive when things change.

When in doubt, go for the most overall impact. That often means choosing the harder problem to solve instead of just going for the low-hanging fruit. That's good. It's what the competition will go for first, anyway. Take the thing that is hard to solve, and do that every time. After a while, you will be so far ahead of anyone else.

Make Your Product Extensible

Software products can be made extensible in two significant ways: by modularizing them and by making them easy to integrate with.

For your own development comfort, modularize your software. This will make it easy to add new components later in the lifetime of the product. Modular software has a high separation of concerns, explicit dependencies, and well-defined interfaces. Every function is neatly wrapped in a package or a module that can be tested and maintained independently. This may not be important when you start, but it will become essential when you start building a team of developers later.

While modularization is an internal attempt at making your

product more extensible, it's required for external extensibility as well. If you want others to be able to interface with your service, it will need to expose usable interfaces. Building modular software will train you to get to the point where you can interface with other services.

The concept behind external extensibility is simple: let others do the work. Build a marketplace for plugins into your product, as Intercom does. Provide an API for your service, as Stripe does. Provide easy-to-replicate integrations into your service so that users who want to embed your product into their own product have an easy time doing it.

Often, this involves extensive documentation. This may seem like a lot of work, but it has two purposes: it will make integrating your service easier for potential partners; and it will also be an asset for when you choose to sell your business. A well-documented pile of software and Standard Operating Procedures with step-by-step instructions and tutorials will work just as well internally for your employees as they will work externally for your partners and integrators.

Successful products are the result of focusing on solving a single problem by providing a lean, long-term-oriented, highly extensible service that grows better for every single user with every carefully added feature.

NOT IN HOUSE: REINVENTING THE WHEEL

As a bootstrapped founder, you will have to be scrappy. You will want to spend as little as you can on expenses, particularly when you're just starting. So, anything you need to do, you want to do by yourself. Anything you need to use, you will want to build yourself. But in my experience, a few things should be excluded from that: if you're not careful, they will blow up in the future, putting the whole business at risk.

Don't Build an Authentication System Yourself

I remember building my first authentication system many years ago while building the MVP for a startup I was involved in. At that point, I was building a lot of software using Node.js, and I was aware of several libraries that would allow me to create this myself. There weren't too many requirements initially: customers should be able to sign up and log in using their email and a password, and that was it. My first mistake was to not spend enough time looking into what authentication really encompasses. It's not just an email and a password, it's an entire web of interconnected processes and assumptions.

First, I noticed that I needed to save my users' passwords. Having worked in software engineering for a while, I knew I couldn't just keep them as plain text. I looked for best practices and found that I needed to implement password hashing and salting using the bcrypt library. I understood that I needed to do this, but I didn't understand why. In the end, I just followed best practices. This is not the level of security your customers will or should ever be happy with. You are dealing with their secret information. They should know that you're doing everything to keep it safe.

Keeping the personally identifiable information of your customers in your database is a giant risk, and will make your system a target. There are entire companies out there that take care of the security and privacy requirements of authentication, with teams of security experts making sure the data is inaccessible to those who shouldn't see it.

Other things pointed at the fact that I had bitten off more than I could chew. After a few days of development, I realized that I would need to build a password reset process for users to recover their passwords. All of a sudden, I needed to integrate transactional emails into what was supposed to be an isolated system. Then, I figured that we were building a B2C product, which could mean that customers would want to log in using their existing social networking providers. It took me almost a week to understand and adequately implement just a few popular OAuth2 providers as a source of authentication.

Building our authentication system made sense before I had realized the complexity I was facing. Even if I were to build it myself, it would not be simple, and definitely not easily maintainable. There were libraries and plugins to make it easier, but it still meant a lot of work that could have gone into building the unique core features of our product.

Ever since that experience, I have recommended using Auth0 and their Identity-as-a-Service offering from the beginning. They have a free plan that will last you a long time without needing to pay, and even with thousands of customers, it will still be less than $100. You will save weeks of development time, and it is a double save: you get to work on your core product, and you don't have to reinvent the wheel. And your customers' data is in good hands.

Don't Build a Payment System Yourself

It's bad enough to have personal information in your database, but having credit card information touch your system offers a strong incentive to steal that precious information. Use a PCI-compliant processor where the card information never gets transmitted to your servers, like Stripe. The great benefit of this is that the payment processors have built-in fraud protection, which will make it easier for you to avoid troublesome customers.

At this point, most founders are already aware that they need to find a suitable solution for payments, and rarely roll out their own. I still hear some first-time entrepreneurs complaining about the fees involved, which can often reach 3–5% of the transacted payment. While this is a lot, it helps to think of this as an infrastructure tax for doing business on the internet, a way to make sure that your recurring revenue will be reliably captured month after month.

Don't Build an Invoicing System Yourself

In the beginning, it may be easy just to generate your own invoices, as you have only a few customers and likely only a few plans or prices. But come tax season, you will find out that you should have added a particular field, for certain kinds of customers from a specific country. Invoicing is complicated, and there are dozens of companies that focus on offering a globally usable invoicing integration into Stripe alone. Leave financial things to the experts, and focus on your strength of providing a great product to your niche audience.

I made this mistake with FeedbackPanda, and never rectified it. It worked well enough, but any change to the system was a pain. Like the authentication systems I had built myself before, I was not aware of the complexities that awaited our business. Most of them were not our own requirements but of a regulatory nature. We had registered our business in a country where invoices needed to be in numerical order, with no gaps. They needed to clearly state postal addresses, and they needed to have valid and appropriate dates as well as specific legal terms.

And then there were taxes! As a German business selling to customers all over the world, we needed to calculate taxes differently depending on the location of every customer. Some had to pay Value-Added Tax, but only if they didn't have a European, non-German VAT ID. The complexity of this resulted in me building a tax calculation system that was very brittle. With tax rates changing every now and then, it also needed to fetch the most recent tax rates every day from a European VAT rate API.

None of this was relevant to the core audience of Feedback-Panda, who were online teachers. They needed help with their daily operations. The time I invested in building the start-of-year invoice number overflow logic (where "#2018-4459" would be followed by "#2019-0001" on the first invoice of January 1st) alone could have meant a few bug fixes or work on a teaching-relevant feature instead. It was such a waste of time.

The Mental Trap of Building Things Yourself

As developers, we are very likely to think that, "If I build it myself, I'll understand it better," and it's true. We do benefit from learning how to solve these problems, to a degree. The problem is that in a bootstrapped business, learning-on-the-job should always result in something highly beneficial. Learning how to build an authentication system like tens of thousands of other developers have learned before won't make your business any better.

Wasting time on building something that others know the complexity of while you are entirely unaware is a foolish thing to do. Your core product is where your expertise lies, it's where you know how much is "enough," and which steps are required to reach that state. You won't have that level of insight into non-core parts of your service. Use the services of experts in those fields.

Wasting time on building something that won't improve your industry expertise will hurt your business. Everything that makes you more of an expert among few others will set you apart from your competition. Building the world's 15,000th invoicing module won't get you any closer to that goal.

The worst part of building things that you don't need to build is that it's distracting you from the primary mission of your business: creating a self-sustaining value engine that helps your customers solve their critical problem. If you're not focusing on making that a reality, you're straying from the path.

Building things that you shouldn't build is often the result of a grandiose underestimation of the time required to get it right enough. For everything that sounds simple enough to build yourself but has many SaaS solutions out there, ask yourself if maybe the people who pay for it know more about the complexity of that feature than you do at this point.

A (Mostly) Unbiased Risk Analysis Framework

It's important to figure out if you can build a feature that you need, or if you need to spend money on an existing SaaS solution.

I will try to give you the least biased perspective on the risks for either choice. They originate from my experiences, reflections, conversations with other founders, and stories I have read on the topic. For every point, make sure you find your own opinion and weigh it accordingly.

If you want to make this a data-driven choice, make a list of all the risks of building and all the risks of buying, then see which list is longer, and take the other option.

The Risks of Building this Yourself

Building things yourself opens up the possibility of waste and distraction. Note all the risks that can negatively impact your focus on the core of your business.

- **Unexpected complexity:** Will building this feature uncover a different order of magnitude of development cost? Are there hidden costs in the amount of time you will have to spend on this? Can you be sure that there is a ceiling? What parts of the feature do you think could turn out to be unusually complex? Have you checked for reports of edge cases?
- **Unexpected compliance:** Are there regulatory requirements for this feature that you may not be aware of? Are there hidden costs in terms of money and effort to be able to comply with them? Have you checked the kinds of compliance that solutions in this space openly advertise? Do they apply to your solution, too?
- **Distraction:** Will building this feature distract you from your mission, or will it lead you to it? Is your focus going to be on the core value generation while you build this?
- **Roadmap littering:** Will this feature add more things

to your own roadmap that push the important stuff further out? Is it worth delivering other features later than anticipated? Are your customers okay with that? Are you?

The Risks of Not Building this Yourself

Buying things makes your systems more fragile and can result in a lack of control. Note all the things that could be a risk to the operations of your business.

- **Unexpected downtime:** How will you react to outages and service degradations? Will your customers understand this? Do you have ways to reach customer support for the service you're buying? Will this cost extra? Is trusting that things will continue working the only way?
- **Unexpected implosion:** What will you do if this service is closing, sold, or pivoting to a different product? Do you have a reliable way of continuing to use it then? Will there be alternatives? Are there migration paths? Can you build abstractions that are good enough to change the underlying service in a hurry?
- **Roadmap misalignment:** Does the service have all the features you need now? Does it have all the features you will need once you scale? If it doesn't, can you be sure it will have those features at that point? Is there a chance this service's roadmap will undergo significant changes in the future?

Finding a Balance

With risks on both sides, how can you make a good decision? I recommend erring on the side of caution. In many cases, I found that to involve buying a solution rather than building it. Established SaaS businesses had run into a lot of the problems that you may encounter long before you even thought of adding this feature.

Know what you're worth. Do the math and weigh the risks carefully. Find the big players in the field that you consider building a solution for, look at their feature set, and see what you think may come back to bite you if you were to build it yourself. Then, plan how long this would take you to engineer. Think of where you'll be in five years. Will this solution still suffice? Or would you rather have other people iron out the kinds and bugs of that part of your solution?

Buying SaaS solutions won't make your business any less sellable either: acquirers have come to understand that the value of a company is in their core offering. Any non-core software they would need to maintain is a liability. Your business will be better off without hard-to-maintain components that other people have solved much better and cheaper somewhere else.

In general, if it's not a part of your core business, consider buying a solution. This means that you will have a large number of small services you'll be paying for over the years. That's fine. Every service you pay for is an overall reduction in the complexity of your solution. Your product should consist of the minimum logic to maximally solve your niche audience's most critical problem. Leave everything else to those who care more about addressing issues like authentication, payment, and invoicing. Concentrate on the things that make your business unique.

MAKING TECH CHOICES: DON'T ADD RISK TO A RISKY BUSINESS

As TECHNICAL FOUNDERS, we're supposed to choose the technology that works best for us and our business. But we often let the cargo-culting around the newest, hottest tech stack get to us. Many technical founders see a new startup as an opportunity to figure out a modern tech stack. That is a dangerous move. Not only do you have to deal with the inherently hazardous nature of creating a new business, but now there is also the chance that the new and mostly untested tech stack may not be able to solve the problem you're trying to solve.

The central question of choosing one particular technology over another is this: "Will you be able to use this well for a long time?"

There are three components to this question: your technical aptitude as a founder, your ability to use the technology for your particular purpose, and how you can minimize the chance of having to replace it later.

Founder-Technology Fit

When in doubt, stick to what you know. If you have built your last four projects with Laravel, the chances are that your business may benefit more from you getting up to speed quickly in Laravel than spending three months figuring out how to learn a different programming language like Golang. With new technology comes new paradigms and best practices, and it takes a long time to assimilate all this information.

When looking at a tech stack or service, ask yourself if you're able to evaluate it properly. You may know a lot about building SaaS tools. Still, you may not have the expertise to judge whether a particular database will perform better for the specific kind of data and query logic you will need for your service. For some technologies, you can run a little experiment. Others you will need to use for more extended periods to develop an understanding. Ask fellow founders about their experiences with any particular technology that you don't have any personal experience with yourself.

It may be tempting to choose to learn a new technology that supposedly is the perfect fit for your project. In rare cases, this is the right course of action, because the fit is just too good to be ignored. In most other cases, however, you're overestimating the technology and underestimating your own skills. If you can code using one technology, you will be able to build almost anything using the knowledge you already have. This will be your advantage. You can jump right into building the product without needing to learn anything new.

Purpose-Technology Fit

Particularly with newly available technology, you will often only see the "happy path," the use cases for which the technology has been developed. This can lead to blind spots in your evaluation: you just don't know what hasn't been discovered yet. Over time, these solutions will encounter edge cases and performance problems, which will eventually be resolved. But it's likely that you don't want to be the one discovering these problems and having to wait for a solution.

The more specific a technical solution, the more likely it will not be optimal for any usage patterns that lie outside this particular niche. Over-optimized solutions could look appealing, but the moment your business requirements change, you may be left with a technology that is unwieldy and unable to do the job.

For data storage systems like databases, use tried and tested systems like PostgreSQL unless your business absolutely needs a different kind of storage. Postgres has been adopting the right parts of NoSQL and Time Series databases over the last few versions, so there is no need to experiment with systems that may not scale well in production. You don't want to encounter performance bottlenecks because the system you're using has not been used at a specific scale before.

I have learned to look at generalists more favorably over time. I'm not talking about one-size-fits-all solutions here; I mean the kinds of technologies that have evolved from their edge-case-only usage toward more adaptable products. Redis, for example, is a generalist in the specialized niche of caching solutions. Most of the time, you recognize the generalists by the simplicity of the interface they offer. The more it looks like a collection of simple building blocks, the better.

I've fallen into the specialist trap before. When we started FeedbackPanda, I was looking for a cloud hosting provider capable of orchestrating Docker containers. I thought the big cloud providers were not specific enough with their hosted Kubernetes offerings, so I picked a small infrastructure startup that promised to allow interacting with Docker containers through their dashboards and GUIs instead of having to use command-line calls. I was thrilled and set up our production system on their platform. For a while, it went well, but then, their service experienced a few problems. Those little hiccups turned into full-on outages, lasting for hours. I had no choice but to move our production system onto a major cloud provider overnight. Ever since then, the system has run without a second of downtime. The more generalist option of a cloud-hosted Kubernetes turned out to be the more stable choice. And it turned out I could integrate the command-line calls much better into our release pipeline than the clicks on dashboards and user interfaces.

Going with a generalist solution could require more work on your end initially, but it will also reduce the number of surprises that may wait for you in the future. Often, generalists have many very different users, and therefore have to build systems that can handle a lot of different ways of being used. This results in resilient systems that can be made to fit individual purposes without making it harder for others to use them differently.

Technology Durability

One of the worst things that can happen to a SaaS business is when a crucial part of your tech stack breaks away at a later stage of your business. That is a risk that you can never fully get rid of, but you can minimize it.

To be on the safe side, choose popular technology. Many developers using a certain framework or stack will mean that more bugs are discovered over time, and this kind of software is often very well-maintained. The best way to quickly find out if a particular piece of software is popular is to look for documentation and educational resources. If there are a lot of tutorials and the technology seems well-documented at first glance, it will likely be around for quite a while.

Look for a vibrant community. I've noticed that in the Elixir/Phoenix community developers are very engaged, and they love spending time educating other developers about the intricacies of this functional programming language and the ecosystem.

When you're new to a programming language or just not as advanced as you need to be to solve your problem, you will have to learn the lay of the land before you can dive into building your product: what are the libraries you will need to use for certain parts? What are the best practices? Why are things done the way they are done? You'll learn all these things very quickly if there are excellent educational resources provided by the makers of the technology and the communities that form around it.

Maturity is also an essential property of good technology. If people have been using something for a few years, you can expect it to be reliable, mostly bug-free, and performant both for low- and high-usage patterns. There are often good indicators for the maturity of a technology: feature-completeness, ability to integrate with other solutions and workflows, and the breadth of use-cases it's been tested in. For databases, you will find that there are some tried and tested options like PostgreSQL, which has been around since 1996 and is being used in businesses of all sizes, including Netflix, Spotify, and Uber.

I made the mistake of building a business on an immaturely selected database once. I picked a fancy, newly developed NoSQL database that was lauded for its real-time capabilities by the early adopters. What I found out a few months into the development was that I really needed a relational database that was performant under a heavy query load. All the real-time features were irrelevant when I noticed that this new technology wasn't designed to handle the kind of usage that our application required. I learned a valuable lesson that day that I carried into FeedbackPanda: for your core technology, boring is better.

In general, I would advise against learning a new technology stack by building a business around it. There are two goals here, and they don't align well: building a stable business that will survive for a long time and learning a technology that may or may not be a passing fad. This extends to the services you use as well.

Remember the Docker hosting startups I mentioned above that we had to migrate away from in a hurry? They exhibited another risky behavior: uncertainty about the future presence of a service. At some point, after we had already migrated away, we received an email stating that they were shutting down the service, with two weeks' notice, urging all current customers to migrate their products elsewhere. Then, a few months later, we received another email stating that they'd found a new investor to help them restart their service. Now they asked customers to come back. While ridiculously unprofessional, this was an important lesson for me. There is a real risk in choosing imma- ture services and technologies.

Guidelines to Pick a Technology

Over the years, I have collected a list of attributes that tech- nology should exhibit to be a good fit. It doesn't have to have them all, but it should hit more marks than it misses. You'll have enough work on your hands from serving a niche audience with a likely ever-changing problem. You don't need to worry about your tech stack at the same time.

Technology that you can use well for a long time has these attributes:

- It can be used to solve your problem. You can find stories of how other businesses have used this technology to fulfill a similar need to yours. You can evaluate the technology without spending months of your time.

- It's popular. You find a lot of resources and opinions about it on the web. There are books on the technology for beginners and experts alike.
- It's surrounded by vibrant communities. There are forums, Twitter communities, whole Slack instances dedicated to the technology, and they're active.
- It's reliable. You can find a lot of established businesses that use it in their production systems without too many disaster stories.
- It's scalable. Small business and big businesses are using this technology.
- It's extensible. You can find a lot of libraries and integrations for the technology. You can also find information on how you can get them to work.
- It's mature. You can find a history of how the technology was adapted to fulfill the real needs of the people using it.
- It's well-maintained. You can find recent and regular updates to the service, either in a changelog or in the source code itself. People who report their problems are responded to, and their concerns addressed.
- It's replaceable. You can find alternatives to the technology that you can use in its stead should it become problematic or ineffective.

If a technology you're looking at checks all or most of these boxes, use it. If not, look for one that does. If you do this for all the choices you will need to make, you'll end up with a very maintainable collection of technologies that will stand the test of time.

FROM PRODUCT TO BUSINESS

A WELL-OILED MACHINE

A PRODUCT IS NOT A BUSINESS—JUST yet. That's an important thing to understand, particularly when you're a technical founder. It's the reason the book *The E-Myth* exists: the entrepreneurial myth is that if you build it, they will come. But they won't unless you put in the effort to create a reliable system to sell the product at a profit continuously: a business.

A business is more than a landing page, a product, and a bank account. A business is a complex system of processes. Building a product may come easy to you if you're technically inclined, but turning it into a value-generating machine is a whole different kind of challenge. Others may have trouble coming up with the product but thrive on building the structures needed to sell it over and over again.

In the initial phase of starting your bootstrapped business, you may think you don't need processes just yet. I argue that there are a few things that you should do strategically from the beginning, and turn future entrepreneurial actions into processes as soon as you can.

I realized this when I read *Built to Sell* by John Warrillow: a sellable business is a well-structured business. Nobody wants to buy a business that isn't easy to run. But you don't actually ever need to sell your sellable business. You can enjoy the benefits of an easy-to-operate company and keep it for yourself.

Ever since I understood that an organized business is a sellable business, I have made every effort to build a well-documented business that my partner Danielle and I could run by ourselves or hand over to someone else at any point. We eventually did that by selling the business after two years, but we could have just hired a few replacements and paid them to keep the business running.

FORGET GOALS, CREATE SYSTEMS: FOUNDATIONS OF A SUSTAINABLE BUSINESS

WHEN YOU'RE STARTING with your business idea, you will be looking at how successful businesses have accomplished their success. You will see a lot of different sizes, markets, and business models. But they all have one thing in common: they've built a system that works. Their long-term and short-term goals may have changed through the years, but the system that has kept them running never has. That system is the core of every business.

A sustainable bootstrapped business is successful when you have found a repeatable, reliable, and resilient system to continuously provide a value-producing product to paying customers at a profit.

Since "system" is such an abstract term: look at it as a set of rules and guidelines, like a recipe. To make a tasty omelet, you will need to mix the right ingredients and cook them for the right time, at the right temperature, using a specific technique. A business is the same. Having a recipe in place will make the transition from the Preparation Stage into the Survival Stage less chaotic. But, it's still important to think of the core growth engine of your business before you start selling your product to your audience.

A business without goals is an aimless venture. But goals are reached and exceeded. New goals arrive in their place, and they often change shape mid-operation. A goal is meant to become obsolete. A system is intended to endure and allow you to reach your goals in the first place.

Building a Repeatable System

When you're building a bootstrapped business, it will usually be just you in the beginning. Maybe you have a co-founder or two, but you won't have an army of salespeople that you can unleash on your audience. Your business needs to be a one-person-show, and that means you will need to sell your product to your customers over and over again yourself. For that, generating revenue needs to be an easily repeatable process.

At best, you're building a way to capture a never-ending stream of recurring revenue. The optimal situation is when you grow every month, and your revenue consistently increases. You will have reached that state when you create a subscription business with negative churn.

In a subscription-based business, churn is the percentage of customers that discontinue their subscriptions month over month. Churn hurts your growth twice. For each churned customer, you need to find a new customer just to get back to a net-zero. To grow, you effectively need two new customers. Negative churn happens when the customers who stay with your business spend more time on upgrades than you lose from customers canceling. That is the holy grail of subscription busi-nesses: when your churn is negative, you don't even need to add more customers to grow. Every new customer is a bonus!

But before you can get there, a lot of work needs to be done. You'll figure out a starting point for your pricing and tweak it over time. At some point, you will need to offer ways for your customers to upgrade their subscriptions. You'll need to keep your retention as high as possible and maximize the influx of new prospects.

All of this is so much easier if the process you need to acquire a new customer is straightforward and repeatable. That usually means automated and self-serve. If not, you'll need to make sales manually, which takes away attention from building your product and creating an automated and well-documented business that is built to sell.

The fewer steps there are to your process of acquiring a new customer, the better. Optimally, they come to your marketing content, sign up to your product, have their "a-ha" moment, and subscribe. Of course, each of these steps is incredibly hard to pull off, and that's the entrepreneurial challenge. Fewer steps mean fewer chances of losing your prospect, so keep the process slim.

Building a Reliable System

Providing a reliable service sounds easier than it is. You may have set up everything to be well-tested and highly available only to find that your payment provider has a small glitch that is affecting customers in a particular state. Or, your email service is being flagged as spam by an email provider like Google Mail so that all those emails you sent out yesterday never arrived in your customers' inboxes. These things happened to us at FeedbackPanda, and we had to find ways to circumvent these issues.

Being reliable doesn't mean being perfect. But it does mean that your product is built with maximizing availability and performance in mind. No customer wants to use a sluggish or unreliable product.

This required two kinds of reliability: architectural and

operational. Architectural reliability measures how well your service is designed to provide uninterrupted access to your product. Operational reliability measures the effectiveness of your systems to cope with external interruptions.

For every external service you use, do some research into their support forums, their status page, or on social media. Find previous occurrences of service outages, and check how quickly they were resolved. Pay particular attention to people complaining about not receiving help on social media, and reach out to them. Ask how they handled that situation. You will learn a lot about what you will need to prepare for that way.

In any case, create a process for reaching out to your customers when something goes wrong, because it will. Prepare a message stating that you're working on it, with an apology and the promise to get back to them as quickly as you can. Keep this message in a note where you can quickly copy it. It has two purposes: it reduces the cognitive effort of responding to customers during an emergency; and it allows your customers to spread a comprehensive message to their peers, reducing the number of incoming messages. Nothing is more distracting when you're trying to restore your production system than hundreds of customers reaching out about your product not working.

You can hope that you will never have a fatal outage. Or, you can prepare and build a reliable product and business. It may take some work, but having the bases covered will give you peace of mind when everything works fine and when things are a bit rough.

Building a Resilient System

Resiliency is different from reliability in that it looks at your business over a long time instead of being focused on mere moments. A resilient business is capable of surviving in an ever-changing market. Today, you may have hundreds of customers, but some regulations make 90% of them cancel tomorrow. If you set up your business to be resilient, you will be able to survive situations like this.

A resilient business is independent. If you have 500 customers, one of them quitting is not a big deal. If you have five customers, a single cancellation can cost you 20% or more of your revenue. It's hard to diversify when you're in a very homogenous niche. You can build resiliency into your niche product by offering yearly subscriptions, as this will capture advance revenue that allows you to make the necessary changes to adapt to different circumstances.

A resilient business is adaptive. If your payment processor shuts down your account or freezes your funds, your system should be able to integrate an alternative processor quickly. You have enough data in your database to restore your revenue: you know which plans your users were on and when they were supposed to renew. They may need to re-enter their payment data, but at least the continuity of their subscription is guaranteed that way. The same is true for authentication. Always have their email address in your database, even if you use an Identity-as-a-Service solution. In case that breaks, you can still reach your customers.

A resilient business is extensible. If you can be integrated easily, your service will become part of the broader ecosystem of tools in your niche. More and more other services will interact with you, bringing with them a steady flow of new leads and reputation within the community. If your processes allow you to quickly build integrations into new and exciting services in your niche as well, your product will provide your customers with additional ways of making their lives easier.

Your business and your product should be around for a long

time. Processes and architectural decisions that increase resilience will make sure it has a chance to endure.

There are several advanced concepts to help entrepreneurs structure their businesses. While most of them are aimed at larger enterprises, the Entrepreneurial Operating System (EOS) has been used successfully in many bootstrapped companies. It aligns and strengthens the six key components of any business: the alignment between your vision; the real-world data; your people; your critical issues; your processes that systemize consistency; and traction to bring discipline and accountability into your business. It's definitely a good system to look into from the beginning to see how you want your future business to be structured in the future, what needs to be prepared, and what kinds of changes you can expect to encounter.

The Evolution of a System

A repeatable, reliable, and resilient system will need to be continuously refined and improved. Your customers will change their methods. New regulations and requirements will need a response. This is the heart of your operation. It must never stop working. Every day, it must deliver as much as or more than the day before.

It will take some fine-tuning. You will never be done making sure it's working correctly. Every time something inside or outside your business changes, you may need to adjust your system. It doesn't always have to be bad: sometimes, you will be able to remove a step because a new technology enables you to fully automate a previously manual action.

As long as you regularly check in with your processes and assumptions, your system will work for you. When you start feeling some friction where there was none before, you're starting to work for the system. Reflect on what has changed, how to respond to it with your current knowledge, and adjust your process. You've been doing your marketing on Facebook, but customers come through Instagram more and more? Adjust. Extend your Facebook campaigns also to be shown on Instagram, or engage a test audience with visual content that you have made particularly for their platform. If that works, you will slowly shift your focus to that new platform, and adjust your content processes to fit that one best.

Over time, the number and complexity of your processes will likely grow. At the beginning of your business, you want to be flexible, but don't mistake that for winging it. Write down what you do and why you do it, so that you can eventually turn your evolving system into a collection of Standard Operating Procedures. Having everything documented that way will make your company a well-oiled machine, and that will make it more sellable, even if you don't intend to sell.

YOUR INITIAL PRICING WILL NEVER
BE RIGHT, BUT TRY ANYWAY

WHEN YOU'RE JUST STARTING, finding the right pricing model for your young business seems very hard and almost entirely arbitrary. That's because, at such an early stage of your business, it is impossible to find the "correct" price for several reasons.

At the beginning of your business, revenue serves one purpose before any other: validation. A paying customer is validating multiple things at the same time. They are saying that your product is good enough to solve their problem, they are saying that it provides more value than it costs, and they are saying that their problem is painful enough to pay for a solution. With that one payment, product, value, and problem are validated.

That's why the price is only secondary. As long as it is not higher than the value of the product, it will be sufficient to allow for business validation. It may not be the perfect price, and you may leave money on the table, but at that stage, it only matters to show that the business works. Early pricing validates your business and initial product. Later pricing optimizes overall revenue.

There are three rules to early pricing: it's never perfect, it can be changed, and it should be aspirational.

Particularly when you are building a complicated product, you will have to start with a slimmed-down version of your final vision. It will only contain the basic features, the functionality that is needed to show what problem the product solves at its core. But your price should reflect the value of your full vision. That is because you are selling to a particular kind of customer: the early adopter.

The Psychology of Pricing for Early Adopters

Regular customers look at a product, calculate the immediate value they would receive, compare that to the price, and purchase if the benefit significantly outweighs the cost. If a product promises to be better in the future, they dismiss this as a purchase risk. "Majority customers" buy in the here and now; they are customers anchored in the present.

Early adopters or their even more radical peers, the innovators, don't think like that. They make purchasing decisions on what things could become. They will buy an electric car even though the charging infrastructure may not yet be there for it: they trust that the network effect will take care of that if enough people get involved. These customers buy for the future; they are anchored in the hope and trust that the things they purchase will turn out to be great.

And that final state is what they see when they look at the first quirky version of your product. They see it for what it could become, not for what it lacks. And they will pay for what they believe it will be. Of course, there is a lot of nuanced thinking going into such a purchasing decision, but you can be sure that the innovators and early adopters in your market will pay a premium for a product that breaks new ground.

Here's the catch: you will have to live up to the expectations you set with your price. And you'll have to do that rather quickly. The early customers may become your biggest supporters and marketing channels if you do it right. If you fail to fulfill your promise, they will soon pack up their things and move to another promising product.

It's important to think of your price as a very fluid number with a lot of flexibility. It is not set in stone. What matters is the value you provide to your customers.

Value Metrics: How to Measure the Value You Provide

Your price should reflect what you think the value of using your product is for your customers. This is tricky, as software products are continually evolving, and the value they generate evolves with the product. A good strategy to measure the value you provide to your customers is to determine their central value metric and measuring that.

What is a value metric? It is the most relevant metric that goes up when your customer's business is doing well. For an image hosting service, it is the number of images uploaded. For a music streaming business, it's the number of times their songs were streamed. For a team-building service, it's the number of team-building exercises successfully finished. If your customers are barbers, it's the number of beards they can shave in a day.

The point is: if that number goes up, they make more money. And if that number goes up, you should make more money, too. If you use tiered pricing, splitting the tiers among certain economically sensible limits of that value metric will make a big difference in your revenue.

Price Acceptance: Purchasing Power and Jobs-to-Be-Done

Be aware that the acceptance of your price levels also depends on the purchasing power of your audience. Selling to large enterprise companies will allow you to charge much more than when you're selling to online teachers who are working two jobs.

What you need to find out is how much it costs them right now to solve this problem. Do they have a solution already? If they do, what are they paying for it? If they don't, how much time does it take them to do it themselves? How much would that be worth?

One approach that always helps with determining this number is the jobs-to-be-done framework. It states that every product or service replaces something else, but not necessarily the same kind of thing. Imagine a software product that provides AI-generated technical drawings. It may not just replace another software, but make a whole position in the company superfluous: that of the technical draftsman. With one purchase, the company could save $100,000 or more in a year. Now imagine a CRM system that has specific features that automate the work that was usually done by unpaid interns or a half-automated task that is run once a month. How much does that save the company?

For FeedbackPanda, we knew that the purchasing power of our customer base was reasonably low. They weren't paying for any solution yet, so they weren't budgeting for a tool like ours. The resource that teachers invested was their free time, which they valued surprisingly little. So, we chose to price our product at a point that reflected what online teachers would make by teaching just one more hour per month. That turned out to be a very acceptable term for teachers, and it held true when we increased our prices by 50% only one year into the business.

Find out the way the problem is solved now, and figure out what resources are invested in it. That will heavily determine if your price is acceptable or not.

The Problem of Underpricing

Significantly underpricing your product will create a few problems down the road. While it will likely get you a lot of customers initially, many of them will be very price-sensitive. In general, bottom-of-the-barrel customers are hard to deal with, as they will want to squeeze the most value out of your customer support and your product for the lowest price.

Once you raise prices later, even a little, those customers could be very vocal about their disappointment. While there are ways to deal with that, like time-limited subscription grandfathering, you'll be limiting yourself from the beginning, and you will surround yourself with customers you don't want.

Price always communicates value. By pricing a product surprisingly low, you are saying that it is worth very little. That will scare away customers who are looking for high-quality products. Those are the customers you want because they are invested in making the product better and allowing it to thrive.

The Problem of Overpricing

Overpricing your product, on the other hand, is not as bad. You're communicating that you think your product is worth it, you indicate that it is a professional tool, something for experts, for the people who know what they are doing.

Don't underestimate the signaling value of price, particularly in crowded markets. The moment you are substantially cheaper than other products, customers who care about quality will think you're worse. The moment you're more expensive, those customers may start paying attention and check out your product.

With a high-price product, you only need a fraction of the number of customers to become sustainable. And you can always lower your prices if customers disagree with your value proposition. Don't be afraid to charge more, particularly in the beginning. You may think that your product isn't fully finished yet, but that is no reason not to charge the full value that people are ready to pay. For your customers, the result of using your product is what they pay for.

Another Thing to Try

If you don't have any customers yet, be bold with your price. Zero customers paying $20 might as well be zero customers paying $50. See if you can find the early adopters that are looking for a quality product in the future by showing them your sincere attempt to build one through a higher price.

Find a good initial price for your product. If you offer subscriptions, be sure to provide a yearly subscription option, at a slightly reduced price, from the beginning. Those subscriptions are an excellent signal for how much people think your product will be part of their lives. The moment someone commits to a year, you know that you are solving a critical problem well enough.

Don't forget that, ultimately, initial pricing is all about validating your business, product, vision, and what your market is willing to pay. Start with a reasonable price that is not too high to be insulting, not too low to suggest low quality, and shows your ambition to build a world-class product to solve the critical problem of your audience.

DO YOU NEED A CO-FOUNDER?

BUILDING a business alone can be daunting. You might lack a few skills; in fact, I am sure you do. There is a lot to learn when you start a company, and you will never stop running into unexpected challenges that require the acquisition of new skills and knowledge.

So, should you find someone to make all of this easier?

A partner, an equal, a co-founder?

Some founders are lone wolves and thrive on overcoming the daily challenges. Other founders want to work on the things they enjoy and leave the other stuff to someone who is better suited to that work.

Some founders want to live a life of responsibility and share none of the spoils, while others want to work in a more relaxed way and split the profit with like-minded people.

Do you need a co-founder? Not necessarily. But your business will benefit immensely from having a co-founder.

If you are a solo founder, you just do what's right. With co-founders, you have to justify your choices, or at least achieve alignment about them. Choosing to build a company with another person can be a challenge. All of a sudden, responsibility and accountability are part of every decision. For some people, that is very easy, while others may have a hard time. It boils down to one core component: communication.

Communicators First, Founders Second

If you are looking for a co-founder, look for someone who can communicate well with you. No matter how different your skill levels are, you can work together well if you know each other's goals and methods. That requires you to make sure that you're aligned regularly. That can only happen if you speak to each other face-to-face.

I had a co-founder once who would only talk to me when they felt that I was lagging behind on my work. Before that, they were incommunicado: they didn't reach out, didn't ask if I needed their input, they seemed not to understand the subtleties of technical work, and they never tried to learn them. As a result, my own frequency of communication decreased, as I got more and more annoyed with their apparent detachment. The business went nowhere.

Communication is a trust-building activity. When you don't understand something in the business, you will need to make sure you talk to your co-founder and find a common understanding. You don't need to be an expert in everything they do. However, you should have a solid grasp of the why and the how of their contributions to your business.

Personality Alignment (and Why It Shouldn't Involve Beer)

There is the saying in the startup community that you should find someone to have a beer with, but this rarely ever translates into an excellent entrepreneurial relationship. Sure, it's great to work with a friend, but there is no connection between socializing and working together successfully. Particularly with entrepreneurial people, social drinking can mean completely different things: a mostly introverted thinker may avoid these events, while an extroverted networker thrives on those situations. If "having a drink" means "having a meaningful discussion about your potential impact on the problems of the world," that's another story. But don't look for someone with whom you can have a beer. You don't want to miss out on a great co-founder because they prefer a glass of wine.

Find someone with whom you can solve a problem. Both of you should get excited at the prospect of tackling a complicated and annoying issue. This tendency is the core indicator of the entrepreneur: we can't look at a problem without wanting to solve it immediately. If your co-founder does not express any kind of interest in solving real problems but is more interested in "playing startup" or toying around with technology, be very careful. Their drive to get through the painful parts of your entrepreneurial journey might fizzle out very quickly.

Find someone who is equally excited when they talk about their work and who will glowingly speak about your business when they're asked what they are doing. Even the most introverted character can capture the attention of a crowd with their enthusiastic portrayal of how you are impacting the lives of hundreds of customers. You want a co-founder that will do this at least as well as you do. If they lack the passion for your business when they speak to others, how much passion can they have for it when they talk to themselves?

Empowerment Alignment

When you start talking to potential co-founders, find out how much they care about empowering people. That's a good indicator for several important things: their willingness to help your customers, their focus on building a problem-solving product, and their perspective on building and enabling a great team inside the business.

Empowering people is at the core of entrepreneurship. Co-founders have to empower each other to do their best work. This is so much easier if they have a burning desire to make the world a better place for everyone.

If your co-founder cares as much as you do, you are aligned along a fundamental axis. They may be more into marketing or development than you are, but their real goal is to build something that lifts everyone. And that is what you want from a business that lasts.

Skill Alignment

When it comes to the skill set, you can go either way. It doesn't matter if you are polar opposites, clones of each other, or anything in between.

Complementary skills are excellent and allow for separation of concern. Now you can work in parallel, with every founder focusing on their strengths. But in the end, you will both need to do work that lies outside your comfort zone. Make sure to lay out the responsibilities for that kind of work from the beginning, so there are no "I thought that is your job" discussions when it comes to working on things you both don't enjoy.

If there is plenty of skill overlap, that can help your business too. Two sales-focused founders can sell twice as much. If both founders like to code, the codebase will be built maintainable and team-compatible from the beginning. The challenge of this constellation is not to step on each other's toes. You will need to be precise in the responsibilities of each founder and how to resolve conflicts, both in work and in the direction of the business. Follow the approach laid out in Michael E. Gerber's *E-Myth Revisited* and create an organizational chart for what you think your business will look like in five years, then add one founder to every position on the chart. That will allow you to pre-determine who has the final say about what.

As long as the lines between the founders are clear, then having excellent communication will allow you to create a company where people respect and listen to each other.

The Perils of Being a Solo Founder

If you want to go at it alone, that is okay, too. Just be aware that there is no one to help you when you're sleeping or sick. As a solo founder, you are the company. Unless you can outsource or delegate work to employees, you are responsible for all things. It could mean a few years of all-day-every-day dedication to your business before you can hire people to help you out with these things.

If you have read the *4-Hour Workweek*, you may have the goal of building an automated business that won't take much of your time. That may be the result of your entrepreneurial journey, but the beginning phases will need much more time and attention. Be prepared to spend significant time on your business when you go at it alone.

You will need to build systems to deal with the high amounts of work much faster than with a co-founder. After all, a co-founder can take over things when you're traveling. They can help out when you're indisposed. Without a co-founder, you won't have that luxury. Automating and documenting your internal processes becomes a front-of-mind action that is highly important to staying sane as a solo founder. It will also make it much easier to hand over the reins of the company at some later stage of the business.

Things to Look Out for When Vetting a Co-Founder

There are a few things to look out for when considering working with another founder. You will both be interested in growing the business and deriving monetary value from it. This can get problematic if you're misaligned on a few axes.

Contribution Asymmetry

If you found a company with someone who has an excellent network for you to sell into, you run into the risk of doing all the work yourself, because they may feel they bring enough to the table by already having the network. Assuming that shares are distributed equally, both founders should work equally hard on the business. This could get quite complicated if your co-founder came into the company as a source of capital. How much work do a few thousand dollars genuinely represent? Be very clear in your communication what is expected of each founder.

Wealth Asymmetry

If there is a noticeable difference in wealth levels between your co-founder and you, your decision-making may be impacted very differently by your drive to generate profits. If you're living on a shoe-string budget yourself, you may want your business to be ramen-profitable as quickly as possible. A co-founder with a sizeable financial safety net may look at more long-term profitability. Neither perspective is necessarily wrong, as both lead to positive business results. Be very clear about the near-term expectations when starting the business. Find something that works for all founders.

Unequal Share Distribution

Often when founders look for co-founders, they already have been thinking about their business for a long time. They may even have built a prototype or have paying customers. At that point, it is quite unlikely that they will opt for a 50/50 share distribution with a new co-founder, as they took a substantial risk in getting the business this far. At that point, no founder is willing to part with half the company easily.

Usually, the co-founder gets a minority of the shares that is large enough to warrant them still being considered founders. I have seen everything from 49.9% down to 5%. Be aware that your co-founder's interest in building the company into a profitable business may not be the same when they only own 5% of the shares. Imagine selling the business for $1million: they would only get $50k while you would get the remaining $950k. These results are worlds apart, and while you may be financially secure for the rest of your life, your co-founder can maybe afford to scrape a few years off their 30-year mortgage. These are entirely different incentives. Be sure that both of you are fine with the distribution of your shares.

Vesting Expectations

At the beginning of a founder relationship, things are usually looking great. You get started working on the business. Things begin to happen, and progress is made. You're confident in your co-founder, and they are working with a lot of passion and drive. But who is to say this will last for more than a few weeks? You can't know, and because of that, you should look into a vesting schedule for their shares. In VC-funded startups, vesting schedules are usually multi-year, as the momentum required to become a unicorn startup with $1 billion or more in valuation takes a few years to aggregate into speeds that allow for explosive growth. For a bootstrapped business, this timeline could be a bit of a stretch: you don't have a runway, your business is a risky endeavor. I recommend a vesting schedule that starts after six months and then vests a part of the shares every quarter. This allows for dealing with contingencies and changes in the business landscape.

Outlook Asymmetry

If you are a bootstrapper, you will be looking for a co-founder that wants to go down the bootstrapped route, too. But what if they change their mind? What if they push for outside investment, derailing your efforts to build a sustainable business that has no investors telling you what to do? This needs to be very clear between the founders. Some entrepreneurs see bootstrapping as the initial phase of a business, and some see it as the optimal state for the lifetime of a company. Make sure you're aligned here before you enter into any agreements.

The same goes for eventually selling the business. While most people entertain the idea of the big exit, some founders don't care about it. This can lead to unpleasant surprises when you get that call or email with a life-changing offer, and your co-founder shrugs it off. Make sure you work toward the same business goals.

Finding a co-founder that shares your passion and sees eye-to-eye with you on the future of the business can be the most incredible thing. Carefully vet your candidates and make sure that you can communicate well. Check for alignment on how vital empowerment is to the both of you.

And, have a beer with them if you must.

THE SURVIVAL STAGE

THE SURVIVAL STAGE AND YOU

RELEASING a product for the first time is like jumping into a lake: the water might be too cold, and you don't know what to expect. But once you've jumped, you'll get used to the temperature quickly, and you'll be having a great time swimming around.

Usually, founders launch their product way too late. They tinker around for months and months, trying to get things perfectly right. Some never start because they always find something else to build, just in case. Several things need to be healthy to build a business that thrives and survives.

A business can only be as healthy as its founder. If you're struggling with stress and anxiety, things will start slipping through the cracks, further increasing the chaos. But you can prepare. You'll learn about the mental traps and uncomfortable conversations you will encounter and how to prepare for them.

The Survival Stage is the time to turn your prototype into a quality product by building the right things and building things right. We'll look into improving your product slowly and deliberately without adding more complexity than absolutely needed. If you work on keeping the product slim and focused, you'll have a much easier time maintaining and extending your product later.

The moment you have customers, they will start talking to you. You'll learn how to help your users most efficiently without getting distracted from working on your product and business. We will also take a look at the kinds of pricing strategies that could work for your business, which ones could be dangerous, and how to find more customers for your services.

In this stage, everything will be a rapid product iteration. Your goal will be to build resilient systems to deal with the complexity of operating a business while looking for reliable and repeatable processes to guarantee a profitable engine of sustainable growth. You will work on helping customers first to find the product and then to find their way through it.

MENTAL HEALTH: IT'S NOT OPTIONAL

WHY YOUR MENTAL HEALTH MATTERS

RUNNING A COMPANY IS HARD. Running a bootstrapped company is particularly hard. Unlike a company with funding, every decision you make has an impact on the immediate survival of your business. That can take a toll if you're not prepared.

You will need to take care of your mental health, at all times. I've made the mistake of ignoring the signs of stress, anxiety, and burnout. It took a lot of effort to dig myself out of that hole. It left a few scars, and I still feel jolts of anxiety when I hear certain notification sounds long after selling my business.

Learning about how to deal with perfectionism, impostor syndrome, and similar psychological hurdles will make you resilient to self-sabotage. In the end, the only person that truly stands in the way of your success is yourself. You will learn how you can give yourself permission to not be perfect, to do things a bit beyond your expertise, and to go against the grain where others don't.

Understanding that your work as an entrepreneur may also lead to social headaches will allow you to prepare for uncomfortable situations and conversations, and to focus on what matters most: building a life-changing bootstrapped business. People around you may not understand what you're trying to do, and there are ways to prepare for those encounters.

When you keep your mind healthy, your business can thrive. Don't fall for the hustle-or-die mentality. You can be a normal human being and run a business. You don't need to be the flawless superhuman that people often project to be. I definitely never felt superhuman when I ran FeedbackPanda with Danielle. Together, we managed to not ruin the business. But we had our down days, our doubts, and our mistakes. That was to be expected, and it was on those occasions that we learned the most, about running a company and about ourselves.

You will be fine. Trust in your abilities and give yourself the mental tools to weather the storms of running a business.

REAL AND IMAGINARY
RESPONSIBILITIES OF A
BOOTSTRAPPED FOUNDER

As a FOUNDER, you will encounter many expectations. Founders have to have a mission. They have to care about their customers genuinely. A great founder is a leader, a visionary, an expert.

Sometimes you just want to be you—the entrepreneur who had a good idea for a business and then worked on it diligently. You don't need to be a hero. You just want to run your business.

And still, you feel like you're not meeting expectations. You feel like you could do more to help your customers. Give more back to your community. Others know so much more about your industry. Everyone else is doing things differently.

Welcome to the world of imaginary responsibilities.

Every founder feels them. They creep into your mind when you see yet another business that is doing better than yours while browsing Twitter.

They invade your dreams because you listened to that podcast with the super-successful guest just before bed. They had so much fun laughing and talking about their successes, and you're sitting there, thinking you're just an impostor.

There are a few main themes that come up once in a while.

Learn to recognize them, learn to focus on what is real, and ignore the imaginary.

Perfectionism

You have been building this cool new feature. It works on your development system, and it will be impressive once you release it. But the user interface can still use some work.

You know that a few of your more technically illiterate users have had trouble with complicated interfaces, and you want to make sure that every single one of your customers gets some value out of the system. So, you spend another week polishing the UI.

Then, you notice that the documentation you wrote for the feature could use a few more clarifying videos. So, you spend another week creating walkthrough videos for every single way customers may use the product.

Then, you notice something else. And another thing. You end up never releasing the feature.

Welcome to perfectionism. It will keep you from achieving your goals.

"I have to build the perfect business."

The perfect business doesn't exist. Any business is a dynamic enterprise, a thing that you do, not a thing you have. Nothing in your business will ever be perfect, as there is always room for improvement.

Rephrase this into "I want to build a sustainable business. I want to live a good life, and provide a solution that will help people." Set your goals to something you can control, not some platonic ideal of a business. A working product does not have to be perfect. It just has to work well enough to be useful.

Don't stress. Approach your business with the Pareto principle, the rule of 80/20: the last 20% of your work will take up 80% of the time. Save yourself from wasting your time like that. Get 80% of it done, and deal with the rest if (and only if) it is needed.

Focus on long-term goals and create traction, both within your own life and with your market. Every action you take needs to have a real impact on whom you want to serve. Don't focus on details that only a few customers may ever see. Work on things that lift all of your customers at the same time.

Usually, the most impactful things are also the hardest things to do. Start with those things. Don't take the low-hanging fruit. It is usually the first thing your competitors will also pick. Go for the things they fear to tackle. Do this often. That is how you will stay ahead even if things don't seem perfect.

"I have to create the ultimate solution for all the problems my customers have."

If there were all-encompassing solutions, we would only drive one car. We would eat one kind of cheese and use one type of shampoo. But we don't. We have choices because we have different priorities, and excellent products take that into account.

Rephrase this into "I want to provide value to my customers that makes their lives easier." They don't expect you to solve all of their problems. A Swiss Army knife is great, but you don't see mechanics use it to repair cars, or chefs to filet a fish. Special tasks need special tools, and that is true for almost everything people do, in both their personal and their professional lives.

Do one thing really well. Focus on the critical problem that your customers have. They may have additional issues, but you should focus on the most critical one. Once that is solved, you can look into other problems. Not before.

The more you're spread out with your products, the less you

will impact the lives of your customers. You will need to make choices about which product deserves your attention, starving all the others. Particularly in the beginning, focus on one specific problem and solve that problem alone. Your attention to detail will be a differentiator to all those Swiss Army knives that look great but are ultimately disappointing.

Impostor Syndrome

You've been thinking a lot about your bootstrapped business. You did the research, built a prototype, talked to prospective customers, and worked their feedback into your MVP.

Then, one day, you read an article about your target industry, and you stop reading in the middle of the page. You know you did all this research, but you feel like you don't have any idea what is going on in the industry. There is so much more you need to learn before you can start your business.

You definitely need to read more books. There are so many podcasts you still need to listen to. You end up learning forever and never start your business.

Welcome to impostor syndrome. It will keep you from achieving your goals.

"I feel like I'm not good enough to create something great."

In a time of life-long learning, we'll never be finished learning. So, we may as well start creating things sooner rather than later. Just like learning never ends, neither does perfecting the product. When you start, it may not be great. But it is something. And that alone sets you apart.

Rephrase this into "I can start with something that works." The fact that you are working on a solution to someone's problem already sets you apart from everyone else. Most people don't even start. They are caught up in the belief that if they learn just one more thing, they will be ready. They never are.

Any improvement over the status quo is good. Don't let the VC siren calls of "it needs to be an order of magnitude better" lull you into thinking that if you don't disrupt the whole industry, you won't be adding value. Value-add starts with the smallest things. If you add enough value enough times, you will make a significant impact on the lives of your customers.

Start with what you know. Create something that you think is useful. Then go out and talk to the customers. Get their feedback and adjust. Repeat until you have found the solution. Repeat this until you have made something great.

"I have to be the most knowledgeable expert in the domain."

Sometimes, you look at your audience and feel intimidated. Here are people who have worked in their positions for decades. They know the ins and outs of their business, and they have seen many vendors come and go. You feel this fear that if you are not just as much an expert as they are, they won't even look at you.

Rephrase this into "I need to know enough to help." Expertise takes time, and it takes experience. You can't read up on experience. You will have to get it yourself by working for your customers.

You will become an expert by trying. If you succeed, that is great. You have a fantastic business, and your life will be improved significantly. If your business fails, you will now be an expert in the field. You know the size of the market. You have developed a sense of where the problems are, what solutions you can create, and how to talk to people in the industry. You can start a new company or consult people who do. It is a win-win situation.

Expertise comes from experience. Do the work. Spend the time. There is no better place to learn than right in the thick of things. Jump into the deep end and keep swimming. You will learn so much in such a short amount of time.

Most importantly: you are not a fraud. Real impostors don't suffer from impostor syndrome.

Cargo-Culting

You read that bootstrapped founders do things a certain way. They never take funding, so you swear you will never take funding. They talk to customers at all times, so you take every opportunity to speak to your customers at all times. This is what bootstrappers do. They iterate quickly on their product, so you try and release a new feature every few days. They go to conferences, so you fly all across the world to talk to your peers. You notice that everyone seems to be crushing it. You redouble your efforts, and you spend more time on your business. This is what bootstrappers do. You have not seen daylight for a few weeks, your children only see you hunched over your laptop, and you haven't called your parents in over three months. You keep doing this until you burn out.

Welcome to cargo-culting. It will keep you from achieving your goals.

"I have to do everything by myself because I'm a solopreneur, and that is what they do."

The term solopreneur is aspirational for many people who want to start a business—keeping all the profits! Never having to explain yourself! Full control over every aspect of the company! And then reality hits, you run into brick walls, your energy levels are depleted, and you don't enjoy work anymore. That's not what you want.

Reframe this as "I can get people to join my cause when I am overwhelmed." Humans love to join things that have a purpose. People want to be part of missions, and they want to help. Don't think you have to do everything alone. You won't, and you can't. At some point, you will need other people.

Delegating work to others can free you up in many ways. It's not just about your time. It is about your focus and your potential. Any task you don't want to do is a task that keeps you from taking care of something that you want to accomplish. Interruptions will slow you down and deter you from reaching your goals.

We waited much too long with hiring people at Feedback-Panda. I was taking care of development and customer service. Incoming help requests constantly interrupted my product work. I still get PTSD-like symptoms from the Intercom notification sound that indicated a new customer service conversation. The moment we hired a customer support person, and they took that workload off me, my head was clear again within days. I could focus again. And it turns out that other people are better at customer service than I am. They would keep calm and help where I frantically apologized and overwhelmed customers with technical details. Delegating will make the experience better for you and your customers.

"I have to risk burnout because successful people work hard."

Hustle porn is everywhere. People show off their accomplishments on social media and in the founder communities. Businesses hit their goals and milestones left, right, and center. Everyone is crushing it, and rarely do you hear of anyone struggling. But you struggle all the time. Is there something wrong with you? No one else seems to have these issues.

Reframe this as "I have to take care of my mental health." A business will struggle if its founder struggles. There will be ups, and there will be downs. People don't usually talk about the bad parts. Only recently have I seen founders share their tales of struggle and defeat in public spaces. It is a great start, but the stories of glory and success still prevail.

Burnout is not a badge of honor. It is a medical condition. It's a state you don't ever want to experience. When you are burned out, you lose your drive. You are exhausted; you lose the joy of your work, and your performance suffers. It takes a long time to get out of that state.

I had experienced burnout twice before, once when I was working for a VC-funded company in Silicon Valley and then later when growing FeedbackPanda. In both cases, it took me a long time to recover. Finding the motivation to work is hard when the sound of an email triggers a mild panic attack. That is not a good place for a founder.

Working hard does not mean working long hours. You can be productive by working smarter. Delegate tasks that irritate you to people who love doing them. Automate away things that don't need your direct involvement. Then move to other repetitive tasks. Repeat until your workload is manageable.

Here is the thing about responsibilities: they are all in your mind. Sure, you may have contracts and obligations, but what you focus your attention on is determined by your thoughts. The expectations you set are all in your head. Once you become aware that the only thing standing in the way of your success is yourself, it becomes so much easier.

Don't fall for being perfect. Don't doubt yourself. Don't do things because that is the way things are or have been done.

Just be your authentic self, ready, and eager to learn. That is an excellent foundation for a sustainable business that helps real people with their real problems.

PRODUCT EVOLUTION: CONTROLLED GROWTH AND SAYING NO

BUILDING A PRODUCT UNDER CONSTRAINTS

Once you have started selling a product, you'll want to make sure it gets better and better at serving your customers.

In theory, that means inventing new features and improving upon the old. In reality, founders that don't focus much on controlling the growth of their product turn it from a slim and focused offer into a bloated monster.

Saying "no" to feature requests becomes a necessary skill to learn. In addition to making sure only the features that genuinely provide more value to the customers make it into the product, you'll also need to make sure you build them in a way that allows you to change or remove them when needed. What is required today may be obsolete or harmful tomorrow. Maintaining the product with that thought in mind requires doing certain things a certain way.

Bootstrapping a business means saying "no" to the non-essential things. Your resources are limited, so you have to prioritize the actions and choices that have the most impact. For your product, that means being aware of all your options, weighing their relative potential, and choosing the ones that provide the most value.

Additionally, setting up your product and infrastructure with a healthy measure of abstractions and flexibility will guarantee that you can make those choices reliably over time. If you take care to establish these practices from the start, evolving your product efficiently will be that much easier.

BUILDING THE RIGHT THINGS

THE EVOLUTION OF THE "WHAT"

WHEN IT COMES to making things better, it's essential to understand where to start. You want to figure out which items are more critical and which requests may sound vital but are not.

The longer you're in business, the more your customers will ask for features. It's just human nature: we want things to improve and are rarely happy with the status quo. For someone with limited resources, this means you will have to prioritize. You will learn about several prioritization frameworks, what they're good at, and how you can use them for your business.

Every product-related decision boils down to whether it adds value to your business, your customers' lives, and your own. Managing a product can be overwhelming, and what seems like a good idea at the time often turns out to not work at all. You will learn how to quickly and easily distinguish value-adding features from vanity projects. That way, you can make sure you're building a business that provides as much value as possible.

FIRST THINGS FIRST: FEATURE PRIORITIZATION FRAMEWORKS

A BUSINESS IS AN EVER-EVOLVING THING. As the founder of your business, you will adjust your processes as needed along the way, and you will improve your product over time.

Often, inspiration strikes at the most random times: when you read an article on an industry blog, or you listen to a podcast with someone who fits your customer profile. Other times, your users contact you and tell you that they need an integration for another service, or that they had to change their workflow due to a new law that came into effect.

At any given time during the course of your business, you will have a long list of things you could build: new functionality, improvements, bug fixes, optimizations. In short, you have a collection of features that don't yet exist.

Often, that list contains work for weeks or even months. But your day only has 24 hours. And if you want to get anywhere, you need to start working on something today.

There are several proven frameworks to help you prioritize which features to build for maximizing your outcomes. These are systems that businesses have developed to deal with features in a structured and methodical way. All these approaches attempt to remove uncertainty and quantify desirability in a way that works for every business.

Why Is Prioritization So Hard?

When you are both the technician and the manager of your business, you will look at problems from two opposing viewpoints. The engineer in you loves a challenging problem—even more so, when it's something you care about. The entrepreneur in you only wants to work on things that add value to the business and the lives of your customers. Engineers don't like boring solutions, and entrepreneurs don't like technical gadgets. That one cool interface component you always wanted to build? It's probably not the most impactful thing you can do for your business right now.

Entrepreneurs are notoriously bad at quantifying effort; we're mostly guessing when it comes to estimates. Cognitive biases make it even harder: our willingness to build something makes it feel more achievable, while features we don't want to work on feel like they require more effort.

Another thing we often discount is how easily we get excited. Entrepreneurs are life-long learners, and we're curious about things that are new and challenging. Projects that we have pondered for a long time start losing their appeal when something new and shiny enters our vision. That's why prioritization systems can help us overcome our prejudices and biases.

Feature Prioritization: Scoring

Many companies use some sort of scoring to prioritize their feature development. For that, a feature is looked at from several perspectives, and given a number. A final score is then aggregated to balance out all the component factors.

Intercom uses the **RICE method**, which scores Reach, Impact, Confidence against Effort.

- **Reach** is measured directly from product metrics, expressed as a number of people or events over time. "Customers per quarter" or "transactions per month" are the units for this score. It expresses how many users this feature will affect.
- **Impact** quantifies how much a given feature enables you to reach a business goal. How much does the feature move the needle? As this is not easily expressed as a continuous number, use normalized figures to represent anything from "massive impact (3)" to "medium (1)" down to "minimal impact (0.25)."
- **Confidence** is a percentage that expresses how confident you are in your estimates about this feature. Do you know exactly what awaits you? 100%. Is it a wild guess? 20%. The more you know about the complexity and expectations related to this feature, the higher the score.
- **Effort** is the time needed for a feature, measured in "person-months," the time a single person needs to work on the project to complete it.

To compute the final RICE score, multiply Reach, Impact, and Confidence, then divide by Effort.

Here's an example table using the RICE score:

Project	Reach	Impact	Confidence	Effort	RICE
Project A	400	2	80%	2	320
Project B	1000	1	100%	2	500
Project C	800	3	90%	2	1080

Project C is the clear victor among all those projects that have an effort of two man-months.

The uncertainty of this model is that Impact and Reach are hard-to-come-by data points. There is a lot of guesswork involved still, and that is common to feature prioritization frameworks: in the end, they are making guesses about the future. They may be educated guesses, but they remain guesses.

Baremetrics uses the **DIE method**, scoring Demand and Impact against Effort in a publicly available spreadsheet.

- **Demand:** On a scale of "High (1)" to "Low (3)," how much pull does the market exhibit? How many customers need this feature?
- **Impact:** On a scale of "High (1)" to "Low (3)," how much will this feature move the needle?
- **Effort:** On a scale of "XS (1)" through S, M, L, XL to "XXL (6)," how much work will this take?

The DIE score is then calculated by adding all the numerical values together. The lower the score, the better.

Here's an example table using the DIE score:

Feature	Demand	Impact	Effort	DIE Score
Feature A	1 — High	2 — Medium	4 — L	7
Feature B	2 — Medium	1 — High	2 — S	5
Feature C	3 — Loww	3 — Low	1 — XS	7

Feature B beats the other features and should be prioritized.

In almost all systems, scoring usually boils down to comparing the potential gains versus the possible effort in creating the feature, weighted for risk. This is an excellent choice for bootstrapped businesses, as including development effort is a real requirement for a company that doesn't have funds for extensive R&D exploration.

Feature Prioritization: The Kano Model

This model attempts to set Customer Delight against Product Function, comparing customer value generation with the investment needed to improve the feature over time. If a feature gets better and better, the more you invest in it, it is a great choice. If it doesn't make your customer much happier but requires a lot of maintenance, it's not a priority.

The Kano model distinguishes between basic features that your product just needs to be useful, called threshold features, and "excitement features," which are the most desirable outcome. When you invest time into these features, they yield a disproportionate increase in the delight of your customers. Once you have them, your customer's joy of using your product skyrockets ever higher the more work you put into them.

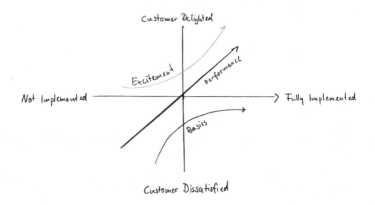

Between the threshold and the excitement features are the performance features. Those increase customer satisfaction proportionally with the time and effort you invest in them. They're useful and provide value, but they can never accomplish the same level of impact that excitement features will.

Two kinds of features are discouraged by this model: indifferent and dissatisfaction features. Anything that customers don't care about or that will upset them should be avoided.

The Kano model gives you a wonderful progression. In essence, you can find the most critical minimum-threshold features that you need to supply, the performance features you can start working on early, and the excitement features that will turn your customers into raving fans.

Feature Prioritization: Story Mapping

Coming from the agile development world, Story Mapping is a way to quickly figure out the order of the steps you need to get a fully working customer workflow implemented from start to finish.

You map out the workflow step by step using a Kanban board or Kanban cards, arranging them in order from the start of the customer experience to the stage that yields the final result.

Then, order the steps by importance, with the most important on the top, with decreasing importance the further down you get.

Finally, create horizontal slices, grouping these steps into releases. Now you have a prioritized list of groups of items, where you can apply further prioritization until you're happy with the order of things.

Prioritizing Prioritization

There are many other systems to prioritize features: Affinity Grouping, Opportunity Scoring, "Buy a Feature," "Value vs.

Complexity Scoring," and many more. Just make sure to stick to one system once you have found it to be usable for your business. Switching around these methods will lead you to prioritization confusion, which will impact your capability to make sound, consistent product evolution choices.

In the end, try to limit the effort you put into prioritizing features. If you spend days working out what you should be working on instead of building features, you won't be able to do any real-world validation. It's tempting to play with the numbers to see which kinds of priority lists you can come up with, but the goal of this process is not to get a perfectly legitimated checklist. Feature prioritization is a guesstimate at best, fed by intuition, preliminary assumptions, and a few metrics. Treat it as a potentially fallible activity.

Spend a few hours on this task, consistently revisit your choices every few weeks as a form of Continuous Validation, and spend most of your time actually working on your product. Incrementally improving a flawed product is better than not having a product at all.

BUILD FOR VALUE, NOT FOR APPLAUSE: PRODUCT MANAGEMENT UNDER HEAVY CONSTRAINTS

A BOOTSTRAPPED FOUNDER will have very little time to devote to building things that don't matter. Everything you do in your bootstrapped business should have a meaningful impact on moving your company toward a state of stability and growth. Bells and whistles are the least of your concerns when you're trying to get to profitability.

To accomplish this, focus on maximizing the value that your product is capable of producing. Three major approaches should go into any product decision:

- It should maximize qualitative impact: "How well does it solve the customer's problem?"
- It should maximize quantitative impact: "How many customers are being helped?"
- It should provide a minimum of usability: "How easy is it for the customer to get their work done?"

As bootstrappers, we have no time to deal with things that don't provide value to our customers and hence our business. It is possible to accomplish all of these three things when you decide how to build features for your product.

Maximal Qualitative Impact

Focus on the "Hot Paths." This is a software engineering term for the parts of your software that are running much more often than others. For a photo upload platform, that would be the part of the software that resizes photos into thumbnails. At the same time, for a social media website, it's likely the algorithm that determines what is shown in your user's social streams. What unites all these software components is that if you speed them up even slightly, it has a significant impact on the whole product.

You can also extend this concept beyond software. What are the hot paths in the workflow of your customers? Which things do they need to do over and over that your product doesn't help with yet? Is there anything you can speed up significantly that would impact the day-to-day activities?

At FeedbackPanda, we found a simple thing that was such a hot path in the workflow of our customers. Many teachers were putting a little sign-off text at the end of the student feedback they created to let the parents of their students know about their availability in the near future. As this changed from day to day, it didn't fit into their feedback templates, as those were meant to contain information about the curriculum, not the teacher. When we noticed that teachers were copying and pasting this little bit of text into their finished feedback, we quickly added a centralized "signature" feature, where they could add their sign-off to their generated feedback automatically, saving them a few seconds every time they used our product. Over a day, that's a few minutes, and it quickly adds up. By adding lots of features like this, we shaved off a few hours a week just by optimizing the hot path.

Within your application, hot paths can be found by looking at performance metrics. If a screen that your users view 100 times a day loads a second faster, that's a few minutes saved at the end of the day. If you measure which parts of your service your customers use most often, you will know where your optimization efforts will be most impactful.

You can accomplish this on the user-experience level by using tools like Hotjar and CrazyEgg, which are called behavior analytics tools, and are mostly recording your users' sessions. They offer heat maps and full session recordings, which are very helpful but also raise many privacy questions. If you integrate these services into your product, consider making them an opt-in choice for your customers. People usually don't like being watched.

A less intrusive way is collecting anonymized metrics from your frontend code by counting how often a particular page or component is instantiated or used. The details will be unique to every product, but the idea is the same: find out what people use most often and make it better. Services like Amplitude, Heap, or Pendo will help.

Consequentially, you will avoid wasting time by ignoring the cold paths. If your users rarely use a non-critical feature, it makes no sense to optimize it, even if that is easier than speeding up another part of the product. Just make sure that the features that are rarely used (but very important) are working well enough, like reliably submitting a report before a deadline after weeks of working in it.

Maximal Quantitative Impact

Whenever you invest time and money into a new feature or an improvement, make sure it impacts as many customers as possible at the same time. It should provide the highest potential value to the largest number of people. Don't focus on something that only 10% of your customers can use. You will be able to add these things at a later point when you're swimming in resources. Notably, in the beginning, any change you make to your product and business has to be a meaningful improvement over the status quo.

Over time, you will likely add a few things that help a few people a lot. But to gain critical mass, you need to start with something that helps a lot of people at least a bit. The idea here is to turn your earliest customers into evangelists for your product, who will shout it from the rooftops. If you only build things that amaze a few of them, that'll be fewer people to do your marketing for you.

There will be the odd exception of a feature that is created for a small but vocal segment of your customers. Be careful not to do this too often, or your product will move too far off the path of being useful to all your customers, it will only be useful to the loud ones.

Measuring quantitative impact works the same way you would measure hot paths since those measurements of a qualitative use are at least partially quantitative as well. For each feature, count and plot how many of your users actually use that feature over reasonable periods. Rank by most-used feature, and look into potential improvements there. For new features, making sure that they will resonate with all of your customers can be checked by adding a mock button for the view/component you don't have yet and present the curious users who click it with a popup promising to implement it. Measure how often people click on that button, and when a threshold is reached, you can consider building it.

Minimum Usability with Maximum Simplicity

When you build features, it's not likely that you will release a fully featured and highly polished version on your first deployment. I would even consider this a waste of time as it would take far too long and would lack any meaningful validation. For that reason, you should release features as soon as they provide the basic functionality they are supposed to perform.

That does not mean your product should be ugly and look scrappy. A usable and clean interface is a valuable feature in itself. However, it isn't necessary to go overboard with the optics. Remember that your solution has to be better than what your customers have used before using your product. It does not have to be the best possible version of itself just yet.

That said, you can make sure you have a baseline of usability by using a UI framework from the beginning. Frameworks like Bootstrap, TailwindUI, or Material Design will allow you to build all of your components, views, and pages using a coordinated and cohesive design approach. With predefined layouts and interface elements, you can be sure to have a good foundation from which to build your features.

Whenever you can, reduce clutter and complexity. If configuration options can be removed from a view and put into a configuration dialog, move them over. If something isn't used most of the time, having it linger in the interface could be more of a distraction than it is helpful. Interfaces should be as simple as possible.

In many cases, this will go against the express wishes of your customers. In my experience, users will always go to "just add a button for X" as a suggested solution to their immediate problems. Well, your users are not designers or product managers. All that this suggestion should do for you is to trigger some research into the underlying problem and how you can best solve it without adding complexity to your interface.

In the Survival Stage of your business, focus your efforts on creating the features that make your service noticeably better for the majority of your users without making the product harder to use. If a feature accomplishes this, go ahead and build it. If it doesn't, stash it for now and build something else that does.

BUILDING THINGS RIGHT

THE EVOLUTION OF THE "HOW"

WHEN IT COMES to making things better, there are a few concepts that will save you a lot of headaches down the road. My grandmother used to say, "If you buy cheap, you'll buy twice." The same is true for software products. If you build your service the scrappy way, you run the risk of having to repair and extend it later, costing you valuable time that could be spent on more productive work.

Building your product with abstractions in mind will allow you to change it more easily and more securely later. Wrapping your external dependencies into abstractions will make switching providers a less risky endeavor. While you likely won't need to make a sweeping change like that too often, it's likely that if you need to make it, it will have to happen quickly. Proper abstractions will prevent you from spending weeks adjusting your product.

At a particular scale, a successful business will need to adopt new systems or processes, so having a flexible product that can easily integrate those will be much easier to manage. The way you deploy your product is one of the most important things to keep flexible, as you never know where your entrepreneurial journey may take you: chances are you'll move your system to another hosting provider after growing to a certain size. Being prepared for that early will save you a lot of hassle.

ABSTRACTIONS

HERE IS a general rule for integrating a third-party-service: never integrate the service directly. A service should always be integrated through an abstraction. While every programming language and accompanying framework works differently, they all provide certain kinds of implementing abstractions, be it through modules, interfaces, macro systems, or packages.

For example, let's say you are integrating MailChimp into your backend server. Instead of using the MailChimp URLs directly in your code, build a class or module responsible for interacting with email list services that handle all the specific calls internally. That way, your email list module can later easily integrate a different service like Email Octopus, raw AWS SNS, or ConvertKit, if you ever feel the need to change.

You would think that some services will never need to be changed. But even in the SaaS world, there are seismic shifts. Companies go out of business, they restructure their pricing to become prohibitively expensive, or they pivot toward solving different problems. Abstracting integrations will prepare you for all of these eventualities.

Abstractions Make Software Easier to Maintain

In addition to being able to change out parts and services when needed, a well-abstracted codebase is very easy to maintain. When all functionality is encapsulated in modules, you effectively have separation of concerns. All payment-related code lives in the payment module or its submodules. Anything related to authentication lives in a different module. Should there be a need for communication between them, there can be either a service bus or a common interface that clearly takes a request from one module and returns the result from the other.

Consequently, you will know exactly where to go when you need to fix a bug or add a new feature. This will help onboard new developers and will speed up your own engineering practice, particularly when you're trying to quickly fix an issue that popped up in production.

Also, abstractions shouldn't only be used for external dependencies. Even internal concerns can be effectively separated. A great consequence of this is that all of a sudden, your code becomes much clearer. It allows you to produce better documentation as well, which helps get new developers working on the code faster, and will be a big asset when you sell the business.

Abstractions Are Easier to Test

Since logic is encapsulated in modules, you can increase your product's resilience and toughness by writing tests that can reliably check if your software produces the correct outputs for your inputs. A well-tested software foundation results in a product that is less prone to errors and outages, and will increase the value of your business because it will be easier for a potential acquirer to take it over.

Once you can reliably test that the internal logic of your abstraction works, you can extend your automated checks to integration tests as well, by mocking the external services or using them directly. This provides you with great opportunities to make sure your abstractions handle the unhappy paths: what will they do when the services are down? How do they handle changes in the data that gets returned? There are whole libraries and packages that can do this kind of testing for you, so plug them into your deployment pipeline as soon as you can.

How to Properly Abstract a Third-Party Service

The basic rule of abstraction is this: never call anything that an external service provides directly. Don't connect to a service API using a hard-coded URL. Don't send an HTTP request to your authentication dependency directly from the logic that handles the login routine.

Always have a layer of indirection between where a service is used and where it's called. Let's imagine you're using Mailchimp and want to add a new email address to your customer email list. Let's also imagine Mailchimp provides an easy-to-integrate SDK or library to connect to their servers, containing a function called `addToList` that will send the email address to their servers to be added to a specific list. In the backend code that is responsible for this, a function called `handleAddEmailToList` gets called. In this function, don't call `Mailchimp.addToList(email, listName)` directly. Instead, create a module that encapsulates all email-list-related logic called `EmailListModule`, and implement a method called `addEmailToList(email, list)`, which itself integrates the `Mailchimp.addToList` call. That way, no matter which email list provider you end up using, calling `Email-ListModule.addEmailToList` will always work.

The Kinds of Services that Should Be Abstracted Away

Make sure you are particularly aware of abstracting away these service categories:

- **Payment providers like Stripe, Chargebee, Paypal:** Treat customer transactions like long-term business relationships that may need to be transferred from one payment provider to another eventually. Don't lock yourself into one provider forever: keep everything you need to migrate your customer to another service in your own database and build your abstraction around the assumption that you could one day need to switch this out for another solution.
- **Authentication providers like Auth0, but also your OAuth2 implementations:** Authentication preferences and best practices change over the years. Before 2019, no one had heard of "Log in with Apple," but Apple made this authentication method mandatory for applications that offered social logins soon after. You will need to extend or completely swap out your authentication logic eventually, so treat your user accounts in the same way you treat your customers' payment history: always keep at least one method to reach out to your customers even if all external services are malfunctioning. For this, I recommend capturing their email, even if they log in using OAuth2-based login systems like Log in with Google or Log in with Facebook.
- **Notifications and chat like Intercom, UserList:** Your marketing and customer communication needs will change over time, but you will always need to be able to reach your customers.

- **Email, including transactional, marketing, and customer communication systems like SendGrid, Mailchimp, and Intercom:** Like its real-time counterpart, asynchronous communication needs to be available to your service, no matter which provider you use.
- **Database connections like MySQL or PostgreSQL:** While these are notoriously hard to change at any point, at a minimum you should abstract away the initialization and configuration steps into their own modules. If you need to migrate your database to another provider at any point, recompiling your code because you can't dynamically change the connection strings is a hassle.
- **Logging:** For your own sanity, use a simple abstraction around your error logging tools. You will have different requirements for your developer compared to your production system, and having things hidden away behind an abstraction reduces the chance of a computation-heavy logger call making it into the production system.
- **Metrics collection:** Like marketing tools, metrics collection services are notoriously expensive. You might have started out with a cheap tier of such a service only to learn a few months later that, for your current needs, this service has become prohibitively expensive. If your metrics collection logic is extensive, replacing the service could take you a few weeks. If you have abstracted the collection and sending logic, it's a matter of minutes.

These services are the most likely ones to change throughout the lifetime of your business. None of those systems should be replaced lightly, but when there is an emergency, you need to be able to swap them out quickly. If you wrap all of them in an abstraction from day one, you'll be prepared for whatever may come.

FLEXIBLE ARCHITECTURE

Particularly when you're building a bootstrapped business, you won't start with a server infrastructure of 20 large servers in a data center somewhere. You will want to start small and cheap, scaling only when necessary.

Containerizing Your Service

I suggest setting up your hosting infrastructure in a cloud-native way: make it compatible with a large number of cloud hosts from the beginning by encapsulating your backend systems in Docker containers. That way, you can run them locally, on your VPC host, on small cloud providers or the big ones, like AWS, Azure, or Google Cloud.

Developing software using containers may seem a bit inflexible due to the added steps. Still, it allows you to conceptualize your software in the same kind of environment that it will run in when you deploy it to your production system. Building software like this will surface dependency and configuration errors much quicker and safer. After all, you will see the errors as they happen on your local computer, and not just after having deployed a new faulty version to production. It's a way to keep your operational peace of mind. You will still need to do ample testing before every deploy.

Having your systems in immutable containers will force them to be mostly stateless, which allows you to save your data in a single source of truth, likely a database or in-memory storage system. Stateless containers will enable you to launch as many as you need to handle the increasing load over time since they can work on different tasks in parallel. Many orchestration systems can auto-scale containers to match the computational demand of your customers.

Once you have multiple containers doing work in parallel, you may want to look into having the containers communicate with each other to distribute tasks and use shared resources evenly. Two technologies stand out here: Cache Data Stores and Message Queues.

Cache Data Stores like Redis or Memcached are semi-permanent and lightning-fast in-memory data structure stores. If you need to access certain kinds of data quickly and often but also need to keep it up-to-date, using a Redis instance that all of your containers access is recommended. Any change in that datastore will immediately be picked up by each container, eliminating the need to synchronize data between the instances. This is useful for things like rate limiting connections for each user, for example. By keeping the current quota and usage statistics in the cache data store, you reduce the load on the database and allow each container to make accurate choices as to whether it should serve a request or not.

Message Queues like RabbitMQ or Apache Kafka allow your system to distribute work between its components. Imagine your application runs in a container, and to keep everything snappy, you want to let a long-running task be executed by another container that runs on a server that is tuned for more performance. A message queue would allow you to hand over the data and wait for the result of the computation or get progress reports. Message Queues are useful to decouple the request from the actual work.

Using containers also allows you to test and quickly deploy new versions of your product without much hassle. In a Google Kubernetes Engine setup, updating the running version of your product is a single change to a configuration file. Reverting to the previous version is just as easy.

When I set up the infrastructure for FeedbackPanda on the Google Cloud, I liked that part the most. With a simple edit to a config file and a shell command, the Kubernetes cluster would fetch the new container from the container repository, start it, and reroute traffic to the new instance. If there were any errors in the container, it would revert to the previously running system. This kind of rolling restart went unnoticed by our customers, and the automated reverts averted many downtimes. The deployment process became effortless. Development, as a result, turned out to be a straightforward and flexible activity.

This flexibility extends to selling the business as well. An easy-to-run system is an easy-to-sell system—the less specific knowledge your acquirer needs to run your product success-fully, the better. If all they need to know is which version number to increase and which command to run to deploy a new version of the software, their perceived deployment complexity is very low. Eventually, your acquirer may want to adjust the process or change it, but for any transitional work, a fully auto-mated system is the best-case scenario.

Making Tough Choices: The Architecture Trilemma and Other Issues

Every structural decision is a tradeoff between two out of three things: high flexibility, high performance, and low complexity. A highly performant and simple system will be very inflexible, and a low-complexity system with a lot of flexibility won't perform very well. In this context, choose the two that will give you the most control as a bootstrapper. In most cases, that will be high flexibility and low complexity. Particularly early on in your business, you will change a few things, sometimes very core parts of your product. To be able to do this, it's okay to give up some performance. Your early customers won't mind— they'd rather have a moderately fast product that fits their needs than a lightning-fast product that doesn't.

You will often need to decide between offering a compelling feature and adding complexity when you consider building new features. Make sure you pick features that create additional value for your business the more you work on them. Using a prioritization framework that takes this into account will help with that.

This doesn't mean you need to adopt long and tedious processes that keep you from freely exploring all possible solutions to a problem. Don't embrace copycat "agile" processes like bloated SCRUM systems just because you've used those in previous jobs or have heard that this is the latest in software engineering. Find the systems that work for you, and keep them as simple as you can.

There's a chance you're a perfectionist. As a software architect, this will make sure you never get anywhere. I had to learn that "good enough" is what things need to be to enable me to run a business. Whenever I was brooding over an architectural choice between multiple options for too long, I evoked a circuit breaker. I made a list of the pro's and con's, listed as many as I could for each decision, and then chose the one with the most favorable ratio. I may not have made the right choice all the time, but at least I made a choice. Analysis paralysis is real, and very dangerous if your most precious resource is your time.

Finally, think about validating your architectural assumption every now and then. This won't be a weekly task, but every year, you should look through all of the services you use, the structures you have built, and the processes you have established within them. If they still help you reach your goal to create and sustain a business that can operate without you, then you can focus on the operational parts of your service.

To enable your architecture to support a "built-to-sell" business, keep an eye on complexity. When the time comes to sell your business, you'll want to have an understandable and straightforward bundle of architectural components to hand over to your acquirer. The simpler, the better.

CUSTOMERS: BUILDING RELATIONSHIPS THAT LAST

WHY RELATIONSHIPS MATTER: MAXIMUM CUSTOMER SERVICE WITH MINIMUM EFFORT

ONCE YOU HAVE PAYING CUSTOMERS, you will notice one thing: it's easier to keep a customer than it is to find a new one.

Before the subscription economy, a transaction was over when the customer left your store. All you needed to do was to get them to buy as much of your inventory as possible. After that, you would likely not see them again, and if they returned in the future, it would take a few times for you to recognize them as a regular customer.

Transactions in the SaaS world are different. For a successful interaction with a customer, maintaining a relationship is critical, as it is an ongoing transaction between your customer and your business. SaaS businesses thrive in the membership economy, where ongoing relationships result in reliable and recurring transactions with long-term customers, over and over again.

In the Survival Stage, your primary goal is to help your customers as much as you can without spending all day doing it. You also want to learn how to retain them as long-term patrons of your business, how to keep them happy, and when to move away from customers that are not right for your business.

When you are running a bootstrapped business, you have to do everything. Build the product, deal with financials, and market your solution.

And customer service is paramount. People are reaching out with questions. Sometimes they are frustrated because they have a deadline. Sometimes they want to chat. In any case, it will eat up your time if you don't find a way of working well with your customers.

Luckily, there are tools and methods for this, even at scale. At FeedbackPanda, I was solely responsible for the technical support of more than 5,000 customers. And, I still had time to develop software.

The Expectations Are Real(-Time)

Emails and tickets are a thing of the past. It used to be the reality for customers of most businesses to send a plea for help and maybe, within a day or two, someone would tell them that they were working on it. A few days or weeks later, someone would resolve their issue or tell them that this was not considered a problem.

Customer service is different today. Solving problems has become a real-time activity as customers expect to receive immediate solutions. They expect there to be a conversation whenever they want to initiate one. Even in enterprise B2B SaaS, where email reigns supreme, people expect immediacy.

As Metha, Steinman, and Murphy say in *Customer Success*: "Customers expect you to make them wildly successful." Every single one of them.

That can easily be an insurmountable resource problem for a bootstrapped founder. You don't have time to talk to your customers all day, every day.

The good news is that there is a crucial distinction. Customers may expect help immediately. But that does not mean they want to talk to a human. They want to have their problem solved. If they can solve their problem themselves and learn how to do it in the future, they will be happier than if someone does the job while they have to wait.

Customers also don't like to be told that they didn't understand the product. Allow them to learn from a variety of materials. Some people like to read, and some want to watch videos.

All of these methods allow for automation and self-serve solutions. Only in rare cases do you need to engage the customer in an actual conversation. If they fail to solve their problem from the self-serve solution, you can still go back to the old "we'll get back to you as soon as we can" or turn the conversation into a real-time, operator-based chat.

At FeedbackPanda, we used Intercom for our customer service. They allow for all three primary modes of customer service: synchronous, asynchronous, and self-help. Tools like Intercom have great integrations into many parts of the tech stack, and you can leverage that to be both responsive to incoming questions, and proactive when you need to reach out to the customer before they even know that there's a problem. You can integrate these tools into the frontend and backend of your SaaS applications, and there are also options for native and hybrid apps on mobile devices and tablets. All these communication paths end up in the Intercom platform, so you can help people wherever they are.

Synchronous Customer Support

Real-time communication with customers is a beautiful thing. Being able to help them right when they need help allows the customer service agent to be empathetic to the pain the customer feels and give them a sense of importance: "A real person is here to help you." For people who are not confident in their ability to solve their problems, this is an enormous relief.

We use the Intercom chat widget in all of our products where our customers can log in. It is integrated into our landing page, the main application, and our mobile applications, too. We initialize the widget with information about the customer, so we can immediately see to whom we are talking. When you have some unique identifier, you can also use the Intercom addon system to create deep links directly into your admin interface or link up their Stripe accounts directly into the Intercom platform. That makes it very easy for the person helping the customer to get to the places from which they can help quickly.

This kind of chat makes the customer service experience personal, both for the customer and the agent. If you are in the early stages of your business, you, as a founder, will be the person dealing with customer support. This channel gives you direct and unfiltered access to your customers and their issues.

You can extract incredible amounts of data from just a single conversation by asking your struggling customers about their goals and motivations. Then, you can use it to fix the issues they are having. At Feedback Panda, we did this multiple times. There is no greater joy than seeing customers' reactions to a new feature or fix that was released within an hour of them having a problem. People don't expect to have any impact on the tools they use, and when you surprise them, you can be sure they will tell their peers about it.

Asynchronous Customer Support

The great thing about having a real-time chat widget is that it can also serve as a delayed messaging system. You can reach out to your customers just as much as they can start a conversation with you. Used correctly, this can be an incredibly useful source of building trust and helping the customer. Used excessively, it turns into spam and a source of annoyance. People are usually okay with marketing emails, but having a message pop up while they are working inside your application will always be a disruption. It should be rare and meaningful to their lives every single time.

At FeedbackPanda, we integrated Intercom into our backend system, and used their Messaging API to send transactional messages to our customers. Only urgent messages would be in-app notifications; the rest of them would be sent via email. Critical messages such as account terminations were sent as both in-app and email messages.

If your customer does not react to an in-app notification, you can always send them an email later. Some customers may take a vacation from their job or be too busy to check your application, so for things that threaten their ability to use their accounts, I recommend always reaching out using both methods.

We also used Intercom for our marketing and onboarding emails. Doing this plays well with having all our customers on their platform already. The onboarding campaign, in particular, can be used to measure conversion rates and engagement profiles. For newsletters and product announcements, the email system will allow your customers to respond immediately, and it will show up as a customer service conversation, with all your added customer data present to help them out.

Self-Help Customer Support

One of the most time-saving tools we have ever used at FeedbackPanda was the Intercom knowledge base feature. Most customers would reach out to us with very similar questions. FeedbackPanda is a tool that does one job well, so for most problems, there is an optimal way to solve them. After communicating that solution to the customer, we would turn the customer service conversation into a knowledge base article immediately. Whenever a future customer would ask the same question or search for the keywords, they would get presented with the article, from which they could then solve their problem themselves. We did this for a few hundred questions whenever customers would first ask about a topic. We ended up with answers to almost all questions people would routinely ask. The number of tickets that required human intervention plummeted and left us the breathing room to run and grow the business.

Video and screenshots are always a good idea when creating knowledge base content. Some people are great readers, but others are very visual or need a narrative to understand a solution. We tried to provide both versions in the same article, and it has been quite well-received.

Another Intercom feature we used to help customers help themselves was AnswerBot. This machine-learning-based feature allows you to have Intercom automatically respond with pre-written answers to specific questions. We would use this for critical problems like "I forgot my login credentials. How do I log in?" or "How can I update my credit card so I can get back into my account?" AnswerBot would pick up these questions and reply with a clear step-by-step solution, sometimes even a video. We also linked deep into our product to the very screen they would need to visit. Being able to help people immediately and automatically allowed us to sleep soundly at night.

Things to Consider

With all these wonderful integrations, you will still have to be aware of a few things. It's not email. It's not just between you and your customers. With Intercom, there is another company in the mix, and your data rests on their servers. That makes it a data-protection and privacy concern. Intercom is compliant with regulations and likely has more security and privacy staff than your business will ever have employees. This is more a question of being aware of what kind of information is absolutely required for your customer service agents to do their work efficiently. It's perfectly fine to give Intercom the unique customer ID so you can create links to your admin interface. (You should never share social security numbers or any other personally identifiable information you have on your customers.)

Price is always a concern for the bootstrapped entrepreneur. Depending on how customer service SaaS tools scale their pricing, you can be perfectly fine or in way over your head. It truly depends. Most subscription-based SaaS businesses will be fine with Intercom as they scale pricing on how many "Active Users" there are. If most of your users are paying customers, that will be alright. If you offer a freemium plan, you will get in trouble if you can't offset the cost of your non-paying users. If you're already struggling with making money with a freemium product, this will hurt your finances even more.

The proliferation of AdBlockers caught some customer service tools by surprise. Depending on how spammy they were perceived, some chat widgets made it onto the blacklists used by AdBlockers. Having your entire customer service built on a system that some people may not be able to see when using certain AdBlockers is a business risk. Customer service tools will likely do their best to stay off those lists, but it could still lead to availability problems from time to time.

As a consequence of the fact that your customer service data is hosted on a third-party platform, which could be impacted by availability problems at any time, it's worth investing time and effort in setting up backups and a migration path. Have the critical information about how you can reach your customers (such as their email address) saved in your account database, as well.

Make regular backups of the data that is held in your customer service system and understand how to access it. There could be a day when you need to migrate from one system to another. It may happen either for business reasons or because of new regulations. Having a reliable backup strategy and the means to move the customer service integrations to another provider will help you to be compliant and avoid being locked in to any one provider.

The Ultimate Goal of Customer Support

Finally, be aware of why you put all of these systems in place: you want to help your customers reach their goals. Focus your energy and ingenuity on building an enormous treasure trove of information for them to solve their problems themselves, jump in when you're needed, and make it a human, relatable experience for your customers.

Excellent customer support is rare. When people encounter a great experience with a customer support agent, they will talk about it. It's a great way to build your reputation as a brand that cares.

YOU MAY BE BARKING UP THE WRONG TREE: RE-EVALUATING YOUR AUDIENCE

WHILE MOST OF your customers will likely enjoy your product, some won't. Some customers will be complaining a lot, asking for features that you don't intend to ever build, or are generally just very hard to please. When you notice that something is wrong, you can usually trace it back to one or more of your assumptions not being aligned with your audience.

This kind of misalignment can be grouped into three types, with conflicts arising from members of your audience not being aligned with which problem you solve, how you solve it, or how your product works.

Audience-Problem Misalignment

The most fundamental misalignment you can experience is when you're solving a problem that your prospective customers don't have. It won't matter if you built the world's most amazing product if it provides no value to your customers. Only a solution to their critical problems can generate that value.

When your prospective customers don't convert or even

show interest in your product, look for these potential product-related reasons:

Maybe you are not looking at the critical problem at all. Have you adequately validated that the problem you're solving is critical? Could you have asked different customers than the ones you're targeting as prospects right now? Double down on your validation efforts. Ask more and different prospects and figure out why what you assumed to be critical is not perceived as such. Do you need to make your prospects aware that they even have a problem?

At FeedbackPanda, we often had to show our prospects that writing student feedback was actually a waste of time when done manually. They just didn't know that it could work any other way. If you need to do customer education before you can show your value proposition, adjust your messaging and marketing efforts accordingly.

Maybe you are not looking at the critical problem anymore (or just yet). Between your problem validation and now, has something changed? Is your prospects' workflow different from the one you assumed they had when you selected which problem to work on? If some of your customers fit that pattern, be extra diligent in figuring out if this is where your customer base is coming from—or where they are going. If their non-critical is turning critical, great. Sit it out. But if it's a critical problem that is turning non-critical, you need to act immediately and figure out which problems you need to solve to retain your customers and keep helping them.

Maybe you are looking at a critical problem, but not theirs. Are you sure you're talking to the right prospects? If you are absolutely sure you're solving a critical problem, then there is someone somewhere who is willing to pay for it. Find those other audiences by looking into adjacent markets. Figure out what differentiates those good prospects from the ones that don't care about the problem you're solving and market exclusively to the ones where you stand a chance.

Audience-Solution Misalignment

Sometimes, you're working on the right problem, but solve it in a way that doesn't resonate with your audience. This is often due to a lack of solution validation, particularly how well you've understood the jobs-to-be-done of your prospective customers, and what they need to get them done.

There are several solution-related reasons that could cause misalignment with your audience:

Maybe your solution doesn't fit your prospects' workflow. Sometimes, the institutional barriers in your prospects' jobs may be too high for you to overcome. If the level of "we work like this here" is incompatible with a new or different solution, your way of solving the problem just won't fit. A lot of restaurants could benefit from a computerized order system. Yet many prefer the time-honored technique of memorizing orders. It just wouldn't fit to use a tablet and painstakingly enter every order where before a mnemonically gifted waiter impressed diners.

Maybe your solution is incomplete. If you owned a fishing equipment store that only sold fishing rods but no fishing lines, would you expect customers to return once they figured out that they can't get everything they need to start fishing? The same is true for your solution. If you help your prospects with their problems insufficiently, then they will likely lose more time using your product than they would by doing it the old way. Find out what shape the input into your solutions will have and what your prospects expect as outputs, and provide means for your solution to work with them. If your customers have Excel files and expect the result of using your solution to be a fully-featured one-file PDF with reports and calculations, you shouldn't ask them to supply you with CSV files and product Word documents. Envision a solution that works with the inputs and outputs that your customers will realistically have.

Maybe your solution is too complicated. Often, this is related to the inputs and outputs and the necessary pre- and post-work that goes into making them compatible with the rest of the workflow your customers have. Other times, your solution involves steps that your customers can't envision taking, either because they don't have the knowledge or permission. In your solution validation calls, make sure that your prospect can take every action they need to use your solution effectively.

Audience–Product Misalignment

Finally, once the problem and solution are aligned, it may come down to the product. Problem and solution are mostly abstract concepts. A product, however, is a real-world implementation of the solution, and it is exposed to the changing needs and preferences of your customers.

Take a look at your product to see if it may be misaligned in one of these ways:

Maybe your product operates in the wrong medium. Are you offering a web-based SaaS where your customers expect a native mobile application? Are you sending emails when your customers would prefer text messages or push notifications? Do your customers have to use your complicated interface on small screens?

This extends to your help-desk as well. Are you offering real-time help when your customers need a paper trail and prefer email? Are you offering tutorial videos when your customers would prefer reading technical documents?

Maybe your product or your messaging is too technical. If your customers are much less technically inclined than you are, your elaborate product could scare them away. Do your customers need an interface with 20 different buttons that allow for all eventualities? Or would a much simpler interface with a few configuration dialogs be a better choice? Can you expect your customers to have your level of technical affinity?

We ran into this issue with FeedbackPanda in the beginning. Some of our customers were very new to online teaching, and they were scared to make mistakes using their computers. It takes a lot of handholding and support to help these kinds of customers to use your product efficiently. And sometimes, it won't work; they'll give up or move to a more straightforward product. At that point, you should stay in close contact with them and see what they need, and if they find something that helps them. Then, learn how you can enable your own product to do that.

Misalignment could be caused by something simple, like the wording of your messaging. For example, do your customers understand the phrase "heuristic-based statistical sentiment analysis," or would "find the tone of a message" be clearer? You don't need to dumb it down, but you also shouldn't overcomplicate it. As an engineer, I feel that I need to be as precise as possible. Customers don't necessarily value this as much as you think.

Maybe your product is confusing. Your customers don't want to be confused. They don't want to be surprised by your product. And they definitely don't want to learn anything new to be able to solve a problem they already had to learn a product or even a manual solution for in the past. Your product should be simpler, easier, and faster than anything they have encountered in the past. If it's not, getting to understand your product is a cognitive load that few are willing to take upon themselves.

That's not to say that people won't learn your product ever. It just means that the simpler your product, the more prospects will play around with it to a point where they can see themselves using it in the future.

How to Handle Audience Misalignment

Here's the worst-case scenario: your product may just not be for them. They may not be your audience. You don't have to bend your product into a shape that works for a market that doesn't value your vision. There will always be people who wish for things to be different and will be vocal about that. They need a different solution, but you are not the one that provides that, which is fine.

Of course, if all of your customers exhibit this behavior, you should stop and reflect if you are talking to the wrong audience altogether. Find the customers that don't complain and see what makes them happy. Focus on finding more of those customers and replace the customers that don't fit your audience anymore.

On the other hand, if you have found that you're serving the right audience but are just a bit misaligned on your perception of the problem, solution, or product, you can fix it. Once again, reach out to your customers to validate your assumptions, and dive deeply into the points of friction you find in those conversations. Engage customers you have asked before as well as new prospects that you haven't talked to in the past. Getting fresh and new opinions into your validation calls is very important at this point, as their absence may have led you to the impasse you're currently facing.

One of the great things about being a bootstrapper is how agile you can be. You can react quickly to changes in the needs and wants of your customers. If an assumption is wrong, you can quickly find a better perspective to take—and you can improve your product and your business immediately. There is no shame in being wrong about your assumptions. They are mostly guesses, after all. Make sure you admit mistakes quickly and focus on making your bootstrapped business better—one assumption at a time.

CHURN, RETENTION, AND REVENUE: WHAT MAKES CUSTOMERS STICK AROUND AND WHY THAT'S IMPORTANT

RETAINING a customer is easier than finding a new one. You already have an open communication channel. They're already interested in hearing from you. You also know their behavior patterns, and you can infer how much and how effectively they use your product from your metrics.

On average, a 5% increase in customer retention leads to a 25%–95% increase in profits. So, keeping customers retained sounds like a great way to keep your business on the right track. If it can impact revenue so significantly, it is definitely worth your time to build a company that focuses on customer retention.

How can you make sure the customer sticks around? What are the goals that you should have to make sure that as few people as possible ever cancel their subscriptions? You'll learn how to focus on the preventable churn and how to keep those customers around. You'll see which kinds of churn are dangerous and which can actually be beneficial to the bottom line of your business.

Why Retention Has Such a Striking Effect on Revenue

The obvious goal is to continuously provide customers with a valuable product throughout their entire journey. The moment your product does not solve their problem anymore, they will find another solution. To prevent them from leaving you for a competitor, you need to solve their problem for them consistently and perpetually. Existing customers get used to the value you deliver; in fact, they start expecting it. That makes them appreciate new features and start complaining when the product doesn't keep up with their critical problem. For as long as you do that, you have a long-term relationship, an ongoing sale.

After all, it's so much easier to sell to a customer you already have. The chance of selling to an existing customer is 60%–70%, whereas a new prospect only buys 5%–20% of the time, according to Marketing Metrics. That means you're looking at three to eight times as high a chance to profit from an existing customer. You'll really want people to stay.

But sometimes, your customers will quit. This can happen for many reasons, and only a few are in your control.

Generally, there is voluntary churn (e.g., when a customer terminates the subscription) and involuntary churn (e.g., when a subscription is terminated due to lack of funds).

Some kinds of churn are preventable. Sometimes, a customer leaving is not the end of your relationship.

Reactivation: How to Talk to Churned Customers

To get a customer to return to your product, you can employ reactivation strategies. After customers have quit, an automated email offering them a free month or a discount is dispatched. That will allow you to reconnect with undecided customers. Often, a conversation with those churned customers will be very enlightening, as it will surface reasons for churn that are still fresh in the minds of your customers. Mainly, in the beginning, reaching out manually will be extremely fruitful to find and resolve the issues that motivate customers to leave.

In some cases, you may get customers to return to the product by reaching out. Don't force it, though. You don't want them to vent their frustration to their peers about your forceful attempts at getting them back, since their peers are very likely potential customers. Respect the choices your customers make, and even though the paid part of the relationship is over, they will continue to talk positively about your product. A business relationship is never really terminated, and if you rely on word of mouth for your marketing, you want all of your customers to feel valued and respected.

Payment Churn: How to Recover Failed Charges

There is also payment-related churn. Credit cards expire every few years, so unless you're using a payment provider that automatically updates credit card details through the Credit Network as Stripe does, for example, you will eventually attempt to charge an expired card. When that happens, you can either integrate a recovery solution like ProfitWell Retain or Baremetrics Recover. These dunning solutions reach out to your customers, prompting them to update their credit card information right after the failed charge occurs. They are, however, not completely customizable. If you're a non-US company, you may run into blocked charges due to your geographical location. Implementing a custom messaging system that tells your customers how to get their bank to unblock the card will eliminate a large percentage of this involuntary churn.

The Surprising Kinds: Empowerment Churn, Temporary Churn, and Welcome Churn

Not all churn is created equal, either. Companies go out of business, or pivot in different ways. A company canceling their subscription with you could be tying up loose ends and stopping operating altogether. This happens particularly often in the freelancing world, where people stop their freelance work to take a full-time job or create a new business.

You may even be seeing a consequence of how much value you've been providing. Your tool could have enabled someone so much that they are now moving up-market, taking a wholly new and higher-paying job. If you set out to help and lift your customers, this could be a bittersweet sign of the real impact of your business.

Some churn is also just temporary. At FeedbackPanda, a large percentage of our customers were new parents. Inevitably, they would go on parental leave and would want to pause their subscriptions for as long as they were not working. Offering a "pause and pick up where you left off" solution was a clear path for us, and something similar could work if your business is in a similar niche with expectable temporary periods of non-use.

Some churn is also welcome. Imagine you have customers who continuously complain or request features you're not willing to accommodate as they don't fit into your vision. As Seth Godin says, these people are not the audience for your art. You should not force a relationship with them just to get some money. Be happy to see them go, and invite the people who like what you do to become your customers instead. They will amplify your voice in their communities; they will rave about the product that you built instead. Toxic customers should be encouraged to churn. Do it nicely, in a friendly fashion. But make sure you don't bend your product to accommodate needs with which you are not aligned.

Customers with short-term needs also don't hurt you when they churn. In the membership economy, you're looking to build long-term relationships. You want a customer lifetime value that is significant, as you invest a lot of time and money into acquiring the right customers. If a customer leaves almost immediately after subscribing, and you're sure they've made this choice because they don't need your product, don't worry. Their customer segment is not relevant to your long-term success, and catering to those needs may lead the product away from being as valuable as possible for your relevant customers.

Value Nurturing: Farm, Don't Hunt

There is also something you can do to prevent churn before it happens: value nurturing. It's all about showing the customer the value they've receiving from your product while they are using it. Show them how much time using your product has saved them this week. Slack sends out an aggregate statistics email every week, making it clear how much using their tool impacts your teams. Find something that reminds your customers why your product is great, and make sure you periodically visualize this to your customers.

The book *Farm, Don't Hunt* by Guy Nirpaz describes the concept of value nurturing in great detail. If you want to work on showing your customers how much value you provide, it will give you many great insights and actionable ideas.

Value Nurturing: Engage and Educate

For example, regularly talking to your customers will help keep your product on their minds. Sending out a newsletter every week with news from the industry, a few tips on how to use the product more efficiently, and sharing a couple of interesting articles will contribute a lot to customer retention. Your brand will be elevated from a product provider to a trusted source of information. When it comes to canceling a subscription, it's much easier to cancel something that is solely providing a tool when you need it compared to a membership in a community that regularly keeps you educated and informed.

Encouraging Annual Plans: Fostering Commitment

A great way to prevent churn is to make the billing cycles longer. If you can churn 12 times per year, the chances are higher than if you only have one payment. It's also a highly psychological issue: annual plans are usually discounted and therefore non-refundable. Purchasing such a plan will make your customers want to get value from their subscription immediately and as fast and for as long as possible. There is a sense of commitment to spending a year's worth of money on a single purchase. While you have to provide the same value you would provide to monthly subscribers, your annual subscribers will feel a stronger commitment to your product and their choice to use it.

Note that a discounted plan or an incentivized early renewal option will cut into your profits. Whenever possible, offset that with expansion revenue, by selling upgrades or one-time products to your customers when there is a chance. Or, price the yearly plan at sustainable levels and charge a premium to your monthly subscribers.

Customer Feedback Tools and Public Roadmaps

There are a few things you can do immediately that will build customer confidence and trust in the future of your business and your product.

Ask your customers methodically. Using a tool like Canny.io allows your customers to suggest features and vote for the ones they find most relevant. It will enable you to figure out which issues are common, and generate a product roadmap from there. Sharing that roadmap will then show your customers where the journey is going. For some, this will be enough information to commit to a long-term relationship. Others will give you valuable insights into their specific needs and requirements.

Intensify Your Onboarding: Find the Magical Moment

Potential long-term customers that churn quickly after adopting your product are your most significant loss in terms of unrealized customer lifetime value. Making sure as many new customers stick around during their trial and after subscribing will significantly impact your bottom line. Spend some time discovering which metric can be used to find out if a customer will stick around or not, and then optimize your onboarding to get your new customers to that point as quickly as you can.

For FeedbackPanda, that metric was writing and using their first feedback template. Users who had created their own templates and generated feedback with them were almost guaranteed to stick around and convert into paying customers. So, we focused our efforts on getting the user to that magical moment when the "a-ha" effect happened. We wanted them to experience this as soon as possible. Once they did, they "got it." And we got them as our customers.

Thank Your Customers

Sometimes, a thank you note can make a difference. Particularly at the beginning of your business, when you're struggling for survival, take the time to reach out to every single customer and say thank you. Thank them for being part of your journey. Thank them for making it possible for you to help them. Be grateful; send them a hand-written postcard if you can. This is particularly powerful when you're selling to a tight-knit community. Seemingly random acts of kindness, particularly when they're not aimed at creating a viral sensation, will make a difference, and your customers will feel valued and respected.

As you can see, most customer retention strategies are focused on showing your customers that they are not just an account number with a credit card attached. Give your customers the feeling that you value them as people, as humans, and they will make sure they repay the favor. Make them feel comfortable and appreciated, and they will stick around.

PRICING: SUBSCRIPTIONS, PLANS, AND OTHER FINANCIAL CHALLENGES

PRICING IS NOT SET IN STONE: STRATEGIES FOR DETERMINING PRODUCT VALUE

THE GREAT THING about revenue is that there are many levers that you can move to improve it. The not-so-great thing about revenue in a bootstrapped business is that it's hard not to move the wrong levers. Customers don't like price changes, as they have budgets to care about and expectations of how much a service is worth. If you irritate them with too many changes or too much pressure to pay more, they will gladly find an alternative to your product that gives them more peace of mind.

Adding more expensive plans could alienate your customers; increasing your prices may upset those who have been with you for a long time. There are many ways to deal with this, and we'll take a look at the ones that work well and the ones that are likely to cause a lot of relationship damage.

Some strategies may work well at the beginning of your business, but prove to be fatal further down the road. This boils down to the makeup of your customer base. In the beginning, the early adopters will understand that nothing is set in stone just yet. Once you sell to mainstream customers, you can't run experiments that easily anymore.

In the Survival Stage, there is a high chance you'll settle with non-optimal pricing plans because the ones you already have work well enough. You can always change your prices. You own your business, and you can change everything about it. Most payment providers allow you to have an infinite number of plans, and you can add (and remove) as many as you like at any given time.

There is no reason to stick with what you initially conceived, or think of it as "good pricing." Don't hesitate to change the prices of your plans just because you picked an arbitrary number of dollars when you first launched the business. But, keep in mind that changes can be disruptive for your customers, so there are a few things to keep in mind.

Honest Pricing and the Perception of Value

Always be transparent about changing prices. Inform every customer who will be affected by this change. If you offer a trial period for your product, make it clear when customers need to subscribe to get the prices they were told when they started their trial. If you raise prices for existing customers, inform them in advance, so they have a chance to commit or complain. Having people frantically scramble to offboard their data because they can't afford your product anymore will create a lot of bad press and sour the long-time relationships you so carefully built.

With enough value nurturing, customers will understand that a continuously maintained and updated SaaS product warrants a price increase. Some may not like it and protest, but in most cases, it will be a net benefit for your business and your customers: you catch up to the value you deliver, while they benefit from the additional resources this revenue increase generates.

Budgets and Price Sensitivity

Keep in mind the budgets of your prospects. There likely is a ceiling, even when you're selling to freelancers and other positions that determine their own budgets. Find out which leadership is involved in this decision and how flexible those budgets are.

Sometimes, what you sell doesn't fit existing budgetary categories, so customers may not know if they have a budget at all, if there is a ceiling, or if they could stretch existing budgets to accommodate paying for your service. You won't know about this until you have talked to your prospective customers in several exploratory conversations.

Price sensitivity is different depending on your customer types. Early adopters buy the product that your service will provide once it's finished; mainstream customers buy the product you sell right now. While you'll want to provide a maximum of value for your price to either group, you can get away with charging higher prices to the group that expects your product to grow into something bigger than it is at the moment they buy it. Don't abuse that trust.

Price Boundaries and the Fallacy of Pricing Too Low Too Early

Early bootstrapped pricing is often too low. Don't discount yourself. Just because you're starting a new business doesn't mean you'll have to scrape the bottom of the barrel. This leads to a big problem in the future. If you believe that raising prices is hard but lowering them is easier, then choosing a low price, in the beginning, will prevent you from ever meaningfully increasing your revenue through price adjustments.

Pricing is strongly correlated with your positioning. If you position yourself as a professional tool, you will be able to charge more, compared to being perceived as a fun distraction. You may reach fewer people, but the relationships you form with B2B customers are much stronger and more reliable than if you were to sell to a B2C market, where you have more customers with higher churn. If you position yourself alongside other high-priced solutions, customers will accept paying more. If you compete with low-priced products, your upper price boundaries will be perceived to be comparatively low.

Pricing Is Always Conversational and Influenced by Expectations

In general, pricing in a vacuum is a questionable approach. In the beginning, you likely don't have much customer data to anchor on. That's fair, and it makes finding a working pricing model quite hard. Customer conversations will help you understand what could work and what could not.

Talking to your customers allows you to find out if they are genuinely committed to buying your product. Pricing feedback from people who wouldn't buy your product anyway is useless and dangerous to follow. You'll need to focus on the prospective customers who will share their expectations with you. You need to understand how they think about the value of software solutions like yours and what they have experienced in the past.

You should price the way people are used to. If they pay per seat for other tools, you're likely to get more conversions offering that, too. If you introduce an unusual pricing model like API-call-based prices in an industry that usually pays a flat fee for services, you will have to spend more time explaining to your prospects why this is better suited to their use cases. Many leads won't materialize because once they see something novel and complicated, they will go with what they already know.

The same goes for your price levels. Your customers will compare your solution to the tools they already use and will evaluate you against the tool, position, or team that your service is supposed to replace. While this is mostly a positioning issue, your customers' prior experience plays into this a lot as well. The more you know about that, the better your messaging can be.

Moving Up-Market

Moving up-market is a common strategy for SaaS businesses: go after bigger and bigger customers. Find the bigger budgets and get your cut. While this is a great strategy when you have a mature company with a stable revenue stream, it is not recommended while you are struggling to survive. There are many risks to what seems like a lucrative path.

Enterprise customers are dangerous beasts: their purchasing processes are opaque, take a long time, and involve levels of commitment you may not be able to make.

Timelines are longer in the enterprise B2B world. The complexity of the corporate sales process makes conversations take a long time and involves more people than a self-service subscription service that generates revenue at the click of a subscription button. You'll have to send emails, follow-ups, explanations, maybe even take a few people in your prospect's company through an extensive demo process. Only go up-market if you know you can still run your business while you or someone in your company does this much more intense sales job.

Subscription Tiers: Paid and Free

If you have a very clear-cut service offering, your product likely allows you to serve the same kinds of customers with the exact same service. While this is great for communicating the value of your product, you are probably leaving money on the table.

At FeedbackPanda, we started our paid monthly subscription offering by having a $5 plan and a $10 plan. The cheaper option had a few limitations around the amounts of data that our customers could store in their databases, while our more expensive plan had no restrictions. From day one, most people chose to purchase an unlimited plan, even though they wouldn't reach the numbers that exceeded the limits of the cheaper plan for months. I attribute this behavior to the fact that we named the more affordable plan "Basic" and the more expensive one "Professional." Our customers were teachers who took great pride in being experts in their field. Their own psychology made them gravitate toward the more expensive option to retain that self-perception.

Tiers are not just tricks to make customers pay more for the same service. They have to make sense. People understand advertising games, and they will harbor very negative feelings toward you if they learn that you're trying to trick them. If you offer tiers, make them comprehensive. Set usage limits, lock away functionality, but always root those choices in business-related reasons. Coercing customers to upgrade to a higher tier without a justified need is not going to help you build a positive relationship with them.

Don't make your pricing too complex to understand. A simple pricing structure allows you to plan better and will lead to fewer surprises. Offering three tiers is what seems to work well in most cases. Only very specific kinds of tools get away with complicated pricing structures. Those tools usually are highly technical and work at large scales, so that different use cases warrant diverging ways of paying for the service.

A popular strategy is to offer a free tier with heavily enforced limits. This allows your customers to make a habit out of using your service before they have to commit to a purchase, which often helps convince prospects of the value of the product. If you offer such a free tier, you will have to pay extra attention to your prices: they need to make sense for those price-sensitive customers, or else they'll migrate away after they start reaching the limits at which you expected them to convert.

Looking at the Intention Behind the Price

At this early stage of your business, ask yourself this question: what is your price supposed to do?

Are you trying to get established first? Are you trying to get your foot in the door? Your very first customers are validation and multiplication opportunities. You'll price differently for those customers than for later customers. Deliver custom prices to the early ones, then reevaluate later.

Are you trying to maximize revenue? Look into the unit economics of your existing customers and find ways to segment the customers that are likely to be highly profitable and offer them more extensive plans with more functionality and better guarantees.

At any point in your business, prices are in motion. Don't set them in stone. Take it as a starting point; don't treat it like a fixed decision. Just like you hope to improve your product, you should look at your prices regularly.

At FeedbackPanda, we increased our prices by 50% a year after going to market. We softened the blow by simultaneously introducing a referral system. We had great success in two ways: our monthly revenue grew as customers agreed to pay more for their monthly plans, and we received a large influx of cash from the customer who chose to lock in their prior pricing by committing to a discounted yearly plan before the deadline.

While it was a scary moment, we were glad to have experimented and increased our prices. Nothing shows that your customers value your product more than when they choose to pay a higher price for it than before.

NOT ALL SUBSCRIBERS ARE EQUAL: DEALING WITH PLANS THAT NO LONGER WORK

YOU MAY HAVE STARTED with subscription plans that turn out to be problematic. At FeedbackPanda, we had started with a $5/month plan. After a few months of offering that, we retired that plan because we noticed that it attracted a kind of customer we did not want to serve: bargain shoppers. The customers on that very cheap plan were using our customer support channels significantly more than those who were on more expensive plans. They complained more and requested more features than anyone else. So, we closed off that plan for new users.

They hated it. Many people who had started their trial assuming that they would get a $5/month plan reached out to us and complained that we took it away before they got a chance to subscribe. While it always hurts to receive such feedback, it was still the right course of action. The voices of those who are bothered will always be much louder than the silence of those who don't mind. We saw in our numbers that our conversion rate didn't suffer from this change.

If you remove a plan, you have a choice: you either upgrade all users to one of the remaining plans, or you "grandfather in" their subscription, which means they get to keep their old plan even though it is no longer offered to new customers.

Upgrading All Affected Customers

Your best chance to increase your MRR immediately is to upgrade all of the customers on the plan that you intend to remove. This will also cause a lot of trouble if you're not giving your customers enough time and options to react to the announcement before an additional dollar changes hands.

Inform your customers far ahead of time. Give them a month or more if you can. At the very least, there should be a few weeks should be between the announcement and the actual change. Special focus should be on communicating this change clearly to your trial customers who started their accounts under the impression that this plan would still be available for them. If you want to be particularly friendly, allow those customers to still subscribe to the plan even while it's already unavailable for other users.

Some customers will cancel. A very effective course of action is to reach out to those who intend to cancel and try to get them to stick around with a discount offer. Often, giving them a month for free is enough of a sign of good faith for them to reconsider their cancellation.

Should they still cancel, think twice if it's worth spending more time and effort at winning them back. If at all, try to reactivate them via email a few days or weeks after they quit. New prospective customers who start a trial even though the lower price is gone are those you want to interact with at this point. These and your existing customers who are willing to pay more for a better product should be the focus of your attention.

Grandfathering All Affected Customers

Grandfathering can be great to keep your early customers around, but there is a risk of underselling your product significantly. It can be a business risk not to be able to claim the real value of your product as revenue just because you think your customers are emotionally attached to a lower price. Expansion revenue is made impossible if the customers who happen to be subscribers already are receiving a life-long discount. An excellent way to allow grandfathering is making it conditional and temporary: allow them to keep the lower price for a year if they upgrade to a yearly subscription. Else, force them to upgrade to the new price. Understand that they should pay for the product they receive today, not the product they signed up for years ago.

When we removed our cheapest plan, we decided to grandfather our $5/month customers. One noticeable consequence was that most customers who reached the limits of their plan eventually upgraded. Only a few customers tried to stay under the limit by deleting data diligently. They would rather save a few dollars a month than have access to their old feedback data. As this number was relatively low, we ignored it and never encouraged them to upgrade, as it wasn't worth our time.

We grandfathered our customers indefinitely, which is something I would not recommend. Give your customers a high but finite amount of time to enjoy their old subscription plan. After a year or so, request that they upgrade to the correspondingly more expensive plan. Your product has grown in terms of value, so all of your subscribers eventually should compensate you accordingly.

NOT ALL SUBSCRIPTIONS ARE EQUAL: OFFERING YEARLY PLANS FROM THE START

Most bootstrapped businesses offer monthly subscription plans. The revenue that is reliably generated from your customers that way is incredibly reliable. If you know how many customers you have, you know exactly how much money will come in this month, next month, and the future, provided you keep the same number of customers.

That's where risk comes into play. If you only offer monthly plans, a wave of cancellations can cut into your revenue substantially, and you will notice within the next 30 days. Yearly subscriptions allow you to lock in a portion of your revenue in a much more reliable way, while providing something valuable beyond dollars: validation.

Yearly Subscriptions and Validation

There is something incredibly satisfying that happens when a customer chooses a yearly plan for your product. Not only do they pay up to 12 times as much as a monthly subscriber, but they also communicate something powerful to you. They trust your business to be around in a year, they trust your product to provide value for at least another year, and they're sure that they won't find anything better until then. That is why having a yearly subscription option is not optional. It should be a choice from the beginning.

It also gives you access to a very interesting subset of your early customers: your future evangelists. Look at it like this: early adopters are already betting on your product for the foreseeable future. If some of them actually commit to paying you for a year, then you can be sure that they will go above and beyond to make sure your business succeeds. They will be the people who talk about your service on social media, introduce it to their peers and the members of the communities they frequent. Leverage that, particularly in the beginning.

Yearly Subscriptions and Cash Flow

Besides the validation component, a yearly plan will allow you to borrow from future profits to invest in your business. Being able to invest the 11 months of advance payments into the growth of your business will liberate you from the month-to-month thinking you would have if you only offered monthly plans.

This will protect you from running out of money too fast. Any meaningful churn will still do financial damage to your business, so unless at least half of your subscribers are on a yearly plan, you will need to iterate your business when people start canceling. Having a few yearly subscribers will allow you to spend a few more days or weeks dealing with the things you need to improve.

Yearly Subscriptions and Discounts

You should also discount your yearly subscriptions, for two reasons. First, a cheaper subscription will incentivize customers who like to save on purchases they would make anyway. Second, and this is a much more critical reason, a discounted plan can come with a (clearly visible and communicated) non-refundable clause. This allows you to use the full amount for investing in your business, alleviating the need to hold funds for possible refunds, should the business run into trouble.

Most customers will understand that discounted plans are not refundable. Make absolutely sure that your refund policy is clearly visible to your customers before they purchase, and have it easily visible in your account settings as well as in your knowledge base and Terms & Conditions.

At FeedbackPanda, we sometimes refunded yearly subscriptions even though we had a no-refund policy. For a handful of hard cases like people who had suddenly lost their jobs or had medical emergencies, we quickly refunded the money. This saved us from chargeback fees that would have occurred had our customers gone through their bank, and it created a lot of goodwill with the people we helped. Many of them became very loyal, loudly talking about our surprisingly helpful customer service and how respected they felt when we made an exception to the terms. To our knowledge, no one ever abused this system, and the loss in revenue was worth all the feedback and gratitude we got from our customers.

SELLER BEWARE: PRICING MODELS THAT CAN BREAK YOUR BUSINESS

THERE ARE a lot of great ideas when it comes to optimizing your pricing to attract more customers or keep them retained. Two pricing models can be hazardous if not implemented carefully: freemium accounts and lifetime accounts.

The Risks of Freemium Accounts

A freemium pricing model can be great to get people to use your product, start integrating it, and eventually start paying for it. It can be very dangerous to your business if the freemium tier offered allows customers to use the product extensively without ever needing to pay for it. Setting clear limits that are easily reached when the product is used in a revenue-generating way is paramount here.

Businesses like Baremetrics almost went out of business because freemium users caused infrastructure costs to skyrocket by using the product in unlimited and unmetered ways. When Baremetrics released their freemium accounts, thousands of businesses signed up and imported their payment provider data into the Baremetrics system. The onslaught of data was so intense that they had to scramble to provision new servers to be able to handle the load. At the same time, customer support queries grew because those new users needed assistance, too. Without making an additional dollar's worth of revenue, they now had to pay more for infrastructure, and their paying customers had to wait longer to get support.

If you try to attract customers using the freemium model, make it hard for them to earn money without paying you. At least that way, once a user derives meaningful value from your service, they have to start paying. You can accomplish that by turning key features into paid-only options or instituting limits that are hard to reach for an amateur but easily reached by a professional. Usually, this scales along with the value metric of a customer, like the amounts of successful purchases in an eCommerce store or the number of photos uploaded to an image upload site.

The risk of freemium increases ten-fold when you need paying customers to offset the cost incurred by your freemium users. That's why I recommend setting limits that keep your customers from making too much money off the free tier of your service, and that keep your customers from overwhelming your infrastructure.

Be advised that many third-party services charge according to the number of active users. Unless your paying users can offset that cost, using the freemium model can be very prohibitive to choosing the right integrations for your service due to the very high number of non-paying customers. Particularly if you implement freemium later during the course of your business, this could cause a lot of financial stress. Whenever you choose to use a customer-facing service, look at what will happen when your user count changes by order of magnitude.

Finally, freemium plans could cannibalize your paid plans. Every free-plan user is a user that could be on a paid plan if you didn't have a freemium option. Think about it like this: if the customer would have paid, you don't capture their revenue. If they wouldn't have paid anyway, why would you want them as a customer?

The Risks of Lifetime Accounts

Lifetime accounts are quite similar, as the danger also lies in resource consumption that, after some time, exceeds the money they paid for the product. For a customer, "lifetime" means their own lives, while for most businesses, the "lifetime" in question is that of the current iteration of the product. This can be quite confusing, and it usually leads to bad blood once the perceived forever-account gets migrated into a monthly plan. These accounts are great to raise initial capital for a business, but they create a lot of pain and become liabilities in the later stages of a business—particularly when you intend to sell the business.

Lifetime accounts often signal that the business is in a bad financial state. If you were confident that your subscribers would stay with you for their "lifetime," why take so comparatively little money up front?

Lifetime accounts also attract less-than-desirable customers. The expectations you set up by offering a paid service for life can become insurmountable. With a recurring subscription fee, you can at least defend that a customer has the right to claim your assistance again and again. But what will happen when a customer who paid what in most cases is just a few hundred dollars for lifetime access to a service reaches out to you every few days, holding your attention for hours? These expectations will be hard to fulfill.

With a lifetime account, be absolutely clear in your Terms & Conditions what "lifetime" means. Is it the lifetime of your customer? Your lifetime? The lifetime of the product in this version? All versions? Is it the lifetime of the lifetime offer? The moment a customer understands "lifetime" to mean something else than what you intend it to be, there will be a very uncomfortable conversation in your future.

It's Not Just Risks

Both Freemium and Lifetime accounts can work for your business. When applied consciously and with the right strategy, either can provide a benefit to a bootstrapped business—when applied temporarily.

Slack uses the power of Freemium to get people to join free self-organizing communities, only to later have the same people carry the paid version into their day jobs. Zapier offers a "Free Forever" plan that similarly converts free users into customers once they require more advanced solutions to their integration problems. Both companies treat their free users as valuable customers, because they know that conversion rates are high, and a single user who works for an organization with 50,000 employees can turn into a lead catalyst.

Some businesses that desperately need cash up front can sell a few lifetime accounts to their earliest customers, and that will give them the funds they need to jumpstart a business that can survive long enough for recurring revenue to establish recurring revenue. But lifetime accounts are just that: a temporary cash injection that, after a while, may turn into a drain on your resources.

Whatever you do, revisit your choice every few months. Keep your eyes on the Customer Acquisition Cost and the Lifetime Value of your users and how those metrics change when you implement these kinds of accounts. Once those metrics show a tendency toward negative revenue, be prepared to phase out those offers.

Generally, adding one more customer to your software service won't cost you much. The marginal cost of SaaS businesses is near zero in many cases. If this is true for your business, you can definitely experiment with these pricing models. Just make sure you don't wipe out potential recurring revenue streams indefinitely by giving customers subscription options that give them a lot of value without compensating your business for providing it.

Both freemium and lifetime accounts can attract the kinds of customers that you may not want to serve. When in doubt, stick with monthly and yearly subscriptions after an extensive trial phase. That way, you'll see if customers are with your business because you continuously provide them enough value. If you're not, they will cancel.

BUSINESS: PULLING LEVERS AND ADJUSTING SCREWS

MAKE THE PRODUCT SELL ITSELF: REFERRAL SYSTEMS

ONE YEAR INTO RUNNING FEEDBACKPANDA, we released a referral system. It was an immediate success, and it stayed that way. When we sold the business, around 40% of new signups came through our referral system.

Immediately after turning on the user-facing parts of the referral system, we started seeing results. Our social media channels quickly filled up with our customers crafting posts that contained their referral links. Signups went up, and churn rates went down. Referral systems benefit everyone involved, and you can set one up efficiently, too.

The FeedbackPanda Referral System

FeedbackPanda had been getting along fine with a steady influx of new customers for over a year. Through the strong word-of-mouth marketing that happened organically within the teacher tribe, our customers were used to their peers talking about our service.

We decided to add a referral system when we raised our prices by 50% only eight months after our public launch. The referral system was supposed to both amplify existing word-of-mouth marketing and give our customers a means to offset the increased price of their subscriptions. It was, in essence, a retention play. That's why we went with a double-sided reward structure: both the referring and the referred customer would get a substantial reward for participating.

It worked like this: for every three customers you referred, you would get a free month of the service. It would be automatically credited to your account the moment the third referred customer purchased a subscription. All referred customers would get a 50% lifetime discount on their subscription. After increasing our prices, this brought their monthly cost right back to where it was before but made the price so much more attractive compared to a non-referred subscription.

This massive discount had an interesting effect: prospects who had heard of our product actively asked for referral codes on social media and were often bombarded with large numbers of responses, each containing a referral link.

As a consequence, we saw our referral links pop up in lots of places on social media, and even in obscure subreddits and on niche blogs. It was a big success, and signups became substantially referral-driven.

How Does a Referral System Work?

Referrals are not a cheap marketing trick. When done right, they can be a great way to grow your business and provide value to new and old customers alike.

The idea is simple: you get a customer to invite a new prospect to your product, and you reward either just the referring customer or both for participating in the transaction.

Most often, a unique referral link is generated for each of your customers so you can track who invited whom. You then encourage your customers to share this link wherever they think new prospects might find it.

The reward of a referral system will vary significantly depending on the kind of service you offer. Dropbox famously used a referral system that gave both the advocate and the referred user increased storage space. At FeedbackPanda, we discounted the subscriptions of both parties. There are many more incentives you can use, such as store credit, coupons, cash, or gift cards.

The math is simple, too: if the discounted advocate revenue plus the discounted revenue from the referred customers is higher than the non-discounted revenue for a user that doesn't participate in the referral system, your system works.

How Can a Referral System Provide Benefits?

Referral systems are economically sensible because the rewards you provide are worth the increased revenue that is generated by customers who invest their time and energy into marketing your product.

This is particularly true in highly tribal niches, which is why we could offer a 50% discount and still significantly impact our MRR with the FeedbackPanda referral system.

When you sell into an interconnected group of people, the built-in virality will give a lot of visibility to community members who recommend your product. By offering a referral system, you add a way for new customers to make substantial savings on a recommendation by a trusted peer. You can't do much better when it comes to incentivizing a conversion.

It becomes a win-win-win situation. The advocate gets rewarded for referring the new customers: both from the service and in the form of trust inside their tribe. The referred customer receives a reward for trusting the advocate. And your business gets a new customer that is inclined to trust the service. This kind of trust projection strengthens business relationships. In the end, this will positively affect your customer retention.

What Benefits Does a Referral System Provide to Advocates?

There are three kinds of benefits that stand out for the customers that refer your service to their peers.

The most visible one is the reward, often some form of cost reduction or improved access to the service. That is something the advocate may enjoy immediately after referring a new customer. This immediacy is essential: it allows customers to turn referring new customers into a planned and scheduled activity.

Our customers at FeedbackPanda were online English teachers. As it turned out, the Chinese online schools they were teaching for had understood the value of a referral system, too. The schools would pay teachers handsomely for referring their friends and family to become teachers on those platforms as well. By making clear at which stage of their teaching journey a referral reward would be paid out, advocates could reliably plan their monthly income around their referrals. Over the years, some teachers stopped teaching altogether and generated their income exclusively from referring teachers. A good referral system can do that.

The second significant advocate benefit is reputational. If you show to your peers and your community that you use an expert tool to do your job expertly, what will your peers think you are? An expert, of course. By embedding the referral link into helpful content, many advocates show that they know what they are talking about, and then benefit from people following their advice by clicking the link.

The third advocate benefit is related to empowerment. It

feels good to help other people, and it forges relationships. I am still in contact with many people who have referred business- and programming-related tools to me. This is not because I saved a few dollars, but because I received their advice and guidance, with the referral being a small part of it. They helped me understand that things can be done better. They helped me grow. I feel good knowing that my advice and suggestions are enabling other founders and developers to become better at their craft.

What Benefits Does a Referral System Provide to New Users?

It is quite likely that your onboarding is not as effective as you think. Prospective customers come to your landing page, some of them sign up, some of those may use your product, and a few of them will eventually subscribe.

Referrals are the duct-tape for your leaky funnel. A referred user comes to your product with the expectation that if the advocate can use it, so can they. There are a few incentives to sticking with a service that comes referred, namely trust in a supposedly good product, the expectation of savings down the line, and, most importantly, knowing that there is a real person somewhere that they can ask if they run into trouble: the advocate.

How Does a Referral System Help Your Business?

The relationship between the new user and the referring advo- cate is important, and shouldn't be underestimated. In fact, it can be incredibly useful to your business.

Let's look at the example of Chinese online schools again. They built a referral system that would show the advocate exactly where their referred teachers were along their journey.

And then, they would allow advocates and new users to communicate through their platform. They encouraged advocates to help and guide new teachers through their journey.

Essentially, they crowdsourced their onboarding to existing customers. If you build a referral system where your experienced customers help the new users get up to speed, you can significantly reduce the workload of your customer service department. If you add a referral system on top of a mature product, you can expect the most basic questions to be answered by your advocates before the questions even make it into your customer service tickets.

We built such a journey-tracking component into the FeedbackPanda referral system. Advocates could see if their referred users accomplished certain milestones, and where they struggled.

This kind of outsourcing also creates a permanent feedback loop about the onboarding process and first-usage problems. Right after we released the FeedbackPanda referral system, our advocates started reaching out, telling us about where they had issues helping their referred users make sense of the product. This allowed us to either change the product quickly or provide better instructions through our knowledge base.

We also noticed higher retention rates in both cohorts, advocates and referred users. We attribute this to the long-term reward for the new users, and the easy-to-reach threshold of three referrals per month to perpetually have a free subscription for advocates.

One of the most significant benefits of having this system turned out to be the added insight we suddenly had into our customer base. With unique referral codes, we could track where our new customers were most receptive to marketing, and who among our customers would most actively share their link in which social networks. That made the previously opaque word-of-mouth marketing much more measurable.

We toyed with the idea of creating different referral codes per social network but never followed through. The idea was to make the tracking even more manageable, but we decided against that. This becomes particularly cumbersome when you don't create random referral codes but use human-readable ones, such as the name of the customer or their business.

The Risk of Fizzling Out: Is Your Service Shareable?

While referral systems are usually opt-in and can be ignored entirely, there are several questions you might want to ask yourself before offering a referral system.

Referral systems don't work for all products or services. In fact, there are many reasons why a referral system wouldn't work well. A referral system may fizzle out for one of these reasons:

- **My precious:** Customers would lose their edge if they shared your service. Think of a marketer finding a tool that allows them to capture new hidden markets. Would they share their secret weapon with other marketers?
- **Training wheels:** Customers would admit to being a beginner if they shared your service. People rarely admit they're not good at something.
- **Empty pockets:** Customers would admit needing the savings from the referral system. We don't like admitting we can't afford something. If sharing a link could make other people think we're cheap, we'd instead not share it.

Conversely, a referral system will work best for these reasons:

- **Network effects:** Customers stand to gain something from another user joining the service.
- **Reputation gain:** Customers can show their peers that they are experts in their industry.
- **Way above the bottom line:** Customers can show that they are doing well using your service.

For FeedbackPanda, we had a powerful network effect built into the product: our customers could share their feedback templates with each other. That meant that every new customer might bring fresh content that the existing customers could use immediately. Inviting a new customer to the website was a way to do less work eventually for our customers, so they had no problem sharing the service. Our service also showed them in a professional light: teachers who used FeedbackPanda were good teachers and cared about their students. And finally, we could disregard the financial aspect, as almost all teachers are well aware of their precarious financial situation and don't mind sharing bargains with each other.

The Risk of Feeling Icky: Will It Impact Genuine Mouth-to-Mouth Marketing?

Once you're sure that your product is inherently shareable, think about how adding a referral system could change the conversations that already happen organically. Often, a recommendation that happened naturally before now can feel forced or sneaky.

If you can live with the fact that some of your prospects may be turned off by incentivized sharing, then go right ahead. But if you have a very sensitive niche, be very careful how and how much you recommend sharing referral links.

And, with sufficiently large groups of people: you won't be able to please everyone. There will always be people who are seemingly allergic to even the slightest sign of self-interest in their communities. We had a few teachers complain about the referral system cheapening the genuine messages of their peers. These kinds of purists cry out whenever they sense the slightest trace of rewarded behavior. They will call their industrious peers "shills," accuse them of being "paid for this," and generally be very vocal about marketing that they think has no place in their community.

If your system works, ignore those people. They are not your audience. Talk to the people who listen. Enable your most excited customers to spread the word and make a little bit extra on the side. If your service is outstanding, people will appreciate it.

We made sure we told our customers very clearly not to turn this into a marketing frenzy. We asked them never to post the link by itself, but always to add some helpful text or explanation of our product. We asked them to respect the rules of their communities regarding product placement and advertisement. In consequence, we received very few complaints from our customers about upsetting their communities.

The Risk of Speaking Too Soon: Is It the Right Time to Add a Referral System?

Earlier, we saw that sharing a referral link is always a risk to your advocate's reputation. What if they refer something of low quality? What if they only share it because they can make a cheap buck? These valid questions appear whenever a prospect is confronted with a referral link.

The best way to alleviate those fears is by providing a reliable product that allows for a great initial experience.

That is not your MVP. Usually, this happens much later in the lifetime of your business. In the Survival Stage, you try to find a repeatable business model and build features into your product that make it better for your customer. This phase is notorious for lots of trial and error. Lots of things change. It's definitely not a good time to have customers onboard other customers, only to find what worked for them not working anymore.

Best wait until your product is stable enough for your user-facing documentation not to change every week. That allows your advocates to support their referred prospects more reliably.

Technical Choices

Like most things SaaS, you can either use an existing solution or build your own. I built the FeedbackPanda referral system myself because I wanted to create a very customizable system. In retrospect, this probably would not have been necessary. Services like ReferralCandy, ReferralRock, SaaSquatch, or Ambassador offer tools that are easy to integrate and allow you to manage not just referrals, but also affiliates and partnerships.

In our case, we only wanted a simple system that was perfect for our customers. This turned out to be quite some work. Not only did I need to implement all the server-side logic to assign subscription extensions correctly and discounted plans, but I also found myself fixing a large number of frontend-related issues that stemmed from the tracking technology needed to tell who referred whom reliably. If you prefer to spend a few weeks building that instead of useful features, go for it. If you'd instead focus on your strengths, use one of the services that already solves all these problems.

If you use a third-party service, make sure you like the way they integrate. Some use widgets, and some offer APIs. Work with a system that fits with your long-term strategy.

When it comes to complexity, take a staggered approach. Your referral system, just like your product, doesn't need to be completely finished to be useful. For example, we initially released the FeedbackPanda referral system to track referrals, but not show the current stage of product adoption to the advocate. It was more critical for us to gather feedback on the overall system than providing every feature immediately.

The most important technical aspect of the system is that it reliably tracks who refers whom. That's all you need to start seeing the benefits.

Encouraging Your Customers to Become Advocates

We launched our referral system publicly, at the same time as increasing our prices. That allowed us to announce both changes at the same time, in tandem. With a month to go, we started reaching out to our customers through an Intercom message and the weekly newsletter, explaining what we'd be introducing and clearly stating the value proposition of using the referral system.

We framed it as a way to help other teachers become better teachers while saving a few dollars. That built sufficiently high anticipation that on the day we released the referral system, there was a noticeable wave of customers sharing their referral links. That prompted a lot of their peers to become interested in what FeedbackPanda was, and those questions summoned our evangelist customers to share their testimonials. People were ready to do our marketing for us, and they did.

In your communication leading up to and after the launch, draw parallels with other referral systems they may already know. It is a trust transfer opportunity that can make a meaningful difference in the adoption of your system. As our customers already knew a similar referral system with the school they taught for, they knew it was in their interest to participate.

We made sure we published clear step-by-step descriptions

of how to find their referral link and how to make it interesting for prospective customers in several knowledge base articles. We used screenshots and video tutorials to make it as easy as possible to understand. We also added a very prominent interface element into the dashboard of our application to make sure that the concept of referring customers was exposed to our customers' field of vision every single day.

We chose that kind of communication over active recruiting. We didn't reach out to people directly, but we put it in front of them wherever we could. A referral system should be optional, and only if a customer really wants to support the service should they do it. We wanted our advocates to refer new customers because they found it the right thing to do.

That doesn't mean you can't reach out to specific customers. In fact, active recruiting is an excellent idea in tribal niches. We talked to a limited number of our most socially active customers and recommended that they try out the system to see if this would give them more insight into their reach. That approach netted us a few excellent placements of links on niche-specific blogs.

A Few Thoughts Regarding Tracking and Privacy

When it comes to tracking, I recommend you capture the whole journey if possible, for maximum insight. Track the channels where your referrals happen and who is most prolific at putting their referral link into those channels. These are opportunities for partnerships that go beyond sharing a link. You can quickly find an influencer that would like you to sponsor their channels.

If you're planning to have your advocates onboard your new customers, make sure you restrict their communication in a way that keeps personally identifiable information from leaking. Don't share email addresses unless your users explicitly agree with such a practice. The best case would be to use an in-app messaging channel that allows you to control who talks to whom.

Remember that not every business can benefit from adding a referral system. It could even make the business look greedy when low-shareability products are pushed through a referral system. Referral systems are meant to support your marketing with an incentivized method of getting new users to try out your product. Make sure your product is shareable, your rewards incentivize your customers, and you provide plenty of information on how they can communicate the benefits to prospective customers.

SURVIVING A RECESSION AS A BOOTSTRAPPED BUSINESS

JUST A FEW WEEKS after the beginning of the Coronavirus outbreak in early 2020, the first SaaS businesses were reporting cancellations. The bootstrapped SaaS world may not have been affected by the pandemic as much as other industries, but we saw second-order effects appearing quickly.

For example, you may not be affected by a temporary closure of bars and restaurants directly. Still, if you're running a business that sells to these establishments or those they rely on, you'll see some changes in the future. For SaaS businesses like OpenTable, this happened very quickly, as they saw bookings going down 50% and more within days. This development had a trickle-down effect into many adjacent industries, in the same sector and beyond.

Online Sports Betting Platforms, a kind of business that did well in prior recessions, found themselves in a tight spot at the beginning of the pandemic. With most sports leagues suspended or canceled, their revenue streams, which usually picked up when the economy tanked, started to dwindle. No recession is the same, and what worked before won't necessarily work reliably this time.

In reflecting on my own experiences of working in SaaS businesses back in 2008 and the years after, I'll make a case for how bootstrappers can approach setting up their businesses to withstand the up and downs of increasingly interconnected global economies. I've compiled this into the AAAH!-Framework, short for Awareness, Anticipation, Adaptation, Healthy Optimism, and Action!: actionable steps to make sure you meet the challenges of a recession.

Awareness: Accepting that Change Is Happening

It all starts with not looking the other way. Things are changing during an economic downturn. The graveyards of the economy are riddled with remnants of businesses that stared change in the face and decided to continue business as usual. Don't try selling the things you already sell for the price they always sold for and wonder why sales go down.

You don't have to understand or directly experience the reason for a recession for it to affect you. Social upheavals happen to large groups of people, and you'll be in it whether you want to be or not. Accept that change is happening.

This is surprisingly hard for entrepreneurs, who are usually quick to embrace change. It's the entrepreneurial curse: our boundless optimism when it comes to the economy. If you think that things will work out eventually, a few years of things not working so well are hard to imagine.

Economic downturns are scary. But just like a booming economy, they are only times of change. You would react to more and more customers knocking on your door when things are looking better and better. So why not respond just as much when things are starting to look worse. Reframe the chilling word "recession" as "things that impact your business that you need to react to like anything else," and you'll know what to do.

Awareness of change starts with you, the founder. If you

have employees, you will need to make sure they also operate from that perspective. It won't do your business any good if you're working on making the business recession-proof when your customer service agents dismiss your customers' worries and questions. Team alignment will be more important than ever, and it starts with operating in the same economic reality.

It is in that reality that your business needs to survive. By accepting that long-term change is ahead of you, you'll be able to address what needs to be done without panicking.

Anticipation: Thinking About the Implications

Long-term changes can manifest in several ways. First and foremost, money dries up in a recession. Budgets shrink, and expenses are cut. Businesses will shrink themselves healthy, and if you're not essential to their operations, you will lose them as a customer. This doesn't mean you won't find different customers who need your product. It just means that you should expect a shift in the composition of your customer portfolio.

Second, people are insecure and frightened of things getting worse. That will translate into their willingness to make long-term commitments, both as customers and as partners. Your customers will be more stressed than usual, and less forgiving when it comes to issues, which will impact your customer service load and the intensity of the work involved. Sales and marketing will become less effective, first because the context in which they happen has changed, and later due to increased risk perception in your prospective customers.

Operational capabilities will change all over the place. In your business, you could experience this in the shape of the team being less effective. Employees may look for safer jobs, and contractors could stop freelancing altogether. Services you depend on may make radical changes. Some could go out of business. Your customers may experience a shift in their needs and requirements that you will have to anticipate.

Here are a few things you might want to pay attention to and the questions you will need to find answers to:

- **Legislative changes:** How are governments reacting to the cause and the consequences of the recession? How does this affect the regulatory landscape?
- **Changes in technology:** Are people using technology differently during or as a result of the cause of the recession? Which outdated preferences do you rely on? Do you need to realign your messaging to reach people using these new technologies?
- **Market movements:** Are purchasing patterns going to change significantly? Will important players in the market thrive or suffer? Is your niche still going to exist a year from now, or is it transforming? Will the market be saturated, or will it expand?
- **Labor:** How will unemployment impact the availability of talent for your business? How quickly will unemployment rise? Are your employees feeling safe with you? Will they look at other jobs?
- **Competition:** Will there be more or less competition in your industry? Are competitors failing? Why? Are there new competitors springing up? What motivates them? Will funding sources in your market dry up, or will investors spend more? What kinds of businesses will they fund? Will businesses that were not generating revenue because they had a lot of funding suddenly have to make a profit in a way that impacts your market? Which default-alive businesses are turning into default-dead?

The COVID-19 pandemic is a good example of how to

anticipate these types of changes. Governments responded to the pandemic with social isolation policies, massively disrupting existing consumption patterns. As a consequence of quarantine efforts, work-from-home became a necessity for many, resulting in an explosive increase in the need for enabling technologies like videoconferencing and collaboration tools. With school-age children being forced to stay home as well, EdTech tools and homeschool-related fields became much more interesting all of a sudden. With people working from home and having their children around, a lack of social connectivity tools designed for this purpose became clear. Companies who had until recently only marginally served these fields started intensifying their efforts to move into that market, increasing competition among the available solutions. Other markets started drying up temporarily, mostly in industries related to tourism and non-virtual entertainment. Virtual entertainment businesses began to see sharp uptakes in usage, and delivery businesses were overrun with orders.

All of this happened within the first few weeks of the COVID-19 pandemic. The long-term repercussions of this event are unclear at this point, but the forces set in motion will result in lasting changes to industries, professions, and personal lives.

Adaptation: Implementing a Response

You'll need to be on your toes to be able to react to changes quickly and reliably during a recession. You can prepare for this by segmenting the actions you'll need to take into two main categories: short-term activities you can take right when a recession hits, and long-term activities that you can expect to take during the downturn.

Short-Term Adaptations

The best antidote against money drying up is having it before it stops moving. Your immediate goal when entering a recession should be to have, or at least quickly build, reserve. Collect revenue as much as you can, as soon as you can. Even if you need to discount them heavily, offer and advertise yearly subscription plans. Give your customers a pay-ahead-of-time offer that they can't refuse. You need more runway than usual over the next months.

Try having at least three months of cash as if you had no revenue on hand. That should be the minimum to aim for in order to buy yourself time for impactful changes. If you're not yet profitable, double this to six months of cash. In this case, turn on your revenue engine as soon as you can. Even if it's terrible at the start, it's better than nothing. If you can get your revenue working while people are spending less and less, it's a testament to your entrepreneurial skill, and it can only improve from there. Get it started as soon as humanly possible.

Focus on sales now, right this moment. You will need to land your customers before they stop spending their money due to budget cuts. Somewhere in the financial and controlling departments, people are dusting off the old emergency budget cut plans. Get in there before the door closes.

Finally, a thing you can do right when you get into a recession is to cut your own expenses. Cut all non-essential subscriptions. Even if it's a bit more extra work, the costs for those services could mean the difference between staying afloat for one more month or having to declare bankruptcy.

This is an excellent opportunity for some reflection: who could be doing to your service what you are doing to all these non-essentials now? Which companies may consider you a "nice-to-have" instead of a "must-have" that is ready to be cut at a moment's notice when things look bleak? Think about why that is, and how you can become the service that your customers decide to keep in moments like this.

Having a reserve, focusing on sales early, and cutting expenses are good practices in any kind of economic climate. When you're entering a recession, these become necessities.

Another thing that is more important than ever at this point is to focus on crystal-clear communication.

Be clear to your customers that you intend to stick around. Be explicit about the measures you're taking to deal with the uncertainties of the immediate future. Some customers may complain about your communication because every service they use has something to say at that point. I believe that as a customer myself, I'd rather ignore one more email than having to wonder if the businesses I depend on are aware of what is happening.

The reason you need to be extra clear is two-fold. Initially, you need to soften the blow for people who are starting to realize that their mental model of the world differs from reality. If you position yourself as someone who began diligently preparing before they even considered the economic change a problem, you will be regarded as a shining beacon of perceptiveness and preparation. Later on, clear communication will be an important indicator of you staying the course: if you're consistent and understandable in your words and actions, you will build relationships of trust with your team and customers. This kind of confidence can make the difference between retaining a customer and having them cancel their subscription. Being straightforward with your team can mean that they don't start looking for other job openings elsewhere.

Long-Term Adaptations

Once you have taken these initial actions, you can start looking at what can be done over the next few months to make sure you stay in good shape and react to the changes that will undoubtedly occur. Here I mean two things: problems and opportunities. Problems are the things we're most concerned with when a recession hits. But opportunities will appear as well, and they will be the antidote to your problems most of the time.

There will still be customers out there looking for solutions to their problems, even when budgets are smaller, and people are cautious about buying. That's why refining your position is vital during this time. Pay close attention to what changes in the day-to-day lives and workflows of your prospective customers. Learn from them about their fears and worries. If those change, you will have to adjust your messaging to include them in the catalog of problems you solve. If your product needs to be adjusted for this, prioritizing that will enable you to help with newly found critical problems.

Look into your customer base to find which industries and customer cohorts generate the most revenue for your business. Then, trace their funding source and assess the risk of that drying up. After that, reach out to customers who are in the groups that are most likely to continue to support your business. In those calls, you find out how you can serve them even better, and then focus on the learnings from those conversations.

During a recession, you want your product to be as simple and focused as possible. Any cruft or untrimmed fat can be detrimental to your prospect's willingness to buy. On the flip side of this, any support and help they can get from you without needing to pay will create trust and goodwill. Often, that translates into referrals and word-of-mouth marketing that circumvents people's purchase risk calculations. If you have already helped a prospect with a valuable piece of content or a free tool, they will be much more likely to do business with you.

There are a few questions that you should reflect on when you're navigating your business through a recession. Many of those questions don't appear as often when things go well, so it could take some research to get to a meaningful answer.

- What are your strengths? Do you have any unfair advantages you could capitalize on? How can you protect your upside?
- What are your weaknesses? Where could competitors sweep in and grab vital market share? How can you protect your downside?
- Which category are you in? Which category should you be in? Has there been a category shift? Will there be? Is your market still in the Goldilocks zone: small enough to escape the competition but big enough to support your business?
- Is your positioning accurately reflecting the value of your service? Could it be misunderstood due to changing circumstances?
- How can your offer be more compelling? Is lowering prices an option? What can you do beyond that to make purchasers feel safe when choosing to buy your product? How can you get existing customers to commit more to your business? What experiments can you do to find these opportunities? Who can you have a conversation with to find new avenues of talking to your customers?

As a safety precaution, start looking into adjacent markets that overlap some with your current model. If your business is threatened, you can pivot and take your customers with you. In other cases, you may find excellent opportunities to partner up and mutually promote each other's projects. In times of need, band together. This is just as true for families as it is for service providers in many industries.

Everything that can reduce the risk for your customers will

help. It means making your product more stable, offering more and better guarantees, and finding alternative suppliers in case your supply chain is impacted. If you see something happening within your niche, move along with it. Don't resist where things are going. Align your business with the trajectory of your customers' needs and requirements. Reduce ambiguity where you can: be the scalpel, not the Swiss Army knife. Do one thing really well, and have a clear value proposition that can help your customers solve their critical problems.

Revisit your strategies and tactics regularly. Things change quickly, particularly during the initial phases of a recession. There are weeks when decades seem to happen. What was the right choice last month could become damaging to your business by next week. Keep your messaging under close observation. The sensibilities of people shift precariously, and your marketing slogans from last week may be ignored today.

Healthy Optimism: Trust in Progress and the Good in Others

"This, too, shall pass." The one good thing about recessions is that they end. They end because things turn around eventually. That doesn't happen by chance. It happens because entrepreneurs believe that it can be done, and then they just do it.

This trust needs to come from within you, the founder. You need to have an inner compass that guides you through these times. Believing that your business is doomed won't help you make the right choices to keep it afloat until things are better. I've always been a very optimistic person myself, and I think it's important to see the good in other people even when times are tough, and they act from a place of fear and uncertainty.

Show empathy for other's plight, guide them to make good long-term choices, and supply the tools to do that. Remind them to focus their energy on the things that provide value to people. Stay away from negativity, and don't join the chorus of the alarmists. Be a voice of reason and productivity that people can follow.

Stay confident in your ability to adapt to changing circumstances. Create processes in anticipation of major shifts: how will you handle increasing customer service workload when new regulations change people's workflows overnight? What happens when your crucial employee gets sick and has to stay home for weeks? Prepare for contingencies like that, and they won't be more than small bumps on the road for your business.

Be generous; don't fire your employees if you can avoid it. Ask for people to take a pay cut, which is often called the "Recession Discount," and pay it back when things are better. Show your workers that you're in this for the long run. They will stick with you if they see a future in your company. With a healthy dose of optimism that resonates through your actions, you will create the required alignment to get through the recession together. Tough times will eventually be over, but tough people remain. Band together even closer with your team and your customers, and you'll be able to weather the storm.

Act Deliberately, But Act

One of the most important things to do when you're entering a recession is to overcome analysis paralysis. Technical founders are particularly prone to decisional perfectionism, and that can ruin your business more than ever when you're facing a recession.

Don't act rashly, but act. Take a day for reflection. Work on your awareness and acceptance of the changes to come. Make sure you have answers to all the questions regarding the future of your niche, your customers, your business, and your own personal life.

Reflect on these things thoroughly, but try to keep yourself from doing mental gymnastics. Nobody knows what the future will hold; we're all giving our best guesses. If you approach your business systematically, you will increase the chance to emerge from this recession successfully.

Make notes on how you came to your conclusions. What could seem perfectly reasonable today may never again be in the future. If possible, make a recording of your train of thought in audio or video form. You may need to revisit a lot of your assumptions later, and it will help to jog your memory at that future point in time.

Let your reflections stay with you for a day or two. Recessions usually last for months and years; there is no harm in giving your brain a day or two to process your thoughts.

After that, get right to work. There will be a lot to do.

MARKETING AND SALES

SPREADING THE WORD: MARKETING ON A SHOESTRING BUDGET

BUILDING A PRODUCT IS NOT ENOUGH. No matter how good your product is, if nobody knows where to find it, you don't have a business. Spreading the word is an essential part of running a business, and so is convincing potential customers to try the product and eventually purchase it.

Many founders are scared of sales and marketing. They feel that customers are out of their league or that an unexperienced approach to marketing might confuse new prospects. "If only the product could speak for itself," they think. Well, it does not. You will have to speak for it. But you can do it on your own terms.

We will look into the proven methods and strategies of marketing your service in the early phases of your business. You will also learn where you can find help and support from other founders, how much of your journey you can safely share, and what benefits you have as a bootstrapper that you may not be aware of yet.

One beautiful thing about a niche is that there is a certain similarity among the people in it. They are likely to frequent the same social media forums, read the same blogs, visit the same websites. They often are organized in communities where word of mouth spreads quickly.

You can leverage the density of these networks by becoming a part of them. Genuinely participate in niche communities. Don't just use them as a marketing platform. Contribute before you advertise. Better, don't advertise at all, create meaningful content around your product, and share that in a way that is helpful to people even without engaging with the product directly.

Three components are essential to spreading the word efficiently, and they all interact with each other: tribes, water coolers, and word of mouth. And they are all quite affordable.

The Power of Tribes

You want to become part of and eventually lead a tribe. Tribes are communities that long for connection and shared interests, and members of a tribe follow the same community leaders. Facilitate more connection or satisfy people's interests, and you will be a voice in the community that your potential customers will listen to.

Tribes form around all kinds of topics. Some are obvious in our day-to-day lives, like fans of sports clubs. Others are extremely niche and highly virtual, like some obscure internet forum of indoor gardeners in Germany. But they are essentially the same: they all revolve around a central interest, and people talk about it with each other.

This makes tribes a great audience for your product. A very homogenous audience can be marketed to quite easily, as you know exactly where you can reach them and what language they speak.

The Power of the Water Cooler

Find the water cooler. The locations where your customers congregate when they are not hard at work can provide insightful information, as people talk more freely there than in professional circles.

Most of these water coolers are found in social networks like Facebook or Twitter. Reddit is a perfect place to look, as the sheer amount of specific subreddits makes it quite likely that there will be a vibrant community for your niche audience. Tribes are notorious for having very active water coolers, and once you find one, becoming a member is very worthwhile.

Listen to what people ask and complain about and offer your product embedded in more general advice. Shameless promotion is usually frowned upon in these communities, so you will need to provide something helpful and meaningful along with your plug. It is beneficial to become an actual member of the community before doing any intentional marketing. This will help you learn the language of the tribe and give you a chance to communicate with people, establishing yourself as a genuine member of their group.

Water coolers are wonderful for your content marketing in two ways. Initially, you will have the opportunity to see what your audience is interested in because that's the content with which they share and engage. Once you've understood what works for them and what does not, you can create content that you can be sure your audience will enjoy. Since you've already been a member of the community for a bit, you can provide quality content and market your product at the same time.

The Power of Word of Mouth

Word of mouth is the highest-converting way of spreading the word. Convince people to convince others and give them the tools to do so. Create easy-to-consume and easy-to-share content that existing customers can forward to new prospects. Allow them to mentor their peers into using your product by adding means to connect inside the product. This works particularly well with a referral system.

Word of mouth works mostly for low-touch businesses. Because these companies have a large number of customers and prospects that can take a look at a product through easy and self-service signups, word of mouth can happen without your intervention or encouragement.

In high-touch businesses, word of mouth works differently. Most of the time in B2B industries, your product is not very shareable because it gives an edge to the businesses that use it. Instead of everyone in the industry talking about your product, you want everyone in the businesses you would like as customers to talk about your solution before you reach out through direct sales.

There is one thing about word of mouth that you need to be aware of. You have almost no means to censor or steer the conversation. If there is something negative about your business, communities and tribes will discuss it. For many founders, hearing people complain about their service feels painful, but it's a normal part of the business. In the end, even a neutral or negative conversation will keep your brand on the minds of your prospects and remind them of the fact that you're at least trying to help.

Your Most Effective Marketing Strategy: Helping Your Tribe

Unlike large agencies, bootstrapped founders usually don't want to spend tens of thousands of dollars per month on social media advertisements. That doesn't mean you can't leverage social media for your marketing. Quite the opposite: a well-executed social media strategy can outperform pay-per-click ads significantly—it definitely did for us at Feed-backPanda.

We also experimented with paid ads, of course. And we didn't see any additional engagement compared to our existing content marketing and outreach strategies. So we doubled down on that, and it was the right choice for us.

And, there was a very basic assumption underpinning all of the marketing efforts: it's not about pushing a message into an audience of receivers, and hoping for signups conversions. It's about fostering a community that is eager to spread your messages, building your brand, and gaining recognition and reputation. To accomplish that, you have to focus on building a community first, and also optimizing your messaging. You need to help your tribe grow stronger, and they will be an amplifier for your messages.

If you're fortunate enough to sell to a very focused niche that is at best a highly active tribe or at worst a loose community, here are a few ways you can help them:

- **Facilitate communication.** Allow for more connections between the people in your niche. Enable existing communities or build one yourself using community software like Circle.so or Tribe.so. Interview leaders in the community on your blog, giving them more reach and their voices more impact. Interview members of your community, showcasing both their uniqueness and their belonging to the tribe at the same time. Syndicate user-generated content on your blog. Turn regular tribe members into influencers through your outlets.
- **Facilitate exchange.** From day one, envision your product to have a component where your users can share something. It can be data, insights, best practices, support, frankly anything. Give your users a

chance to empower each other, and they will be sure to increase their impact radius by carrying your service to their peers. Offer free resources from inside the community, and share your content with other outlets in the niche.

- **Produce and syndicate valuable content.** No matter if you're producing a podcast, regular blog posts, a video series, or you write articles with ratings, reviews, and testimonials: as long as you provide helpful and meaningful content for your niche, you will have followers that spread it. As your content is written for your customers, any new reader will likely be an excellent candidate to become a new customer as well.

All of this generates trust. Trust is the currency of tribes, and with enough trust, people want to listen to you. You don't need to spend money on marketing, and frankly, you couldn't buy this kind of relationship with your customers if you wanted to.

Use the fact that you're selling to a niche audience to your advantage and become a leader in your tribe. Help it grow, help your community members to learn and get ahead. This way, you'll end up with a never-ending stream of eager customers who trust you and amplify your messages.

SELLING AS A BOOTSTRAPPER: BEWARE OF THE WHALES

SALES WORKS DIFFERENTLY for bootstrapped founders. There are many useful resources out there like the *SalesForFounders Course* by Louis Nicholls, and often, effective sales can be condensed into a few main points. I'll leave this to the experts, and only talk about a few learnings that I personally had when it came to sales.

You don't have time or the resources to sell prospective customers what they want. You will need to sell them *what they will buy*. Big companies with huge R&D budgets can afford to sell their prospective customers a vision and then turn that into reality. As a bootstrapper, you will need to sell what you already have.

The only exception to this is early adopter customers. They are more likely to accept that a newly created product is missing a few features. Your early customers often understand that certain things are unfinished when they sign up. But don't get complacent: the moment you market to mainstream customers, you will only be able to sell what is there.

Don't promise the world to customers just to get their

money: with limited resources, you run the risk of overcommitting. The agility of your bootstrapped business comes from your ability to change course and quickly respond to customer needs. If you're locking in a roadmap for your customers just to get them on board, you risk being unable to pivot and adapt to new circumstances.

Many small businesses have been derailed by selling to just a few big customers, only to turn into their personal custom development shops. If you value your independence, go after a large number of smaller customers instead of just a few big ones. While it's a great joy to see a single customer pay thousands of dollars at once, it puts you at their mercy.

If a single customer can threaten to destroy half of your business's revenue by talking about canceling, are you sure you can still make the choice that is best for your business instead of caving in and fulfilling their wishes? Having so many customers that a few of them canceling barely makes a dent in your revenue is a great way to de-risk your business, and it completely changes your sales conversations. Where before you would throw yourself at new customers, blinded by the great increase in revenue they may bring, you take a soberer stance when a single customer only marginally increases your MRR. There will be much less pressure, and a much less pronounced power distance.

Like all things in your bootstrapped business, you want your sales process to be as streamlined as possible. Learn from every sales call you conduct. Assess if your process is still optimal for your business whenever you get a "yes" or a "no." It is the interaction with real people that will give you insight into what's working or what isn't. Getting a "no" is great: here goes a customer that would not get enough value from your product if they had said "yes."

Every "no" shows you what people need that you don't yet provide. The more conversations like that you conduct, the more you learn. If your target audience only consists of a few large customers, you have very few opportunities ever to get this kind of information. This form of direct validation is very valuable and is only accessible if you're actually talking to your prospective customers.

BEING SMALL IS A BENEFIT: LEVERAGING SIZE AS A BOOTSTRAPPER

MANY FOUNDERS FEEL they need to act bigger than they are. They expect only to be taken seriously when they appear to be a mature company. It turns out that this is no longer the case in many industries.

Depending on the size of your customers, the fact that you are a small business with few, if any, employees can be incredibly useful. If you are selling to individual customers or are in a B2BC market where your customers are tiny companies or freelancers, the fact that you're not just another faceless corporate entity will be a most welcome surprise. People treat you differently when you show that you're in the market because you care.

At FeedbackPanda, we communicated clearly from the beginning that it was just Danielle and me running the company. Our customers even took up the work of correcting other people publicly when they assumed we were a larger business. That always kept the founders relatable. We were just like our customers: real people solving real problems. This kind of relationship allowed us to mess up from time to time, only to encounter a lot of goodwill and understanding.

Bootstrapped founders and their businesses are different from other enterprises in a few key ways, and each of those can be used to your maximum advantage.

Bootstrappers have skin in the game. They can't hide behind a corporate facade. Reputation is important to them and the success of their businesses. Customers understand that once they are dealing with a bootstrapped, they can expect more than "business as usual."

If you're selling to a niche that understands the bootstrapping life, such as the startup market, you will also encounter this behavior. In the end, it boils down to honesty. Can you reliably deliver the levels of service that your customers expect? If you explain from the beginning that you are a solopreneur and that may mean that the service can be shaky when you're not there to fix it, you will allow your prospects to pre-sort themselves. You wouldn't want to have a customer you cannot yet serve anyway. Once the business enters the Stability Stage, you can change your messaging to attract those customers.

Leverage having skin in the game like this:

- **Be clear about being a bootstrapper.** Don't go for sympathy; go for comprehension. When a customer complains about a bug, don't say, "It's just me, so this will take a while," instead tell them that you'll personally get on it right after the conversation. Convey that their direct feedback matters.
- **Appeal to early adopters by using their language.** In the early stages of your journey, using labels like "pre-release," "beta," and "prototype" will attract innovators and early adopters while it will keep mainstream customers at bay.
- **Be public about your journey.** Talk to other founders, no matter if they are your audience or not. Share your story, leave traces. People who care to find

them will follow your journey and support you because they know how important this is for you. They will respond to your questions when you need an external perspective, and they will spread information about your journey to those who will listen.

Bootstrappers have nothing to lose. We don't have insane amounts of capital. We don't have hordes of employees we need to employ securely. We are flexible and can adapt to changing circumstances in the industry we serve much faster than established companies that cling to the status quo. If a prospect chooses your service, they can be assured that you will do whatever it takes to keep making your product better at solving their critical problems.

Leverage having nothing to lose like this:

- **Show the journey of your product proudly.** Document and publish the evolution of your product, your business, and your entrepreneurial perspective.
- **Celebrate features, pivots, and improvements.** Blog about things that make a difference in your customers' lives, and be proud of it. Your agility is your advantage. Communicate this with your prospects.

Bootstrappers have everything to lose. While our agility makes us very adaptable, it also prohibits us from entrenching ourselves too much: other bootstrapped businesses may spring up and start competition. For that reason, we're forced to build as stable and reliable a business as possible. For many founders, that means dedicating every minute of the day to the product and its customers. If a prospect chooses to buy from you, they can expect you to work your hardest to get and retain their business.

Leverage having everything to lose like this:

- **Celebrate your challenges.** Don't hide the bad and only talk about the good. Share what worked and what didn't with the founder community. Customers will do their research, and when they find that you work hard on finding the best way to go forward, that will create a lot of goodwill.
- **Share your struggles and growth as an entrepreneur.** You don't have a gigantic safety cushion and utopian exit bonuses when you leave the business. If your business fails, so will you. By showing how you deal with problems and reliably overcome them, you're projecting confidence and that you're in it for the long run.

Bootstrappers are laser-focused experts. One consequence of having access to very little capital and no employees in the beginning is that a bootstrapped business usually solves one thing really well and nothing else. For that, the founders have to be or become experts in their fields. When your prospects see your business, they don't see a giant corporation with dozens of unrelated products that it's trying to force on every possible customer, whether they need it or not. They see a purpose-built business that is working tirelessly on offering a product that solves a critical problem for a well-defined audience, with a founder that knows what they are doing.

Leverage being a laser-focused expert like this:

- **Show your expertise by writing.** Have a blog, write regularly, and write about what you know. Be a voice in your niche audience that people will follow.

- **Get interviewed on podcasts.** Nothing shows your expertise level more than a fruitful discussion with another expert in the industry you serve. Promote the episodes when they get released with your audience.

Bootstrappers are steering the ship. Founders not only envisioned the business they run, but they are operating and improving it every day. Often, a customer reaching out to customer service will be talking to the founder of the company. Unlike a rank-and-file employee at a large faceless corporation, founders have a large stake in the outcome of every interaction with customers, so they will pour their heart into every single interaction with each customer. You can use your direct connection with customers to turn a stressful customer service chat into a delightful trust-building opportunity.

Leverage steering the ship like this:

- **Be present and empathetic every time.** A great customer service interaction will stay on people's minds for a long time, and they will talk about it to their peers.
- **Follow through on promises.** When interacting with partners and large customers, you, as the founder, can use your command of the business as a credible argument as to why you can guarantee certain things. No confirmations and verifications are needed when you're the one both promising and delivering things.

Bootstrappers are relatable. In most families, you can find an entrepreneur. It's a grandfather who was laid off from a job in the factory and started his own business. It's an aunt who decided to turn a hobby into a business and is now employing a handful of people. We all know someone, a relationship or an acquaintance, who decided to start their own thing. Your customers will, too. By making it clear that you are a person running a business, their expectations and capacity for understanding will increase significantly. In a way, you are an underdog, just like their dad was when he started the family business. You're someone who cares, like their sister-in-law, when she quit her high-paid-but-unfulfilling office job to start a project that helped real people with real problems.

Leverage this level of relatability like this:

- **Prominently show the person behind the business, directly on your landing page or in an About page.** Make the business about yourself; use your personal brand and motivation to be more relatable.
- **Share the origin story of the business both through your business communication and outside of it, in interviews and on social media.** People love narratives, and nothing is more attractive than a rags-to-riches underdog story in the making.
- **When interacting with your customers, use a real-life picture for your user avatar and use your full name.** Engage with people on a personal level, as the engaged founder, not the distant business owner.

Use your agility and nimbleness as a bootstrapper to your advantage. Present yourself to the world as a real person, with all the shortcomings and problems that every one of your customers encounters in their own lives.

TOO MANY EYES: WHY BOOTSTRAPPED COMPANIES STOP BEING TRANSPARENT (EVENTUALLY)

WHEN BUFFER STARTED BEING RADICALLY transparent, the entrepreneurial community was enthusiastic. A brighter future of collaboration, shared learning, openness, and lifting the disadvantaged was on the horizon. Revenue, Salaries, Compensation: everything was made public for everyone to see. Recently, Buffer closed off their public revenue dashboard. Other bootstrapped companies such as Transistor.fm have gone through the same progression of opening and later closing off their revenue data. Why is that?

Two common patterns emerge when you read the explanations and comments made by those who resorted to turning off their public dashboards. Either the data is incomplete and paints a picture that is distorting the reality of the business, or the publicly available information gives the competition a one-sided information advantage.

Transparency in the bootstrapped world became a widely appreciated topic when Buffer made their salary and revenue information public starting in 2013, talking publicly about their numbers and values on the Open Buffer blog. Many interviews and news articles followed, lauding the bold move toward transparency as a blueprint for how a successful business should be talking about how much it pays its employees and how much revenue it generates.

Many companies followed their example. The Baremetrics Open Startups page filled up with other SaaS businesses committing to publicly sharing their revenue information.

Yet, after a while, some businesses stopped sharing their numbers. Some of those reversions have happened in recent months. The most prominent example is Buffer, who dropped from the Baremetrics Open Startups page. It most recently happened again when Transistor.fm made their revenue information private after having shared it publicly for over a year.

While Buffer have been almost ironically private about not being public anymore, Transistor.fm were much more transparent about not being transparent anymore. On their podcast, Build Your SaaS, Justin and Jon talked about going public with their revenue information in May 2018. Then, in November 2019, they laid out the arguments about why they turned off their publicly available dashboard and revenue numbers.

The Transistor.fm story sheds some interesting light on why companies choose to be radically transparent. The motivation to start sharing business internals with the public happens for a few reasons:

- **Social proof:** Fellow entrepreneurs, potential customers, and even investors can see that your numbers are real: your financials are right there for everyone to see. This builds a lot of trust in a world where everyone is inflating their numbers to appear bigger and more successful than they truly are.
- **Public accountability:** You're motivated to increase the numbers, not to have growth stalling. Someone, somewhere, is watching you. People will keep up with your success or lack thereof. If you commit to goals

publicly, stakeholders have the means to track your progress. While this can be the source of high anxiety, it can also energize and encourage you to work toward your goals even more.

- **People love underdogs:** You will find a lot of goodwill and support when people can see that your little company is doing its best to grow and become an established business. Advice and help will appear in unexpected ways. Customers will root for you, as they may also be a small business trying to make it. In the end, this kind of transparency is marketing. You're marketing the business as a real company led by a real person. This kind of intimacy does not exist for most business relationships, and people will relate to your business differently than to an opaque, faceless, anonymous company.
- **The "whisper network" effect:** By being transparent about your numbers, you equalize the playing field: historically disadvantaged groups and minorities benefit from things being in the open. This is particularly effective if you share salary information, as well. When Buffer opened up their salary information to the public, they were overwhelmed with resumes. People love an employer who is publicly transparent.

With all these benefits, what then would cause a business to stop sharing? Wherever you look, it seems to be one unifying problem: competition.

Every single one of your competitors can look into your numbers. They can see what happened when you pushed out your big marketing campaign, as they will see the immediate impact in your numbers. They can find out if your recent pricing changes worked for you or didn't work.

Essentially, you are giving your non-transparent competition the information advantage. You can only see your own numbers, but they get to see yours and their own. They get your learnings without sharing their own struggles.

Transparency may even encourage people to start a competing business because they see you not paying attention to a part of your business. A segment of your customers may be churning more than others because the product does not fully align with their needs. Competitors may find that information in your data before you do.

It may even encourage copycats that will chip away at your primary customer base. While copycat businesses don't have the same drive, determination, and experience that you have, giving people actionable information such as how your subscription plan levels are working for your audience is a risk. You paid dearly experimenting with your plans, just for someone to copy your business model with all those learnings for free.

That is a lot of risk for minimal upside. It breeds anxiety if you always wonder who may be scheming against you after having analyzed your data. Don't mistake this for paranoia. In a time where a SaaS business is easy to set up, this is a realistic scenario. It's just too many eyes looking at and probing your business. It is a distraction for founders who would prefer to work on their business instead of wondering who may be inspecting their numbers.

That's what happened to Transistor.fm. For Jon and Justin, it felt like they had to justify having their numbers in the open. With public scrutiny come expectations. Justin didn't want to be a performer anymore, caring more about the public image than the actual value the business provided.

I can understand this completely. At FeedbackPanda, we did share our revenue numbers on IndieHackers. Still, we never went fully public with all of our revenue, churn, retention, and subscription details being available like on the Baremetrics

Open Startup page. The public MRR was enough for us to attract interested parties. However, any would-be competition didn't have any additional insight.

Sometimes, it's the nature of the business that makes accurate and comprehensible transparency practically impossible. When Tyler Tringas had the business metrics for Storemapper in the open, it quickly became apparent that they were showing an incomplete picture. So, he turned off the public dashboard again.

There can also be too much transparency. Not just because there is competition, but also because numbers don't exist in a vacuum. Let's say you have a 16% churn over a 30-day period. What does this mean? Did a large number of customers cancel? Did you weed out a few accounts that were abusing the system? Did you increase prices, and while a lot of people churned, you still made 200% profit on the ones that stayed?

The numbers are not enough. They can be misleading or meaningless. Radical transparency is highly contextual, and without knowing the context, the figures can lead to misunderstandings. For a young bootstrapped business, this context may be quite clear, as most bootstrapped entrepreneurs go through the same struggle. However, once you grow to a specific size, some factors are unique to your business, your niche, your customer base. Those may not be apparent to you, so how could a person who knows very little about your business understand those complex interactions?

So what should a bootstrapped founder do?

I recommend being transparent but in a measured way. Share your Stripe-verified revenue on IndieHackers, and regularly communicate what's going on in your business. Create a narrative that gives context to the numbers. Share successes and failures. Keep people who are interested in the business updated with regular summaries. Every month, talk about what worked, what didn't, how the important numbers moved.

Make sure having those numbers out there does not detract from your overall goal of building a sustainable, life-changing business. Because in the end, transparency is not the goal. It is secondary to you achieving a life of independence and control.

Transparency is a great way to show that you are a real person working on a sustainable business. Let the numbers work for you instead of you working for the numbers. Just like you want the business to work for you instead of you working for the business.

THE STABILITY STAGE

THE STABILITY STAGE AND YOU

THERE WILL BE a point when your business starts getting along fine. You have built a product that works well for your customers. You've found a pricing model that generates sufficient revenue to pay for the business. Maybe you've committed to the business full-time, and you can already pay yourself a salary.

The important part is that you've built a business that has survived long enough to establish repeatable processes around your product and your business. Now is the time to optimize those processes for scaling. You will need to develop methods and approaches that can deal with much larger numbers of interactions and transactions at this stage.

Developing processes is scary for first-time entrepreneurs, and it feels like something that would reduce your agility and capacity to adapt to changes. You'll learn that it's quite the opposite: by implementing processes and Standard Operating Procedures, you will turn your business into a more flexible, less mistake-prone, and altogether more sellable company.

In this stage, you will work on automating the internal processes of the business. You'll be streamlining these operations into resilient and transferable processes so that you can have a well-positioned company that looks good to potential partners and has opportunities for sustainable growth. Finally, you will build long-term relationships with customers and turn the business into a brand with a tribe.

BUILDING RELATIONSHIPS: WORKING WITH CUSTOMERS

In the beginning, you had a few customers, your innovators and early adopters. They were with you from the start, and they understood your business at that point: a work-in-progress, with things that worked and things that didn't. These customers came for your vision and stayed because you continued to deliver.

Throughout the Survival Stage, you will have added many more to your customer base, and you will find more and more customers who don't share the early-adopter sentiment anymore. These mainstream customers expect things to be perfect at all times. They will threaten to cancel if their needs are not fulfilled as soon as they voice them. Mainstream customers will require you to talk to them differently.

Altogether, your customer base will grow both in size and in diversity. You will have to deal with diverging expectations and requirements and still deliver the value you've been delivering so far.

You will need to implement systems that will allow you to

stay in touch with your customers in a meaningful way without distracting you from growing your business. Customer service, customer success, and customer retention are very important to get right during this stage.

CUSTOMER SERVICE AT SCALE: HELPING THOSE WHO HELPS THEMSELVES

WITH AN INCREASING number of people paying for your product, your way of interacting with them will also change: you can't reach out to every single customer individually anymore. Where you were able to chat at length with your earliest customers, you will now have to be brief.

It's great to have a conversation with someone if you are trying to find out how your first version of the product is perceived. You don't need to talk about this at length if you already have 500 customers who have been paying for that product for months. While you still want to check in regularly, it's not required every single time you talk to a customer.

Every customer will still expect to be taken as seriously as your earliest adopters, likely even more. But your attention only goes so far. While real-time support was easy to manage when the likelihood of parallel conversations was low, it becomes very hard to manage at scale.

Transitioning from Synchronous to Asynchronous and Self-Help

If you run a business that has a lot of incoming help requests, your best bet is to look extensively at asynchronous and self-help-based support systems.

A knowledge base is an incredibly helpful tool at any scale, but it is required once you reach a certain size. Being able to explain a problem once and making the solution available to all who ask the same question in the future is very valuable. If you do this for every question that is often asked, it will significantly reduce the time spent on responding to those requests.

At FeedbackPanda, we made a point of turning answers to questions that could be answered with step-by-step instructions into knowledge base articles immediately after the conversations were over. Every day, one or two new articles would appear in the knowledge base. Using Intercom, these articles would be automatically suggested whenever the next customer would ask a question related to the words in the title.

Additionally, we trained the Intercom AnswerBot feature to respond to particularly pressing questions with automated step-by-step responses. That helped us help users who needed immediate assistance with login issues, payment failures, or blocked accounts. For a company that never hired a customer service representative for the night shift, this automation let us sleep at night—until it didn't.

Speaking the Language

You and your employees must understand the subtleties of your customer niche's psychology. Accountants approach solving problems differently than artists. Aligning the customer service voice to the customers' psychology will prevent a lot of misunderstandings and allow you to continue building your brand even when customers are frustrated and helpless.

You can learn this customer-side language fairly quickly by doing a customer interview in which you ask them to use your software and explain what they are doing. Complete a couple of interviews, and you'll see overlaps in how certain actions are described, what words are used, and how processes are conceptualized. Be sure to make this available to everyone in the business who is in regular contact with customers. Having access to material that allows your team to be more empathetic to your customers will be of massive benefit to your external presentation.

Getting Help

Never hiring help at FeedbackPanda was a mistake. With more customers signing up for our service, the count of those who didn't get their questions answered by the automation or couldn't find adequate help through the knowledge base increased. Every morning, there were a few unanswered messages, often portraying the desperation with which customers had tried to reach out only to not find help. I thought we could deal with this alone, but in retrospect, it was a mistake. Just because it's not a full-time job just yet doesn't mean you can't look for help.

It is essential to hire a customer service representative eventually. Find the time of day that statistically has the most incoming tickets, find a person whose working hours fall into the that time zone. If you can find your customer support rep from within your existing customer base, you can be sure they understand both the product and the customer perspective. If not, allow your newly hired customer service rep to spend some time with your customers.

With someone taking all the customer service conversations,

you will have peace of mind, in two ways: first, you know that your customers are taken care of, and second, you know that if there is any problem that requires your intervention, a person will try to get in touch with you. While automated systems are often used for alerts, nothing beats someone who can contextualize a situation while they inform you about it.

We didn't hire for customer service until after we had sold FeedbackPanda. During the transition phase, as we handed over the company, we had to hire replacements for our position. When I trained the customer service rep that our acquirer hired, all the preparations we had made paid off. With all our help-desk articles and documented processes, it only took a few days to get them up to speed. It was a revelation to me when my anxiety about getting the customer service done dropped to zero within a few days of having someone else dealing with it. We should've hired much earlier.

CUSTOMER EXPLORATION: SEEING THROUGH YOUR CUSTOMER'S EYES

AT THIS STAGE of your business, you have a mostly mature product that is used by many customers. You can expect that for most of their use cases, it is good enough. But instead of guessing, I recommend setting aside some time every few months to do some customer exploration.

Consider it to be Continuous Validation of the customer-facing properties of your service. Just like you need to make sure your expenses are not growing beyond what you can afford, you need to regularly check if your product still solves your customers' critical problem sufficiently.

This is best done by incentivizing customers to jump on a screen-share-based video call that you can record. Service credit or an Amazon gift card can work wonders here, depending on the kind of customer. As long as it's something valuable to them, either money, time, or reputation, it will help you get them on board.

The Good, the Bad, and the Unaware

It's hard to find the right customers to make sure the feedback you'll receive is as unbiased as possible. That's where the three-pronged approach works well as it allows you to find the extremes and the overlaps. First, find the customers that had the most trouble with your product and watch them use it for a while. Then, do the same with volunteer customers who have not reached out about problems. Finally, talk to a few customers who usually rave about the product and share it with their peers.

You will find a lot of known issues, but there will also be surprising ones: often, the customers who don't complain may still be struggling and using the product in strange, unexpected ways. You will never find those behavior patterns unless you catch your customers exhibiting them.

This method often surfaces any disconnects in feature presence and feature usage. It allows you to revise your roadmap and fine-tune your feature prioritization framework.

It will allow you to improve the affordance that your features show, and it will lead to a better user interface.

Be sure to include the customers who exposed the problem in the deliberation about potential solutions. That level of involvement will often turn them into brand ambassadors, providing a powerful brand reinforcement effect in your niche community.

What to Ask During a Customer Exploration Call

I suggest taking every call as a completely fresh opportunity to look into the life of this particular customer. It's a form of qualitative analysis, so don't expect to get any meaningful numbers. What you're looking for are imbalances and opportunities.

Set expectations. The first thing you should tell your

customers after thanking them for joining is that this is a space where they can be as critical as they want to be. You're looking for things that don't work, not for praise. Just like with your audience, problem, and validation calls in the Preparation Stage, you need your customers to point out the malfunctions, pains, and issues. Make sure they understand that they can help you most by pointing out as many problems as possible.

Ask for an unbiased walkthrough. Make your customers use the product to solve their problem under your observation, best through screen sharing. Ask them to explain to you what they're doing. Act as if you were someone who is seeing the product for the first time. What works well here is asking your customer to explain it as if you were a colleague. The idea here is to remove any bias toward you. The video part of this will be incredibly useful. You can see how quickly customers pick up interface actions and how they interact with your product.

After the walkthrough, ask what pains them. Which needs are not fulfilled? Where are costs too high? Where do they spend more time than they'd like? This is an excellent opportunity for them to reflect on the actions they just took and discover where reality was disconnected from the expectations they might have had.

Ask for alternatives. Are there alternative products that offer a solution to their problems? If so, how do they differ from your product? If your product didn't exist, how would your customer solve their problem right now? You're trying to find out everything you can about the job-to-be-done. Beware that this is likely speculation and not overly realistic, but it should give you some insight into the order of magnitude that your product is helping them. If their alternative is just a little bit harder to accomplish, you'll need to step up your game.

Ask for missing critical features. Most of the time, customers will be content with the scope of your product. But then there are the times when everything changes. A new law requires providing a new report or document, and your current solution doesn't yet offer it. A good example of this is offering downloadable invoices. This won't be a first-rate feature when you start your business, but it definitely will become critical come tax season. Listening to your customers voice their dissatisfaction with the absence of some features can guide you into how much they need something.

Ask for nice-to-haves last. Often, those features are quickly built or already in the works. It's a good way to end a conversation with a customer, as the focus is on something positive yet non-critical. The chances of something important surfacing here are low, but you never know: your customer may have particular needs they are unaware of, and what they'd like to see may uncover something new.

Repetition Is Key

So how often should you do this? It depends on how many resources you want to invest in this kind of research. It's beneficial, but it also takes your attention away for a few hours per call, both with preparation, the call itself, and making meaningful notes during and after the call. I recommend you take a day for this activity with three or four customers every two months.

Try talking to the same customers multiple times throughout a year. What new problems did they encounter since your last call? Did you solve the problems they complained about in the meantime? This is a great opportunity for you to show how accountable you can be. If you can make a customer's life easier, it's likely they will share their experience with their peers.

CUSTOMER RETENTION: KEEPING THEM AROUND

WHEN IT COMES to customer relationships, momentum is on your side: it is much easier to retain a customer than it is to find a new one. Once the initial inertia is surpassed, the effort that needs to be put into keeping a customer is significantly lower than acquiring and onboarding a new customer. And a churned customer is a double loss: not only do you have to find a new customer to replace them; to grow, you will need to find two new customers. That's why customer retention is of utmost importance when growing a business.

This focus on retaining a customer at all costs is somewhat new. Before the subscription economy, a repeat customer was a nice-to-have, but most of the time, the relationship with the customer was over after the first transaction. Processes were optimized to get the customer through the order process and stop them from abandoning their cart. But once they ordered, it was over.

The membership economy is very different. Customer retention is more important than getting new customers, as churn is the silent killer. Retention can be measured in renewal or cancellation rates, and keeping it as close to 100% as possible will determine if your business is sustainable or not.

Luckily, there are several proven strategies to increase retention, and they all center around your relationship with your customers.

Value Nurturing

Value nurturing strategies increase the customer's perceived value of your product, making the cancellation feel like a more significant loss. Showing your customers how much they benefit from your product will make them stick around longer.

Your goal is to confirm again, over and over, your customers' belief that choosing your service was a smart choice. Not only does it have to feel right, but it should also clearly be a good economic decision, both on their first day and right now.

In an ideal world, customers would continuously notice what a fantastic product you provide them. They would flood your customer service channels with thank you messages, and they would write long blog posts about how everyone should be a customer of your business, forever. Sadly, life gets in the way, and other things are much more important to your customers.

That's why it's up to you to show them what they get. Show them their progress, how much they have improved ever since they used your service. Show them how well they do compared to other users, how much impact your service has in their lives. In short: make the value they receive visible to them inside your product and in your communication.

It's not only limited to this, though. The goal is to retain a customer, and showing them what they get is just one way of keeping them around. You want your product to be something on which they depend. When times are tough, you want your service to be the last one to be canceled. This is best accomplished by creating voluntary dependency: offer something on which your customers want to depend. Provide so much value compared to the alternatives that they willingly take the risks inherent in every choice of using an external product.

A word about value: we are not just talking about your revenue here. For your customers to stick around, your business needs to provide them with benefits and advantages every single time they use it. Your customer lifetime value is inextricably linked to the perceived value of your customers.

Here's the trick to customer success: increasing their revenue will increase yours. Make them successful, help them grow the lifetime value of their customers, and their LTV will expand as well.

Expectation Management

Managing expectations is a significant factor, too. Being able to occasionally over-deliver will delight your customers as it is an unexpected bonus. I'm not saying you should consistently undersell your product. But surprising a customer with something good they didn't expect is a rare occurrence in the business world. Those who succeed at that will be remembered.

Customers will tell a few people about a positive experience, but they will tell a few dozen about a negative one. Keeping customers above the baseline will reduce the chance of them ranting to their peers, who may often be potential customers.

Every impression counts. At any touchpoint, you can synchronize expectations. Find out what your customers are concerned with and adjust your priorities when expectations change. From your customer's perspective, it's a magical thing to see a feature suggestion become an actual feature.

The level of trust in the brand and the decisions you make are incredibly important for renewal. By aligning what your customers expect you to do with your actions, trust grows, and value generation will happen along with the expectations of your customers.

Those expectations change over time. In the beginning, customers often have to find their footing, and they expect ease of use and being able to integrate your product into their work-flow. After a few years, focus shifts to perceived value, as your service has become a regular part of your customers' work routine. Unless they're really needed, customers will ask less and less for new features, and they will shift their focus onto existing parts of your offer and how the current set of features can be improved even more.

Throughout a customer's lifetime, get a feel for the acceptance of and desire for self-service in your customer base. In the beginning, you can respond to every support query yourself. When you scale, more of your support will shift toward more asynchronous and self-help solutions. It's important to take your customers with you on that journey. The early adopter that you talked to every few days through your real-time chat will have to understand that your attention is more divided. Their expectations will need to change with your structural changes.

Find the At-Risk-of-Leaving Customers

In the best case, a customer stays with you for many years. They love your product, their every wish comes true every time, and they become catalysts for your marketing.

This is, of course, utopian. Every single customer of yours has different problems and hardships, and what works for one may not work for another. Inevitably, at some point, a few customers will think about canceling. If you want your retention to remain high, there are two things you can do:

Convince them to stay if they're about to leave. The hard part is to figure out who is about to cancel. You can track people clicking the button that starts the cancellation process and trigger a customer service conversation. Tag this customer as someone who should receive a follow-up email asking what you can do for them. You can track other things than clear cancellation intent: do they stop using the product for a long time? Stay clear of acting too quickly, as this is often a result of vacation, maternal leave, or just other priorities. But it is worth measuring so that you have an indicator you can use to inform your communication strategy.

Convince them to come back after they leave. This is your last chance to retain them as a customer. After someone cancels, give them a grace period of a few days or hours, but re-engage them. Depending on how shameless you want to be, ask them to return with a free month, or even extend them the offer of a lifetime discount for returning on a paid subscription. As long as it fits into your economic calculations, keeping a customer is worth more than losing them, even with reduced revenue.

There is a difference in what makes customers leave, and it is connected to how long they have been with you. Early customers are more likely to quit because of lower switching costs and less dependency on your service within their established workflows. They're more jittery, so expect their cohorts to cancel more. Long-term customers quit for different reasons: either their perceived value decreases or the problem–solution fit of your service is misaligned. Take your customer's business size and age into account when you craft your messaging for each cohort, and find something that works for each of them.

Actionable Retention

Here are a few things we did at FeedbackPanda to keep customer retention as high as possible.

Staying in touch with your customers will keep them engaged. Offering a weekly newsletter to expose them to things that have happened in their industry will do two things: first, it will associate your business with a trusted source of information, and second, it will also show that you know what you're talking about. Building trust and reputation goes a long way toward retaining a customer.

Tighten and focus your onboarding. A customer who "gets it" quickly after signing up will stay with you longer and think of your business as a dependable service. If you can reduce the number of steps until your prospective customer reaches the "a-ha" effect, go for it. There is nothing better than a customer telling their peers that your service is "a no-brainer."

Do things that don't scale. Send a postcard. Delight your customers with surprises on their birthdays. Send them a gift after they've been with you for a year. Host a meetup in the city where most of them live. Surprise them in ways that other businesses can't—and wouldn't. Not only will this make those customers stick around, but word will travel, and you will benefit from your customers sharing their delight and surprise with each other. When we had our first 100 customers, we sent out postcards to all of them. A lot of customers shared photos of receiving those postcards in the mail, and consequently, a lot of prospects signed up for our service.

Ask your customers for testimonials. Use them on your marketing site, in app-stores, or any other platform where they can share it with their peers. This gives your reputation and your customer a feeling of being appreciated; after all, they are asked about their opinion. At FeedbackPanda, we often did this after intense customer service interactions where we solved a customer's problem successfully. A happy customer gives great reviews.

In every interaction, focus on building a respectful relationship with your customer. It's the one currency that is worth more than the money they pay you every month.

BUILDING A MATURE BUSINESS

CONTINUOUS VALIDATION: STAYING IN TOUCH WITH YOUR MARKET

I FIRST FELT that we truly had a validated business when we had our very first yearly subscriber. That level of commitment for a young product such as FeedbackPanda two months into our existence showed us that people wanted what we made and were ready to put their money on it.

However, validation is always a temporary state. Your business can be validated only "for the time being." Competition, a changing regulatory landscape, human error, bad press, changing preferences can all derail a working business. That's why we always kept an ear on the pulse of our community. We screened public forums and groups for complaints and new developments.

In the SaaS world, we have Continuous Integration. I think we should also have the concept of Continuous Validation. Regularly and frequently, assess where you are in terms of still being in touch with the market. Are you still solving their most painful problem? Did that change? Are there new issues that you didn't encounter before? That will keep you on your toes— and keep your customers happy.

Continuous Validation of a Business

Continuous Validation is the practice of assuming that every product is an iteration of trying to solve a shape-shifting problem.

Within that cycle, processes and goals need to be realigned from time to time. If you're continuously validating your business, you will avoid making large pivots or becoming outdated.

Today, a business may need to solve a specific problem (let's say Selling Time Machines). Still, a few months or years later, it may need to shift its core business and product strategy (let's say to Grandfather-Paradox-Resolution as a Service). Or maybe, a regulatory agency (let's say the Ministry of Time Travel and Tobacco) issues new guidelines and requirements (let's say "No Time Travel on Sundays"), to which the business needs to adapt (let's say by providing a Time Travel Permission API and selling that as a plan upgrade).

What was once a flourishing business model can turn into an adjacent-yet-different enterprise over time. How can you make sure that you're still aligned with the needs and requirements of your customers?

Check for Problem/Solution Alignment

Every few months, determine if your business is still solving the problem it set out to solve.

Most products are engineered for particular use cases. Those use cases could transform over time. Industries adopt new practices, and workflows change. Your tool may be front and center right now, but a change to the business process or a regulatory requirement may make your product less effective.

Talk to your customers and see if they find friction where there was none before:

- Do they still deal with the problem frequently?
- Does the product provide as much value as it used to a few months ago?
- Have they noticed that your product has become harder to use for certain tasks? (This usually implies a change in the task, not necessarily the product.)
- Are there other tools that they use before and after using your product to get to their results?

Check for "Eisenhower Alignment"

Every few months, determine if you are still solving the most significant problem your customers have. Was something introduced that makes your solution less important? Is their problem less urgent?

This check is named after the Eisenhower Matrix, a method designed to shine a light on the tasks that need to be prioritized. It applies to any audience and industry. People find it easy to use as it only asks if a task is important, urgent, both, or neither. Regularly checking to see if the problem you are solving still exhibits the qualities of a critical problem and fits the Important/Urgent quadrant of the Eisenhower Matrix will allow you to pivot to a different issue if that one is gaining more prevalence.

If you have a way to track how much value your product creates for your customers (as a lead generation tool would track the number of leads generated per day), make sure you look into the historical development of that metric. Is it going up for most users or just a few? What's the overall trend? Find the outliers and talk to them to see what happened to impact their usage of your product.

How to Check

With these two performance checks every once in a while, you are continuously validating your business. But how can you get this information?

It boils down to talking to your customers, either face-to-face or through a survey. I would recommend direct conversations with a few select customers instead of blasting everyone with surveys, but both methods have their benefits. The important part is to reach out to customers who care about their work, and talk to them about the problems they face and if you're still solving them adequately. Like in any good conversation with customers, try to be a good listener. Don't talk about the product, but ask them about how they solve their problems.

If you have the opportunity to talk to the same people again and again over a few years, take it. There is a lot to be learned from the changing perspective of a customer. You will be able to see a difference in what is important to them at different points during their professional journey, which will provide insight into retention strategies along the way. This kind of interaction will also turn your customers into advocates for your business. Being taken seriously will create a solid bond between customer and brand, and the benefits of those kinds of relationships cannot be overstated.

If you create surveys, make sure you don't limit your customers' responses. You are not trying to find surprising, unexpected information. If you already knew of a shift in their problem space, you would have already reacted to it. While we are talking about validation, your primary goal is to explore the unknown, detecting the unexpected changes that you have so far missed. Give survey participants a lot of opportunities to write free-form text, and ask open questions.

Continuous Validation: Check for Founder Alignment

Every few months, look inside yourself to see if you are still feeling passionate about your vision. You set out to make the world a better place for someone in a particular way. Do you still care about the same people? Is there a subgroup or a new audience that you discovered that is even more relatable? Is there another way of getting them to the goals that you have found while solving their problems? Are you still excited about how you help your customers? Have you been brooding over a new idea, but work on your current business goals is keeping you from reflecting on it?

A running business requires commitment and weathering the storms of day-to-day operations. If you're feeling burned out or disinterested, think about delegating the work that is the most tedious. You're a founder; focus on your vision whenever you can. That is the one thing you can't delegate.

When you reflect on founder alignment, envision where you want to be in a few years. From that perspective, take a look at your business. Is it a vehicle that will get you there? Or is it a barrier on the path to where you want to go? Adjust how you run your business accordingly.

Continuous Validation: How Much Is Too Much?

While it's great to check your business every now and then, you should not do that too often. Just like looking at the stock market every day will drive any long-term investor crazy, you don't benefit from continually brooding over the validity of your business, particularly when you have paying customers. Building relationships with the customers you have today is more important than wondering if you will still have them a year from now. The former enables the latter, while the latter hinders the former.

I recommend taking a day each quarter to reflect and go through the validation checks outlined earlier. By validating the problem–solution fit, answering the biggest-problem question by using the Eisenhower Matrix, and checking your passion for how you work and for whom you want to work, you will make sure that you continue to do meaningful, valuable, and impactful work.

You May Not Be Validating Enough (or Correctly)

If you've built a company that is highly automated, you're running the risk of losing touch with your customers. At Feed-backPanda, we had a lot of self-service help material, so many customers would not talk to us through our customer service channels. We would make sure that the help-desk system would contact them and if there was anything the system didn't solve for them, we would learn of what customers were searching for unsuccessfully. Like that, the more complicated problems would eventually be surfaced to us, the humans behind the operation.

You may not need to talk to people at all times, but make sure you talk to them when you're stepping through the valida-tion tasks set out above.

Having a lot of metrics and KPIs is becoming more and more common. Don't just look at the numbers for your deci-sion-making. Use those numbers to see downward trends, but reach out to customers to confirm your observations and get to your conclusions.

All in all, your best bet is to keep your communication chan-nels open to your customers. I've written about how to offer maximum customer service with minimum effort. Try setting up synchronous, asynchronous, and self-help systems that will allow you to reach out to your customers from time to time.

Keep those channels open, and note when people suddenly start to complain or point out things that are lacking when they were not before. Your customers will make sure you continue to provide a product that they need to solve their ever-changing problems.

Finally, there is a risk of validating only features and new developments while leaving out the assumptions. This can be called second-order validation: validate not only the choices you made but also the underlying concepts. An example would be validating a newly introduced tabular view of some data. The first-order question is "Does this tabular view display the data in a meaningful way that helps our customers solve their problem?" The second-order question would be "Is the problem that this data can help solve still the relevant problem, or should we focus on showing different data, potentially in a tabular view?" It's a version of the 5 Whys, applied to customer needs and desires.

Try digging as deep as you can. You will accomplish the best degree of validation by asking real customers about their real problems, figuring out the reasons behind their actions, and making sure you have a clear understanding what has the most impact on their lives.

ROADMAPS AND YOU: BUILDING A FUTURE TOGETHER

IT'S great to know where you are going. It's even better to know that your customers approve of that.

Both goals can be reached by establishing roadmaps. Usually, that's a document that plans what you want to do in the future, ordered by when you want to do it, with more or less accurate guesses on how long it will take. When a feature prioritization framework is a compass, then a roadmap is... well, a map.

The purpose of this roadmap is two-fold: to give you a clear plan for the future, and to help your customer trust that your service will be useful to them for a long time.

One Roadmap, Two Roadmaps

You will encounter founders who tell you that you should have an internal roadmap and a different external roadmap so you can manage expectations. You will also meet founders who tell you that, for transparency's sake, you should only have one solitary roadmap.

This is a question of how much you want to communicate

with your customers, and it will heavily depend on the industry you're in, your competition, and how much transparency you're going for.

I think that a workable solution is somewhere in the middle: have an internal roadmap with all the details, and show a slightly redacted version to the public. For the internal roadmap, use your best estimates and detailed descriptions; for the external roadmap, use generalized date ranges and fewer details. The customer-facing map should always be a limited view of the original. That way, you retain control over what is visible, but it's never too far from your internal roadmap.

Internal Roadmaps

For every single project I've worked on in the past, I eventually had a road map. Sometimes it existed before I started working on the product; other times, it was established months after the project already had paying customers. It's one of many tools that help to structure and plan your work in a dynamic and often-changing company.

You'll benefit from having a plan, even if you don't necessarily stick with it all the time. After all, you're an agile bootstrapper, everything is essentially an experiment, and no decision is set in stone, particularly not the things you'll be doing a few years from now. So, treat it as a flexible guideline.

Internal roadmaps should contain goals and dates for all sections of your business: product milestones, sales and marketing goals, and your plans for operative activities like building a team, integrations, and partnerships. Don't limit a roadmap to features or releases; it can reflect the future of your whole business. In fact, the more different sections of your business are involved, the more insight you might glean into the connection between things.

There are several formats for roadmaps, and they all have their pros and cons:

- **Timeline roadmaps:** These are great when you're one of those founders who needs deadlines for motivation and peace of mind. You can see which things need to be done in parallel at what time, allowing you to know when and where to focus your attention. You can easily miss those dates, though, so better use high-level terms like "by April" instead of "April 21st."
- **Roadmaps without dates:** I personally really like these, and it's best if they come in the form of a Gantt chart. Roadmaps like this show dependencies and connections between tasks more than any discrete date when they should be accomplished. "It's done when it's done, and here is what needs to happen to get there"—what a bootstrapped-compatible sentiment.
- **Kanban-style roadmaps:** Unlike the more common timeline-based roadmaps, Kanban-style roadmaps categorize your planned activities and features into groups, like "Backlog," "To Do," "Doing," and "Done." This is a great way of sorting things if you don't want to commit to any particular order but still want to keep an outline of what the future holds.

No matter which style you choose, you will benefit from having a document that outlines the steps you can and should take with your business. You don't have to keep all the information in your head.

Public Roadmaps (and More)

There is another useful side of roadmaps: making them available to your customers. Future revenue is much more likely to happen when those who pay are happy to continue to do so. If you involve the people who use your product in its development, you will be able to get immediate feedback about the desirability of your planned features. The best way to do this is to have a public feature roadmap (like the one offered by the Roadmap SaaS Canny).

A benefit of a public product roadmap is that it could incentivize customers to commit to yearly plans both as a sign of confidence in your product and to lock in your commitment to provide it for at least a year. While it's great to have those funds available, be aware that this also sets expectations. If you don't deliver on your promise, there will be some damage to the trustworthiness of your brand.

In addition to the roadmap, allowing your customers to suggest features and vote on them is also an excellent idea to measure what people are looking for (and which of those problems are commonly felt). It doesn't absolve you of doing your own research though. The suggestions generated through these tools should start your research process, not conclude it.

A warning about public roadmaps: they become a commitment once you show them to your customers. Once you communicate intent, customers see it as a promise. If you don't follow through, your public roadmap is pointless. If you have dates on your public roadmap, customers expect things to be finished by then. People are drawn to concrete figures, and nothing is more concrete than a date.

Keep in mind that the public roadmap is completely optional. You are at perfect liberty to tell people that your plans are your own, and you won't share them. If you think that this may give your competitors too much information, don't make it public. Just know that customers are used to not being told what is going to happen, and your service could stand out as being the one that does share its plans for the future.

BUILDING A SELLABLE BUSINESS

IN HIS BOOK *Built to Sell,* John Warrillow talks about how to set up a company so it's easy to sell. The great thing about structuring your business like that is that even if you never sell it, you will be able to benefit from it. The reason for this is that the *Built-to-Sell* method focuses on removing the need for the founders to work in the company.

We took this approach with FeedbackPanda, and it literally paid off. After running our business for about 18 months, we had grown it to a mid-five-figure monthly revenue figure, and since we had been sharing this revenue on our IndieHackers product page, the first potential acquirers started reaching out to us.

At that point, we had a very sellable company but no intention to sell. It was very apparent to us that we had a valuable business on our hands—after all, we had done everything we could to make it sustainable. But after a few emails, we were negotiating a deal with a prospective acquirer. Less than two years after launching the business, we had sold it. Transitioning the business was extremely painless, much more than we had thought it would be because we had done everything right to make FeedbackPanda sellable.

What Makes a Business Sellable?

Every business that generates a profit is sellable. In fact, even the ones that don't are sellable—to the right buyer. But the kind of "sellable" I am talking about is not a fire-sale or a bargain-bin acquisition. When I say that a business is sellable, I mean that it will allow you to elevate yourself into a position of previously unattainable financial security and professional success. It did for me, so I will share as much as I can of my experience and learnings.

To sell your business for a life-changing amount of money, it will have to be worth at least that much to potential acquirers. This value will always be highly subjective, so take any numbers and figures you encounter with a grain of salt: if the same business can have a significantly different value between multiple acquirers, then it will be even more pronounced between unrelated businesses from unconnected industries. And that's before taking into account the economic environment.

However, one fact remains true no matter how you look at it: selling a well-structured, sustainable business will always net you a premium. Acquirers will always be interested in companies and products that are doing well and were built with intent.

A Sellable Business Is Focused

When someone is interested in buying your company, they are looking into how much revenue they can expect to receive and how much work it would be to run it. If your business offers one specialized service to a clearly defined niche audience, an acquirer only needs to be trained in one area of expertise. If you provide six different products to a much more general audience, running the company will be more complicated. It will mean more resources, more training, and less profit.

A specialized business is a business built by experts. Your business will have a reputational advantage, and it will be structured to be as efficient as possible because of the expert insights that went into building it. To an acquirer, it comes pre-optimized. For you, it means that your business is the best version of itself: it's the sharpest blade you can forge.

The most attractive businesses have standardized offerings. Most modern SaaS businesses already do that, as standardizing is the only means to achieve economies of scale. For a buyer, "bespoke" is not an indicator of quality; it's a source of trouble. By delivering the same service to all of your customers, any improvement for a single customer will be an improvement for all of them. That will net the business a premium when it is sold.

A Sellable Business Can Run without You

A business that can run without you is sellable. When you are still needed for the day-to-day operations of your company, potential buyers will be scared away. What if you won't stay onboard? What if they can't find someone to replace you? That's why you want to become replaceable, or better yet, replace yourself while running the business already.

The idea is that once you make yourself completely replaceable, you can either hire someone to do your work or hand over the business for a hefty pile of money. Either way, you will be able to benefit from the company without needing to work. This is best done by automating as much of the work as possible and delegating the rest.

The trick is to structure the business for a successful acquisition from the beginning. Both the formal shell of the business and the actual services and offerings can be optimized to be made easy and lucrative to sell. The more you automate the processes of your business, the less your acquirer will have to train new employees. The more you document your processes, the easier the training of the people who replace you will be.

High levels of automation and documentation also make your business run much more smoothly while you own and operate it. Every automation is one less task that you could make mistakes in. Every documented process is a means to easily onboard an employee. The fewer tasks you have to do yourself manually, the more you can spend your time working on things that significantly improve your business, making it more valuable.

A Sellable Business Is Independent

If you have a lot of customers, you will distribute the risk of cancellations. If you only have a few big clients, not only does a single client quitting take a big chunk out of your revenue, it also puts you at the mercy of their internal processes and politics. Don't be dependent.

Acquirers will not buy a business that will implode if a particular customer should cancel. If this risk is too high for a potential buyer, it should be too high for you as well. Diversify your customers. Churn will happen, for reasons that are beyond your control. What is in your control is how you structure your business to deal with the consequences of that situation.

A Sellable Business Does Not Have to Be Sold

This is the best part about making your business sellable: you don't have to sell it to receive the benefits. You can just keep it for as long as you like, and see its value grow. As long as you enjoy running your business, you can ignore or defer the acquisition offers. Most buyers will want to buy your business even more at a later point if you show that you could keep growing it after they first contacted you. After all, you just validated their belief that your business could be further expanded.

Before we founded FeedbackPanda, I spent a lot of time reading startup-related books and listening to podcasts published by the founder community. I was fortunate to learn from the book *Built to Sell* early on, which gave us the opportunity to build FeedbackPanda as a sellable business from the very start.

We probably would have focused on different things had we not been aware of the future benefits of building a sellable business. Over time, focusing on automation and documentation allowed us to keep running a SaaS business with thousands of customers and a two-person team.

STANDARD OPERATING PROCEDURES: MANAGING YOUR FUTURE SELF

DELEGATION IS MOST effective if there is an Operations Manual for the company. Michael E. Gerber calls this the "Turnkey Revolution" in his book *The E-Myth Revisited:* the idea of documenting your business like a franchise. Build your business in a way that you could hand it over to someone else, and it would still keep running.

That's where documentation comes in, in the form of Standard Operating Procedures (SOPs). This sounds like a very bureaucratic construct, but it can be as flexible as you want it to be. After all, it's your business, and your processes will be structured in any way you prefer.

What Are SOPs and Why Are They Useful?

Standard Operating Procedures describe every activity that needs to be done in great detail. They do so in a—surprise—standardized way so that you can easily hand them over to someone else without needing additional information.

By documenting all kinds of processes in your business, you're effectively writing a handbook. This handbook will be worth its virtual weight in gold when you sell your business eventually, and it's already highly valuable while you're still running your business. No matter if it's your replacement, an employee, or yourself, following SOPs will allow you to work

- **More reliably:** Any well-documented process can be executed with fewer errors. After all, you have nothing to remember if all the steps involved are in front of you in a bullet-point list with screenshots and warning labels. SOPs include crucial information to contextualize the process, so even if an employee performs a task for the first time, they know the why and the how.
- **Faster:** Any well-documented process can be executed more quickly, as there is no confusion as to what will need to happen next. It's all there, in black and white.
- **More effectively:** Any process that's well-documented can be executed more efficiently, both at the moment it's performed and over time. Any Standard Operating Procedure can evolve over time, and when a central process receives improvements, any future implementation will benefit from the changes. It's built-in quality control.

Remember that one time a customer asked you to send them their invoice because they couldn't download it from your application for some reason? Imagine, instead of just doing it, you'd written it down. Imagine you'd taken screenshots of every step, creating a clear recipe for getting from the customer reaching out to the moment when you can tell them to check their email.

Repeat this for all positions in your company, and you will end up with a long list of Standard Operating Procedures that you can hand to any new hire and expect them to be able to produce results quickly. That first customer-service-employee-onboarding journey just turned from an odyssey into a pleasure cruise.

Operating procedures de-risk the business as they take actions that have proven results and describe how to do them correctly. Potential harmful side-effects or mistakes are mentioned in SOPs, so as to raise awareness of why things are done the way they are done.

Standard Operating Procedure Building Blocks

Documenting your processes starts with the right tool. That can be as simple as a Word Document or a collaborative Google Doc, something intermediary like an Evernote project or a Notion workspace, or a specific tool for SOPs like SweetProcess or Trainual, which are focused on providing a collaborative business handbook solution.

I recommend you start out with a collaborative Google Doc until you have found a format that works for you and then transfer it to a more elaborate solution should you ever need it.

Look at the processes you already have in place but not yet documented. Figure out which format would work best for them. Are step-by-step checklists workable? Would flowcharts work better? Written full-length instructions? Find something that works for you, as you'll be the first and frankly most important person to work with these in the future.

Do a trial run and try to document one particular process using multiple formats. Pick something that is representative of the majority of your processes for this exercise. Once you have created an SOP in a few different styles, you will know which one appeals to you most. Stick with that one for the kinds of processes that are compatible. Over the long term, keeping your documentation in a unified style will make your procedures even faster and more efficient.

If you're already privileged enough to have employees, get them on board. Show them the formats and your examples. They will be the ones working with those procedures most, so their input is indispensable at this point.

When you write an SOP, put yourself into the shoes of someone else doing the job. This fictional person just joined your business and is eager to work for you. What would they need to know to make this a positive and productive experience? What can you give them in terms of context and guidance that would allow them to solve this problem without your help the first time they encounter it?

When in doubt, be detailed. When it comes to SOPs, there can't be "Too Much Information." Your employees can skip reading things they already know, but they can't divine what you may or may not have meant if it's not there.

Implementing Standard Operating Procedures

Writing documentation is one thing, but getting yourself and your employees to follow the procedures is a whole other thing. It's a balancing act between allowing for creativity and having people performing the tasks as they are defined.

Although the point of having Standard Operating Procedures is to codify processes into clearly defined steps, as a bootstrapper, you can have exceptions here and there. Thinking out of the box is what got you here, so keep it going, even when you're dealing with documentation.

Updating Standard Operating Procedures

Just like your business is a changing entity, so is your documentation of its processes. At least once a year, but best every few months, do a quick read-through and see if anything stands out as a procedure in need of updating.

Often, you will notice that a procedure needs to be updated right when you're performing the task it describes. I recommend deferring this work a few hours to avoid heat-of-the-moment changes that lack reflection. At the same time, you should update it soon after doing the task, or else the perceived need and urgency are lost, and what remains is a procedure that could have been improved but was not.

The Side-Effects of Standard Operating Procedures

Some SOPs will also be appealing starting points for automation. If you do a task a few times a week and it takes you an hour each time, spending a few days on building automation for it is worth it if you know you'll have to do it for another year.

Searching your SOPs for automation opportunities regularly is a great way of making the company leaner and less dependent on reminders and tedious labor. Good documentation and automation go hand in hand in making a business sellable. If one informs the other, that's even better.

A set of good SOPs is great to hand over to new hires. But it will also help you speed up the tasks that you repeatedly have to do yourself. By following a prepared checklist that is the same every time you work on a task, you accelerate the non-automatable functions, giving you more time to work on the creative parts of your business.

BUILDING A MATURE PRODUCT

With a business that is getting more and more organized, your product will also need to be improved in the Stability Stage. You have proven that you can build a solution to deal with a critical problem. Now is the time to allow more and more people to work with this product.

As you scale your customer base, you may want to look into providing new and interoperable ways of interacting with your product. An extensible product increases the opportunity surface for it to become an important part of your customers' workflows by integrating into other solutions and being integrable itself.

It's quite likely that at this stage, your product is mostly complete. It may even have a few features that made sense at the time but are now lying around unused, cluttering the interface and your codebase. While removing features could go against most conventional product management advice, it's worth considering. After all, it may make your product better: it would be faster, easier to use, and more maintainable.

MADE TO STICK: SHAPING AN EXTENSIBLE PRODUCT

IT WON'T TAKE LONG before customers start asking for one particular kind of feature: integrating into other tools that they use all the time. They have adopted your product into their routine and their workflow, only to notice that something is missing. Some steps need to be taken to get your product to seamlessly join into the range of other tools your customers use to solve their problems.

You are looking for product–workflow fit. While it's great to be able to use your product as a standalone solution to their problem, your customers will value it much higher if it comes with two kinds of integrations: input integration and output integration. To provide a basic level of both, build your product to accept and return data in commonly used data formats (such as the eternally requested CSV format). If the workflow requires interactions with cloud services, you will find that most of them provide easily used and well-documented APIs.

Input Integrations

Find out the shape of your customers' data at the outset of their problem.

Let's say your audience is plumbers who need help requisitioning new inventory of their pipefitting supplies. Do they already have an inventory management system that has an API? Are they maybe using an Excel sheet or a Google spreadsheet? Do they have such a system at all, or do they "go and check" regularly?

Whatever it is, you will need to allow your customers to use the system they already have in place. Forcing them to adopt another system just because your product only works with that is a surefire way to build a tool that your prospective customers won't even try.

Every kind of additional input format you support will open your product to more potential customers. This requires research and expert knowledge of the field you're operating in. Of course, at some point, the fraction of customers will be tiny, a niche within the niche, and their potential revenue will be lower than what it costs you to build and maintain an integration. That, too, requires insight into your market.

Whenever you work with data imports, here are a few basic ideas:

- **Integrate the industry-standard format.** Many industries have developed common interchange data formats over time, and they usually are specified in great detail. This is an easy choice if you want to support the biggest number of customers.
- **Integrate comma-separated values.** This is the lingua franca of data. Almost every software tool eventually understands and produces comma-separated values, the CSV format.

- **Integrate Excel files and Google sheets.** Often, that's the highest stage that your prospects will reach with their self-invented and self-organized systems. These are the systems you intend to replace, so make it easy to migrate the existing data into your product.
- **Integrate JSON and/or XML.** When there are already existing services and APIs in your space, make your product compatible with their outputs. Remember, your product exists in a landscape of other services, and fitting into your customers' workflow is the way to adoption.

Output Integration

What is true for your customers' workflow before they use your product is also true for when you've solved their critical problem successfully: they need to continue with other steps. Allowing their data to be easily utilized right after using your service will significantly increase your customer retention and turn your product from a nice-to-have into a must-have.

When you look into which data formats your customers expect, look into both the immediate steps that follow and the final outcome of your customers' task. If you can supply data in a shape that allows for both to be maximally valuable, you're helping twice. If you can enrich your customers' data with something they can use later down the road, your product delivers value even when they're done using it.

When you're exploring what shape your result data should have, here are a few thoughts:

- **Produce the industry-standard format.** As with the input data, this will give you access to the largest group of prospective customers. It will also make sure that other tools that eventually integrate with your solution implement this format, further normalizing the industry standard.

- **Allow for CSV data export.** Your customers may not need it all the time, but this data format is surprisingly relevant for retention. It's commonly used when your customers want to experiment with what using your data with another tool would be like. If you allow them to do this easily, it can further consolidate your product as an essential part of completing tasks.

- **Produce machine-readable data like JSON.** A service that can be accessed by humans and machines is twice as valuable as one that can only be used by people. Allow your more technical customers to use your product in a programmatical way, and the impact of your solution will increase significantly. After all, the types of solutions that other businesses can create by integrating your service as one of many are thousand-fold and extraordinary!

- **Facilitate reporting.** Whatever problem your service solves, it's likely that someone has to report what they have been doing and how well they've done it. For that, make it easy for your customers to export their transactional data, like how often and how much they have used your service. This is also a selling point when you're trying to convince managers and team leads to purchase your product. That way, the problem solves your customers' critical problems as well as allowing their managers to measure their performance—a win-win-win situation.

Integrating Beyond Data Formats

Input and output integrations cover the basic data workflow that your customers have. For deeper integrations, you can build extensions that integrate other SaaS or standalone software products that make up parts of the daily operations of your customers.

Many SaaS products can be integrated programmatically, usually using OAuth or API-key-based credentials. Either way, they can provide a number of interesting opportunities. The most basic integrations enable you to access some subset of your customers' data stored on another SaaS service, either temporarily or until the access is revoked. More advanced integrations will make things like data synchronization, manipulation, and reporting a highly automatable and time-saving endeavor—all of which are highly valued as additional side-effects of a tool that solves your customers' critical problem.

Think about how you can enable other businesses to integrate with your product as well. How would offering a programmatic interface enable other services to provide additional benefits to their customers? How could a service at another part of your customers' workflow benefit from a direct integration? Could that remove superfluous steps like data conversion or export/import? If you can provide a means for developers to integrate your product into theirs, you amplify the reach into your audience by overlapping it with theirs.

On the user-experience side of your customers, consider supplying browser extensions. Often, a little button or link placed into another website can make all the difference. This was the first integration we built at FeedbackPanda. We added a little panda face, already our logo at the time, into the online classrooms by having our customers install a Chrome browser extension. Clicking that button would open a new tab, transmit a bit of information about the classroom to an endpoint on our site, and our frontend would automatically import that information into a form. This was very simple, but it saved our customers a few dozen clicks and a few seconds of typing every time they needed to create a new record. It wasn't very hard to convince people that this was valuable: a 10-second video was all we needed.

Browser extensions are easy to create and deploy, as browser vendors have established browser extension stores that allow for automatic deployments and updates. Building an extension is straightforward, as there is a lot of good documentation available.

A word of warning about browser integrations into third-party websites and services. At FeedbackPanda, we integrated into a lot of online schools' web portals. Those businesses changed their products a lot and without notifying anyone in advance. Since we never partnered with them, there was no way for us to ever learn about this before it happened. Any changes to the data that our extension needed to work would break it, and we would have to release a fixed version. Consequentially, we had to implement continuous automated tests and alarm systems that would tell us immediately when such a change happened so that we could react quickly. As the browser extension stores can take a few hours to distribute an updated version, being quick to deploy a fix is essential to have as few customers as possible impacted by such issues.

If the browser environment has certain limitations that prevent you from fully solving your customers' problems (such as blocking notifications or native filesystem access), you can build and offer dedicated desktop or mobile applications. Only do this if it's required to use your product efficiently. Building, maintaining, and deploying installable applications is a herculean effort compared to a SaaS product. All of a sudden, you have three different codebases and have to support different versions of different operating systems, all with their own update schedules and idiosyncrasies. If you can, restrict your product to a SaaS solution as long as you don't have the resources to build a standalone application.

To make your product easier to integrate with other programs, provide a machine-accessible interface such as a REST API or any other way to automatically ingest data, using a commonly used and trusted authentication method. This also allows you to monetize your product at scale: by offering pricing based on API usage, you can create new subscription tiers that are much more interesting to your more technical users.

The Risks of Integrations

There is a risk of relying too much on these kinds of integrations, which is platform dependence. If integrating with another tool is the only way your product is usable, then any change to that product will be something you have to deal with immediately. If they adjust their product, you will need to make sure your product still integrates. If their business fails, all the customers you gained through that integration may not need your product anymore.

Whenever possible, aim to integrate with multiple competing solutions. Do you integrate with MailChimp? Offer integrations into EmailOctopus, GetResponse, and ConvertKit as well. Should one of these providers go away, you can even help your users migrate to another one that you support.

Be very conscious that whenever you integrate into a service or another service integrates into your product, both services become a slightly more interesting target for a cyberattack. There is value in customer information, both the personally identifiable information of your customers and the business data they keep with you. Be extremely cautious of making any such information easily retrievable through automated means.

Always imagine the worst way an integration could be exploited, and protect your customers and their data with a level of attention that borders on paranoia.

Make sure you're legally allowed to integrate with the services and sites you choose. Although web-scraping content has been declared legal in many jurisdictions, not every business appreciates automated integrations into their products or data. Be ready to ask for permission and study the Terms & Conditions of the service with which you interface.

When you allow for integrations into your service, keep a close eye on the performance impact they have on your infrastructure. While you have complete control over your own software, the interactions caused by third-party products cannot be easily influenced. If a service is hammering your backend with hundreds of thousands of requests per second due to a misconfiguration, you need to be able to maintain a stable system. Be prepared to cut off access to your service for specific consumers, and build a resilient infrastructure that can deal with heavy spikes of traffic. You don't know how easily the delicate interconnectivity of services can be upset by a simple programming error somewhere in one of the systems.

In short, think of the institutional risks of integrating with other services. It's perfectly fine not to integrate with a service if you fear that it could cost you dearly in the future. Integrations are supposed to amplify the usefulness of your product, not bury a time-bomb beneath the foundations of your business.

Made to Stick: Fostering Extensibility

There are a few ways to make a product that sticks around. You can make it an integral part of a vital workflow, or you can make it so compelling that people will change their workflows to fit the product. A way to do both of them at the same time is to create an extensible product.

There are two main ways of extending your product: extending the interface or extending the service itself.

Interface extensions will allow your users to create, use, and manage widgets that integrate into your service and will enable them to do specific, non-generalizable tasks directly in your product. An example of this would be a widget that displays industry-specific time-series graphs drawn from your data.

Service extensions will allow your users to integrate plugins that enable them to use specific, non-generalizable functionality to manipulate the data that your product uses. An example of this would be a plugin that would pull in weather data from a public API into your supply chain management service.

If you understand your product to be a source and a target for integrations from the start, opportunities for extensibility will appear all over the place. Take the ones with the highest impact on most users and implement them first. In some cases, you can enter partnerships with the companies that sell the service with which you integrate. This allows for cross-marketing and mutual value add.

THE POWER OF OMISSION: KILLING FEATURES FOR FUN AND PROFIT

IF YOU ADD features to your product indiscriminately, you will end up with a gigantic bloated mess of software. One way to deal with this is to be very careful when deciding if new features should be added. Another rarely used approach is to remove unused and outdated features. Removing the cruft from your SaaS product is akin to pruning a hedge: you will end up with a more recognizable shape and a clearer vision of what your product is all about.

How Customers React When You Remove Features

Here's the thing with change: there will always be people who hate it, with or without reason. While notorious complainers can be safely ignored, pay close attention to people who react negatively to product removal. Your target customers should be the ones that you delight with your product, and you never know how people use your product in weird ways until you break a workflow that you never expected to be possible. You want to remove a file upload button because everyone drags their files into the browser? There will be that one user who uses their keyboard only. Removing the feature makes the whole product unusable to them all of a sudden.

Make sure never to remove accessibility features because you don't see the need for them yourself. Impaired users rely on these things to be able to use your product. Build as much accessibility as possible into the product from the beginning.

When to Remove a Feature

In some way or another, every reason to remove a feature from your product boils down to feature creep. Here are a few examples, both with reasons why they should be removed and how they come to happen.

Remove unused features. When customers stop using features, they either found a better solution to their problem or they have a different problem to solve. As a result, unused features clutter the user interface of your product, not providing any value to your users. At best, they are a visual nuisance; at worst, they produce unintended side-effects, confusing your customers by their presence. Your codebase will also show signs of bloat when unused features stick around for too long.

We removed such a feature at FeedbackPanda. It was initially introduced to allow our customers to migrate and amend their data from one product version to another. As some of our customers were rather slow to adopt the new version, we left the interface component in for a long time and forgot about it. Half a year after the last customer finished migrating, we finally removed the feature. While doing that, we figured out that some of our customers had misused that feature to change their data in weird ways that we didn't understand before. Talk about a side-effect!

Remove features that distract from product focus. Sometimes, you build things because you think your customers need them, but they turn out to be misaligned with your purpose of solving your customers' critical problem. Those features can make other features less effective or at least harder to find and use. This is the ultimate incarnation of feature creep. It's what will turn your product into a tangled mess if you don't regularly trim the fat.

Remove features that make the product too complex. Very similar to features that distract your users are features that overwhelm them. Many products have seen their customers churn because they became hopelessly complicated to use. It all starts with the intent to provide more value, but it eventually turns into feature overload.

Remove features that are expensive to maintain. This removal opportunity is often overlooked. Some things that are part of your product may, at some point, cause performance issues or incur higher monetary costs than you're willing to pay. Often, it's easy to engineer and maintain heavy-duty features at the beginning of a business with only a few customers. Examples of this would be heavy background-processing of customer data, complicated imports, or extensive export scenarios. While limiting access to this feature may work, removing it is also an option if it's do-or-die.

Why Does Feature Creep Happen?

Feature creep happens for many reasons, and all come from a genuine belief that, at the moment when you conceptualize and build the feature, it's useful and providing value to your business and your customers. But, of course, just because you believe so doesn't make it real. I have built many features that I felt to be absolutely necessary only to shamefully admit defeat and remove them a few months after launching them.

Here are a few situations where I should not have added a feature but did anyway:

I just wanted to build it. Sometimes, you're only interested in understanding how things work, and you think you need to build it. I did so with the FeedbackPanda invoicing system. What started as a simple part of the application, not much more than a list, ended up being a PDF-generating monster and tax-calculating monster of a feature. In retrospect, that's a rabbit hole I should have never even looked at from a distance.

I just wanted to get and convert a big customer. In a prior startup, I built several features for a prospective customer who promised to sign up if only those features were implemented. Of course, they never signed up even when I had deployed the changes, but we kept the feature in the application because we hoped that other customers could benefit from it somehow. They never did.

I thought it was the one feature I needed to release for things to start happening. This is an example of the classical "Next Feature Fallacy": the thinking that the next thing you do will have the big impact you're waiting for. But it usually doesn't. Usually, it will be yet another attempt at making a big difference and failing. This is a great opportunity to dust yourself off and try again. Just make sure you remove the feature that has proven not to work. Don't keep it hanging around.

There are a number of other reasons that can cause you to build things you shouldn't have:

- **"Premature Optimization"-like integrations.** You thought you could use this eventually, and you'd better already have it in the product before you need it. Maybe you intend to eventually partner with a service, so you build an integration ahead of time. And then the partnership falls through, and you never need it. Many technical founders then fall prone to the sunk cost fallacy, thinking that since they already invested their time, the functionality needs to stay there.

- **You're trying to capitalize on trends.** Ever implemented social-media-like functionality even if your customers never interact? I built a Facebook-like social stream with messages and comments for farmers who never took the time to use it because they were too busy harvesting their vegetables. But social media feeds were everywhere, so we just had to have something like this, too. It was not required at all, and completely unused, but we believed that we could pull it off.

- **You saw it somewhere else, and it looked rather cool.** Founders get inspired by other software all the time, and then build something very similar in their own products. What they forget is that every feature exists within the context of a product. That cool overlay animation you see on a social network for designers will completely confuse your almost technically illiterate users. Try to avoid things that are not essential to your product.

- **You needed to release something, and it was quick to build.** Sometimes, you feel like you just need to do something. You haven't released a new feature in weeks, and customers have always asked for something simple. It's not on your roadmap, and you didn't put it on there because it wasn't essential, but you know it will only take an hour or two. Now you have wasted your time twice. You didn't work on anything meaningful, and you will have to remove it again in the future.

No matter what your reasons were then, you need a slim and efficient product now. So, trim the fat, and start removing those obsolete features.

Removing a Feature the Empathetic Way

If you want to remove a feature, sunset it. Make a public announcement about the removal close to when people who use the feature would read it. Then, turn it into an optional feature, using a configuration toggle. Change that toggle to default to an "off" state, and measure how many people react to it. Inform them how to re-enable it and how to work with your product without that feature. If you feel confident that removing the feature won't impact a significant amount of your target customers, remove it.

Feature removal has multiple impacts: you can fully remove a feature, slowly wean customers off over a number of weeks, or phase out the feature via options until the last customer has stopped using it.

No matter what speed you choose, the most important thing to remember is to communicate the changes to your users before and after you remove anything. This will reduce friction between you and your customers. It prepares them for an impending change and reduces the likelihood of them getting confused when it finally happens. By keeping your customers in the loop, you're reducing the customer service load you'll have when you remove the feature. Also, once they know about the change, they can look for alternative ways to solve their problem if they were users of the feature before.

Use all the instruments at your disposal to communicate the removal to your customers. Tell them in-app and through an email. You never know where they are right now, and you need them to know both in advance through a thoughtful email and right when they are in the product, best in the location where the feature used to be. Update your knowledge base and prepare a transitionary video that clearly shows how to solve the problem alternatively if ever needed. The more you invest in communicating a feature removal, the less work you'll have on the customer service front.

There Will Be Consequences

Sometimes, you will learn that some features are part of very hard-to-change workflows for some of your users. Removing the feature will cause you to lose the customer in these cases. Sometimes, that is okay if the removal reduces complexity for everyone else. It's a balancing act. Be clear in your messaging, and insist on making the product a distinctive, slim, focused version of itself instead of succumbing to featuritis.

If people ask why you removed a feature they used before, give them good reasons. Customers will understand when you say, "less is more, and this is making the product better." For your customers, the overall usefulness of your product will trump individual features when they have a chance to think about it. They may complain, but unless they cancel their subscription, they will see it as a viable move.

Finally, by talking to customers before you remove a feature, you spread out the haters. The complainers will complain over a few days, sometimes to you, sometimes on social media, but their cries and yells will be sparse and manageable. Much better than when all hell breaks loose at the same time when you remove a feature without telling anyone.

All in all, slimming down your product can have a net positive effect on the business, your customers, and the value they receive. Keep this tool handy when you're doing some business introspection. Not all questions have to be answered with a "What if we build this?"—some deserve a "We don't really need this!"

BUILDING A TEAM

As the business grows, so will your responsibilities. More and more customers will reach out with questions, and more and more bugs need to be squashed and features designed.

What once filled an hour or two can quickly turn into an entire day. It happens gradually, and you may miss the point when it turns from additional work into a source of stress. What was easy to handle in the beginning could turn into a destructive and insurmountable task later in the course of your business.

If you want to stay sane and still have a balanced life, you will need help. While some outliers can run their million-dollar businesses alone, you will likely need a few people to take care of some things for you eventually. I waited far too long to hire at FeedbackPanda, and it impacted me more than the business. Think of hiring as an opportunity to accelerate the growth of your business, at any level.

WHEN YOU REACH YOUR LIMITS: GROWING A COMPANY BEYOND THE FOUNDER(S)

IF YOU'RE COMING from a professional background in salaried positions, the chances are that you've never hired anyone before. And even if you have, hiring someone for your own business will be a daunting task.

It certainly was for me. I thought that I could manage all that work by myself just fine, so why bother hiring. But I limited myself by doing things that kept me from doing more meaningful work. I was spreading myself too thin, trying to multitask when each task would have deserved my full attention.

Sure, it's great to help customers through live chat. But should I not have spent the time fixing the very issues they complained about? Could someone else not have a friendly conversation and show them a link to the article in the knowledge base where all the steps were laid out? Most importantly, did it really need to be me?

The Mistakes I Made When I Thought I Didn't Need to Hire

My first mistake was to think that it would only be reasonable to hire when there would be enough work for a full-time position. To this day, I don't know why I didn't think of hiring someone part-time, but to me, a job was a full-time endeavor. This resulted in a strange scenario: I never felt it would be enough work for a hire, because not only could I do it myself, but I would also fit other things into my workday. The fact that I worked 12 hours or more every day of the week seemed to not have registered in my entrepreneurial brain.

Hiring someone could have saved me countless hours of work every day, freeing my mind from focusing on the mundane parts of the business at all times. Sometimes, in between customer service chats, I would get a glimpse of what that life could be. I just shrugged it off, but I should have acted on that initial feeling and hired someone to help me.

My second mistake was to think that onboarding a new hire would be too much work. It turned out that waiting to onboard a new hire is even more work, as it just adds all the tasks you don't get to delegate on top of the onboarding efforts. I completely misjudged how effective other people can be at learning a new task. I also underestimated the impact of being well-prepared by having built a sellable business.

If you're using Standard Operating Procedures in your business, the effort of onboarding will be rather low, as you can just give the new employee access to the relevant processes and documentation. Provided that you created meaningful, exhaustive, and instructive documentation, your new hire can explore the scope of their job and prepare for what is to come.

How and Whom to Hire

You always hear that you should hire slowly. That's true; you don't want to waste resources when you could do it yourself or build automation to take care of it. But once you see that you're stuck doing work you don't enjoy that others could do for you, hire quickly.

Choosing what position to hire for will be a very subjective decision. After all, your preferences and tolerance for doing certain jobs are uniquely yours. Only you know when enough is enough.

In most SaaS businesses, customer service positions will be the first ones for which you may want to hire. While software can scale indefinitely, you can't. Once your customer base grows, you can automate as much as possible, but there will still be unforeseen problems at random points in time. Finding someone to triage these issues and sending only the most important ones through to you will free up significant space on your calendar and in your mind.

Marketing and sales positions can also be hired for quite early. For all three roles, you, as a founder, must instill the voice and tone of the messaging into your early employees. Until now, you have always been yourself, speaking to the customers the way you speak. It's essential to keep this style consistent.

Hire someone for the work that annoys you most. Repeat until you enjoy all the work you do.

How to Find Your Perfect Hire

There are two places that I recommend checking out before you head over to the regular job portals and recruiting agencies: expert communities and within your customer base. I've found both to yield excellent results in multiple startups I've been with.

Expert communities work extremely well for finding developers, designers, and marketers. As a bootstrapped founder, you are at least partially a developer, designer, and marketer. During your entrepreneurial journey, you will have encountered the communities where other professionals hang out. You will likely even have asked a few questions or chatted with other founders. When you are looking into hiring someone, go into the communities that you found most inviting, and offer the job there first. You'll pre-filter your applicants that way, and have a much higher chance of finding someone who will fit your culture.

Your customers can be a hunting ground for potential employees as well. Particularly for marketing and customer service positions, there are a lot of opportunities when searching for candidates among your customers. No one knows more about the struggles and needs of your customers than your customers themselves. That makes them ideal candidates to take over the jobs that involve talking to prospective or existing patrons of your business. They speak their language, and they know their pain even more than you. They are destined to build bridges and foster relationships with people they innately understand.

I had great success with both kinds of communities both within FeedbackPanda and at a previous startup. Hiring customer service experts from within our customer base was particularly effective in both cases. If you find a person who is looking for something new and is already aware of your company, all it takes is for them to have a background in the field. As people change jobs every few years, it's not uncommon to find a marketing expert who has become a teacher or a customer service professional who also is interested in local food logistics. You don't know what talent slumbers among your customers until you ask.

It will always be hard to convince people to join a small business. You'll need to have a good pitch ready, as you will need to convey your vision of the business and the part that your new employee will play. You'll need to make clear how they can grow professionally in their new position. This may be a hard thing to verbalize, particularly when you're looking for someone to take over tasks that you find tedious. But don't worry, people love all kinds of work. That's why we have accountants who actually enjoy their jobs. And after all, that's what you want for your business: everyone should love all the work they're doing. That's why you're hiring. You're giving people who crave certain tasks a chance to do them for you, for your business, and ultimately for their own enjoyment and livelihood.

BUILDING A BRAND

With a growing business comes growing awareness. The more people know about your product, the more they will talk to their peers, increase your reach, and help you recruit new customers. To benefit from that, you will need to create a brand around your product and business: you need to have a compelling story, ready to be shared by an engaged and passionate audience.

You will need to start selling more than just a service at this point. Once you start partnerships with other businesses and reach out into a less eager segment of your market (than the early adopters you were talking to before), your messaging moves from providing problem-solving functionality toward creating superior value and helping customers reach their goals.

But what do you say, and how do you spread the word? A well-positioned brand with a unified voice takes care of the what, and a tribe will take care of the how.

YOU WANT A TRIBE

ACCORDING TO SETH GODIN, a tribe is a group of people that are connected to each other, an idea, and a leader. Tribes are supercharged communities. They are dense networks of people who bond over specific interests or goals. These interests range from the mundane to the most personal and exciting topics. No matter if you're into a certain line of shampoos, love drag racing, or want to help the homeless, there will be a tribe of people dedicated to that activity somewhere.

What makes them so special? What makes tribes so incredibly attractive for bootstrapped businesses? To flourish, a tribe really only needs the means to communicate and a shared interest. Tribes leverage social media and networks to find a platform and allow their members to provide insights and distribute knowledge specific to their shared interests among the community.

Tribes and You

There are two ways of participating in a tribe. As a member of any tribe, you can be a follower or a leader. Both roles allow you to be involved and benefit from the interconnected nature of tribes in different ways.

To build a tribe around your business, you can step up as a leader, enabling your customers and those who could become customers to connect with each other, while centering it around your product. But even as a follower of the thought leaders inside a tribe, you will benefit from the knowledge and expertise you'll accumulate. You will learn how people tick, what metaphorical language they speak, and what their needs and desires are. No matter if you lead or follow, being part of a tribe will give you valuable insights.

People have an innate need for connection on every level of their lives. As a business, you can tap into a few of those, but be careful never to exploit them. There is no faster way of losing your customers' trust than to surprise them with actions that conflict with their understanding of belonging and connection. Don't go for the quick win. People are extremely sensitive to interactions where they are at risk of being exploited. Even a harmless remark can cause them to be at high alert, and it will be impossible to make a case for whatever you're selling if your prospect is skeptical of your honesty and reliability. Let people find your service; don't force it on them. Leave traces by providing valuable content; don't throw yourself at your niche audience with discounts and savings.

Tribal Network Effects

The network effects in tribal communities are powerful, as people share a large number of commonalities. When you reach out with a question, you can be sure that you will receive an avalanche of responses. They may be very different, as a tribe is not homogenous. But they will all be aimed at accomplishing a shared desire, a common goal. Setting that goal is the job of a leader. Transforming the shared interests of your tribe's members into a common goal that your product can help accomplish is why marketing works so well in tribes.

A tribe is a grapevine. You will hear about little things quickly, as they cause ripples, which spread quickly through an engaged community. At FeedbackPanda, the teacher tribe would often relay rumors and insider information from within their employers' internal workgroups and forums. That often allowed us to anticipate changes long before they were implemented. Often, we had weeks to build features and fixes to cope with new Chinese educational legislation that affected the schools where our teachers taught. We often had implemented and deployed our solution before the schools were done with their implementations, even though they typically had hundreds of developers.

The speed with which information travels in tribes served us well when our product experienced problems, either due to performance issues on our end or when our integrations broke. First, any sign of trouble resulted in a noticeable number of messages that showed up on our radar. When individual members started talking about things getting slow, others would chime in and state if they were affected, too. That way, we could quickly gauge if this was a problem that was caused by our systems or a slow internet connection. In any case, tribe members would try and help each other immediately, which decreased the load on our customer service desk.

Another great result of being a part of the online teacher tribe was that our most vocal evangelists were also among the most active members of that community. Whenever something happened, good or bad, they would amplify the message and color it in a way that would serve us. Something good happened, and they would tell their peers how we were constantly improving our product and their lives. Something bad happened, and they would tell their peers that it wouldn't be a problem for long as we always strived to fix issues quickly and provide as much value as we possibly could. This way, any message that would make its way through the tribe would effectively be positive and shine a favorable light on our business without our involvement.

While there are many tribes already, you can also play a part in creating one. Find people who share the same interests but are disconnected. Facilitate them coming together and freely exchanging information without any coercion or expectations. A tribe evolves slowly, and by guiding people to build a community, you and your business can be an important pillar of a long-term association of like-minded people.

Building a Tribe

It takes time to build a tribe. People don't trust easily, and they will be skeptical of business leaders engaging them in their communities. Many communities have experienced opportunistic advertisers coming in and trying to sell them their products. As a consequence, almost all of those communities have adopted policies that may look overprotective and overly cautious, but they are the hard-learned lessons of keeping the community from being spammed and falling into disarray.

That's why it's crucial to be a genuine contributor first. Don't rush in, expecting that people will crown you as their leader within days. It often takes a long time to establish a reputation of a trusted and valued member of a tribe.

Play the long game here. Better yet, don't play any game at all: be in it for the people, not for the money. Even if your business should fail, you will still be in an excellent spot to try something else as a leader of a tribe of passionate people centered around an idea.

A tribe is a commitment beyond your business. It's a community of people who look beyond products and services. Even if you manage to sell your product to lots of tribe members, their overarching interest is still bigger than your product. Understand that you're in this for a long time, and act accordingly. A good tribe will be a fertile ground for your ideas and offerings for a long time, so you may as well get comfortable and take part in growing and stabilizing your community.

POSITIONING IS WHERE IT'S AT

YOU CAN POSITION your product in different ways in many different markets. You may have started describing your product in a certain way, only to find that your customers understand it very differently.

Many first-time founders make the mistake of iterating on their product but keeping their positioning the same. Even if they're capable enough of describing their product correctly the first time around so that customers really "get it," they then miss their opportunities to keep the distance as small as possible between what their product does and how their customers perceive it.

April Dunford has an exceptional approach that will help you align how you position your product with what your customers can understand. Find the competitive alternatives first, then highlight the unique features you have that they don't. Show how those features produce value for your customers in fields that they care about, then contextualize it within the market segment. You will end up with a comprehensive narrative that ties together your unique offering and your customers' needs.

Competitive Alternatives Are Not Just Competitors

The term "competitive alternatives" is intriguing. Competitors are not just competing businesses doing more or less the same things you do. Excel, Word, and plain old Post-its can be the current way a problem is solved. Anything that provides your prospective customers some level of help when solving a problem is a competitive alternative.

Making sure you know what is "comparable" to your product will be necessary for highlighting the differentiators of your product. Look for things that are very different from your product. It may not be a SaaS, but an installable piece of software. It may not be software at all, but just a few sheets of paper and a grid. It may even be something completely different, like an intern or the work being outsourced to an agency of sorts. All these things have entirely different value generation potentials and economics. Make sure that the positioning of your service is clearly better than all those alternatives.

Positioning and Value

Know who your product is for and speak their language, understand their problems. Having domain expertise is very helpful here, and you should validate your messaging before you apply it at scale. It's another rendition of "talk to your customers." You'll be surprised by how something that's perfectly clear to you can be confusing to someone in the industry you serve if you don't know the intricacies of the domain-specific language.

When you want to convince a customer to buy a product, you usually show them your value propositions. Value propositions can be leading or lagging. That means some features have an immediate impact when being used, and others will only show themselves in the long tail of using a service. There are retention value propositions that you only use in customer service situations (think of a conversation that contains the phrase "See how easy this was? Next time you'll use this, it won't take more than a minute") that are not going to sell the product to someone who is just browsing. Make sure you use leading value propositions early and discuss long-term benefits later in the customer journey.

I recommend listening to Andy Raskin's talk about storytelling. He recommends laying out the stakes: make your customers wonder why they are on the road to ruin if they continue to do what they're doing. Show them what the losers are moving away from, so they can understand that the winners are moving toward your product. What does it take to win? What do winners move toward? Answer those questions with your service, and you'll have a strongly positioned product.

Talk about the problems you solve as obstacles to the goals of your customers, not just disembodied issues. Give evidence that your solution fosters belonging to the group of winners and believers. This results in great opportunities for conversational marketing. An authentic message gets spread for free.

There is nothing wrong with being specific. Going narrow could feel like you're excluding parts of the market that could be your customers, but it's an illusion. By making your positioning so compelling that your best-fitting customers "get it" completely, you allow them to rephrase it most fittingly when they talk to their peers. Trust that once you have conveyed the value you provide to those who can most use it, they will take care to explore the ways it can be described to a larger customer base for you. You will see this in their public communication, in the social media posts they create, and in the way they describe your product to other people in the market. Find those conversations, and you can learn incredibly useful terms and phrases that you can then leverage in your marketing.

The Context of Positioning Is Competition

When you position your product, don't obscure your competition. It may feel dangerous to show your customers alternatives to your product, but it really isn't, as long as you focus on what makes your product unique. That way, you will allow people who use your competitors' products to have a frame of reference and see if your service is a better fit for them. Additionally, by talking about competitors, you will find that people reach out to you and ask if you can also do something that services that you would never have expected to be competitors allow them to do.

At FeedbackPanda, I never thought to encroach on the territory of text-expansion products by building our own text snippet templating with keyboard shortcuts. It was only after several customers asked if our product had that capability that I noticed this was a competitive alternative to our fully featured text templating application. The fact that we offered "something like TextExpander" for their feedback attracted a number of teachers who previously had not understood the use of our product. We wouldn't even have needed to implement similar functionality: the category alone made a number of prospective customers check out our product.

Positioning Is an Ongoing Process

Once you have your positioning working for your product, don't stop there. There are two kinds of events that will require you to revisit your positioning: product evolution and changes in the environment surrounding your business.

Your product will change over time, either gradually or through a major pivot. No matter how fast you get to this point, there will be a time when the description you use in your positioning needs to be adjusted to fit the service. Features come and go, and your product is a different beast at launch than it will be a few years later. What started as a very niche product could expand into a suite of tools, or what is learned from operating your product for years will result in positioning or product changes later. A previous startup that I co-founded pivoted from being a marketplace for local food into local food subscription services for small businesses and agencies. We had to adjust our positioning completely, as our audience shifted substantially, which required an entirely different approach to product, marketing, and sales.

Markets can change, as well. The longer you're around, the more the business landscape will have moved. Things that were once unique to your product may become commonplace, with competitors adopting them in their own products. Regulation could cause your prospects to focus on things that you never had to advertise in the beginning. When GDPR was announced, all publishing services suddenly had to show that they were compliant with the European privacy regulation, or else they would be a risky service for their customers to use. When those businesses were founded, none of them had to position themselves as a GDPR-compliant service. Yet they all were forced to emphasize that part of their business—and had to scramble and heavily adjust their products accordingly.

The important thing is to regularly update your positioning. At least, take a look at your product, your business, and the landscape around it a few times a year, or when things noticeably change. At those points, schedule some time to reflect on whether your messaging is still aligned with what you offer.

A UNIFIED VOICE: STAYING CONSISTENT WHEN YOU GROW

AT A CERTAIN POINT, it won't be just you talking to your customers anymore. Your employees will be the first touch-points for customer interactions, co-founders and directors, and partners and other businesses. What once was a unified voice—your voice—is now a chorus. If you want to have a company that is consistent and aligned, you'll need to be the conductor of that chorus.

The reason that a chorus of 100 singers can create incredibly elegant harmonies is that they have a central source of truth: a score written in commonly readable music notation, and a conductor to help them keep in sync. You will need to be all of that for your employees and co-founders.

Building a Source of Truth

Create a vision and mission document. Set the tone by explaining the "Why" and the "How" in your own authentic voice. This document will be the point of reference for any question that could crop up in the future. Whenever an employee, co-founder, or a potential acquirer needs to learn about the voice of your business, you can refer them to this writeup, as it will settle any dispute and answer any question.

Write it down in extensive prose, or create a video in which you explain your motivation and your aspirations. Share this with everyone who joins the company, make it clear to them that this is the source of truth whenever someone wonders how they should communicate the means and goals of the business.

At FeedbackPanda, I stated in that document something along the lines of "At FeedbackPanda, we want to enable our teachers who are likely to come from fragile financial backgrounds. When they are in trouble, we help them teach more by using our product until they can catch up."

If you are a customer service representative tasked with deciding if a customer should get a few weeks' extension because their credit card is overdrawn, you don't have to think twice after reading this paragraph. This is how you set the tone.

We outlined from where our desire to help online teachers came, how we understood the product to help and enable them, and what we expected their goals and aspirations to be. In the mission and vision document, the most important topic to cover is your relationship with your customers. Are you a friend? A colleague? Do you teach them? Do you help them with work that they would otherwise have to do themselves?

In a way, this document reflects your internal positioning. Depending on how you understand and communicate your relationship with your customers, your actions and goals will change. Giving new employees and partners the opportunity to see how you understand yourself and your business is very valuable to prevent misunderstandings and misaligned expectations.

Taking Care of the "How"

Echo the voice of your customers. Talk about them as they would talk among themselves. Foster an understanding of the language used in the industry you serve. Your customer service people should be able to understand clearly what your customers are trying to do and be just as easily understood.

This is particularly helpful for new hires in fields that interact a lot with customers, such as customer support and sales. Giving those employees a glimpse into the world of your customers is very helpful. For this, consider describing in a page or two how your customers use your product, and how they would solve their problem if they didn't have your product. Contextualize the workflow of your customers for those employees who may not know much about your industry. Give them the opportunity to look into the tribal niche communities to get a feeling for the communication patterns that dominate your customer base.

What happens when you move upmarket and the language of the industry changes? You will need to adapt. The mission and vision document is not an operations manual. It's a spiritual guide, in some way. Change into a new consistency by revisiting the vision/mission documents, and educate your employees about the differences they're likely to encounter. Never lose track of your original vision, but focus on where you are at this very moment.

THE GROWTH STAGE

SHOULD YOU SELL YOUR COMPANY?

ONCE YOU CAN COMFORTABLY RUN your business without needing to pivot, hire employees, and expand into new segments of the market, you have arrived at the Growth Stage. For many founders, this turns out to be quite a dull phase of the business, as things tend to slow down. Processes are introduced, dependencies are harder to avoid; communication complexity makes decisions harder and takes more time.

If you've been working hard at automating and delegating, you will have ended up with a business that runs like a well-oiled machine. You barely have to spend any time on the operations, and you're left with making the company grow even more. You may be exploring new markets, new products, or partnerships. At some point, you'll find that things have slowed down significantly. The days of frantically pushing out new releases are over. Your MRR is likely in the high five figures, and you can afford to pay your employees a solid salary. What now?

Unless you want to inject your bootstrapped business with millions of venture capital suddenly, you have two options: stay in the company and make it even bigger; or leave the company and sell it to someone interested in growing the company further. Whatever choice you make, you can set the foundations to make the most of it, both financially and professionally.

If you choose the "growth" option, you'll spend the next couple of years focusing on growing the team, building out a legacy, and eventually replacing yourself with someone to do the work for you. You'll receive dividends over time, and you'll retain ownership of the business.

If you choose the "exit" option, you'll spend your time making yourself replaceable as fast as you can, growing your wealth in a singular event, the fabled exit, and then doing something else after a while.

Both options will lead to a life of wealth and doing what you want, just on slightly different timelines. It boils down to your interest in being the leader of a company that won't be recognizable as a startup anymore: processes and hierarchies will need to be put in place. Capable people who can operate at scale will need to fill positions that were previously held by quick learners who thrive on solving small-scale problems. Things will change, and your choice is between being there to supervise the change or putting the work and the risks of it in someone else's hands entirely.

SELLING YOUR COMPANY

THE END OF AN ERA

THERE ARE three main reasons for wanting to sell a company: you've hit a skill ceiling, you want to de-risk yourself, or you want to move on to another project. Each of these reasons is in itself fueled by the unique goals and aspirations of every founder, and they may appear at the same time.

In addition to those main three that occur for almost every founder at some point, there will be any number of personal reasons unique to your own situation. Some of them may not have anything to do with you, but may be caused by the state of the economy around you.

Whatever the reasons may be, you should listen to the feeling inside yourself. If selling the company feels like a viable option, examine that feeling further and try to find the underlying motivation for the thought. While often, it's a fleeting opportunistic feeling, it may also hint at some deeply felt struggle within yourself.

Selling a company is a great way to capture the value you have built in your company within a very short time. You will likely make a lot of money in that sale, and it can change your life significantly.

The obvious drawback is that once you sell the company, any future profits will go to the new owner of the business. If you keep running the company, you will at least retain ownership, even if you replace yourself as the operator of the business. But it will take much longer to generate and extract the same amount of money that you could receive in a sale.

Every deal is different. There are many reasons why someone would want to buy and how much they are willing to pay for a company. However, there are many things you can do to maximize the value of the business and make the selling process enjoyable and profitable.

AT A CROSSROADS: THE DIFFERENT
KINDS OF EXITS

COMPANIES GET ACQUIRED for a few reasons: they're interesting economically, they're interesting strategically, their employees are attractive, or they are a thorn in the eye of the acquirer, a foe to be vanquished. Depending on why someone wants to buy your company, the deal and the whole process of selling the company may be radically different.

In any case, you will likely sell for quite some money. Usually, that money arrives in two parts: one directly when you hand over the company, and another when the transition is completed. The first part is usually a big lump sum, while the second part is a safety retainer, a means to keep the founder engaged and motivated. As you will need to transition the company over to the acquirer, there will be a period of time when you will need to train the team that takes over. In many cases, an earn-out may be part of the exit, which means that your second part of the money is conditional to reaching several business goals for the acquirer over a set period of time.

The Financially Motivated Acquisition

If someone wants to buy your company because your financial outlook is impressive, your growth rates are high, and the future looks bright, they will want to buy as soon as possible and keep the business running as-is as much as they can. This is the most interesting kind of acquisition for a bootstrapped founder. If buyers reach out to buy your business for financial reasons, you know you have done everything right.

Your company will be a diversified income source, and the acquiring company will likely need to find someone to fill your position as the owner and operator of your business. The more documentation and automation you have, the better. If you've been structuring and running your business the "Built to Sell" way, you'll be in a very good position to hand it over easily.

The value of your company will be determined purely by the numbers: how much can your acquirer expect to make by running the company for a few years? How easy will it be to continue to grow the business without the founder? How easy will it be to transition the business into their organization? The more value and the less work are involved here, the higher the price.

Acquirers who buy businesses for this reason usually want to get the deal done quickly, as a growing profitable business gets more valuable every day. The earlier they can get their hands on it, the better. This will affect the amount of money they will be willing to spend. To entice you to sell it to them sooner than later, they may pay a premium for your business.

The Strategically Motivated Acquisition

Some companies acquire strategically. Your business may have an excellent customer base for a segment into which they want to expand, or you have some technology that they would rather buy than build themselves. It's likely that significant changes will be made to your product. Many of your customers will be nudged to buy different products, or they will see dramatic price increases. Unlike a financial acquisition, it's not likely that things will just go on as they did before.

As the founder, you will need to stick around for a bit, making sure that the strategic benefit of the acquisition is realized for the company that bought your business. As things change, you have to be comfortable seeing your vision distorted and realigned with the strategy of another business. Some founders have no trouble getting back into an employee-like position, and others can't handle it. Be aware that there will be work, discussions, and decisions that may be contrary to your beliefs, while large amounts of your compensation could be locked up in the requirement that you stick around for a long time.

The amount of money for which you can sell your company is less easily calculated in this case, as this depends on the unique relationship between the two businesses and the context of the market in which this happens. Be prepared to receive completely different offers from different interested parties. The differentiator you'll have to look out for more than the money is the conditions of transitioning your business.

Be very aware of earn-out conditions (discussed later), which means you have to stay on as the manager of the business and reach certain business goals that someone else will set for you. Many founders fulfill their earn-out obligations without issues, but there is a large number of entrepreneurs who experience a number of complications.

The Talent-Motivated Acquisition

In rarer cases, a company may want to buy your company to get access to your talent, usually called "acquihire." This supposes a certain size of your business, but particularly with the skilled technical talent that surfaces through the bootstrapping scene, it could happen at any size. If you're reliably present in the bootstrapper and indie maker scene, certain companies will look at you and your spirited efforts as a potential addition to their equally ambitious team.

If you're a solo founder, this can put you in an interesting situation. A company may want to hire you for several reasons, and some can work very well for founders. Look at Stripe and their acquisition of the Indie Hackers forums. They got a great entrepreneur, developer, and community leader in Courtland Allen, and the Indie Hackers community can trust in the fact that Stripe will keep the community running for a long time. A win for the acquirer, a win for Courtland, and a big win for the community.

This kind of acquisition happens most often for businesses who are quite young or aren't very profitable yet. At a certain point, the value of the business in question will shift acquirers to put in an offer for financial reasons, as the business itself, not just its owner, becomes an interesting thing to have access to.

The Nuclear Option

Finally, a competitor may want to buy your company, take over your customers, and shut down your product, while binding you to a non-compete for a few years. Usually, founders like this option the least, as nobody wants to see the business they built so carefully being eliminated and forgotten. This kind of exit is a last-resort option, and it will usually come at a hefty discount for the buyer. They understand that if you don't have any other offers, they can offer whatever they want, and you'll take it. Try to find a strategic buyer so that you at least have some leverage in negotiating your price.

. . .

Whatever kind of offer comes your way, understand that they are all signs of interest in your business, nothing more. You don't have to fear missing out on the perfect offer. If your business has value, you will get multiple offers eventually. You can actively seek out buyers yourself, have a broker do the work for you, or just wait for offers to come in. In the end, it's all optional, and you don't have to sell your business if you don't want to.

If you want to, try finding an acquirer who wants to acquire your business for financial reasons. This kind of exit will have the clearest alignment between buyer and seller interests, and there is a lot of useful information available from other founders. And it will quite likely yield the highest offers you could get.

PREPARING FOR THE SALE FROM DAY ONE: GETTING THE DOCUMENTATION RIGHT

Before any acquisition can happen, many prerequisites need to be in place. There will be an extensive due diligence process. Commonly, "buyer-side due diligence" is the procedure of an acquirer making sure that everything is in order with the business they are about to acquire. It's a detailed investigation, making sure that everything you claimed and promised about your business is actually true.

You can prepare your company for this process to happen as smoothly as possible by following a few principles as you run your business. If you need to scramble to get everything ready for due diligence only days before it starts, you'll add a lot of extra work at a time when you're already under twice the workload: you'll have to sort through a huge number of documents and conversations as well as keep running your business at the same time.

Selling the company can require a lot of work if you're unprepared. It can be surprisingly easy and painless if you structure your business and operations as if you intend to easily hand it over one day. This is the moment when building the company in the "Built to Sell" way truly pays off. With all the automation and documentation efforts that you will have put into your business to make yourself as replaceable as possible, an acquirer will take a look into your business and see a well-structured and easy-to-transition company.

There are a number of steps that I have found particularly helpful, which led to the successful sale of our startup Feed-backPanda.

Document Location

It starts with having all your relevant documents and resources securely stored in cloud-based data storage such as Dropbox or Google Drive. This allows you to access your own documents from anywhere, and it makes it easy to deliver access to the storage service when you sell. Many businesses will have their own document cloud solutions, so allowing them to integrate all of your business documents into their systems rather than manually importing everything is attractive.

Structure that storage in a way that makes it clear what each document is, what it's for, and who may need to use it. Using extensive naming conventions is useful, as you want yourself and any future owner to be able to find relevant documents quickly. Keep your essential assets, such as logos and social media templates, in that storage as well. Ideally, all your non-code assets are securely locked up in the same storage service.

Financial Account Separation

Keep your business and your personal accounts separate. This starts with bank accounts. If you want to make sure you have a flawless separation between your private funds and the funds of your business, get a business bank account as soon as you can.

While this will incur some fees in most cases, it is also good practice, and it will protect you from diminishing your personal accounts in case something goes wrong with your business.

Depending on what legal form your business takes, you will be required to have such a separation anyway. If you don't exercise caution from the beginning, any audit of your books will raise concerns in some jurisdictions, and that can lead to hefty fines. If an acquirer purchases your entire business, they also acquire this particular risk. You can prevent this from having an impact on the purchase price by ensuring the personal and business records are cleanly separated .

This may be the most important thing to get right from the beginning. You can always untangle usernames and passwords at a later point, but a transaction that hit the wrong account and was taxed differently than it should have been cannot be reversed easily after the fact.

Service Account Separation

It's also recommended that you keep your service accounts separate. Create a separate Google account for your business and use that to log into the services you use for your company via OAuth2, or use your business email and a strong password.

Keep all of the login details in a separate 1Password vault, and keep only logins and secure notes related to your business in there. That way, when you hand over your business, all you need to do is to invite your acquirer into that vault, and all relevant credentials will be available to them immediately.

In the beginning, you will likely have just one email address, like "firstname@yourdomain.com." Mostly, because you don't need another, but also, because if you're using Google Accounts, you will pay per account. I recommend at least making an alias like "services@yourdomain.com" and logging into services using email and password whenever possible. The convenience of logging in with your founder account could be alluring in the beginning, but just like with your bank accounts, it will pay off to have everything separated from any account that is linked to you as a person.

Thorough Documentation

It's important to document everything—even how you're documenting things. I don't think there is a way to over-document when it comes to something as important as the inner workings of a business. Superfluous documentation can be ignored if it's not needed. Still, there is no way to reconstruct what the original founder of the business did or meant to do when there is no trace of any document or instruction.

Write an extensive Operations Manual from day one. If you do something more than once in your business, write a Standard Operating Procedure for it. It'll be great for transitioning your business over to your successor. Even the smallest task will need to be mentioned or explained, and creating an SOP as soon as you're done with a new task will make sure it won't be forgotten.

If you answer a question in your customer service tool, turn it into a knowledge base article and link to it in your Operations Manual. The more advanced knowledge base system will integrate with your customer service chat systems and suggest articles when they detect certain search terms. This will save you countless hours of customer support, and having the documentation in place will be a great training opportunity for your acquirer's customer service agents, as it gives you the opportunity to gauge what types of problems your customers may experience.

Handing over such a document will be almost like a franchise: the new owner will know exactly how to deal with all parts of the business. They can immediately start running it and training their employees to take over critical functions. The more you document, the faster you can be replaced.

PRIMING YOUR BUSINESS FOR DUE DILIGENCE

IN PREPARATION for a due diligence process, there are a few things you can routinely update and use. Most of these things have to do with financial and business metrics, while others are legal requirements.

The Profit & Loss Sheet

One of the first things any interested party will expect you to provide is a Profit & Loss Sheet, often called the P&L. In its most basic form, it's a spreadsheet outlining your expenses and revenue history, month over month. Some P&L sheets are highly detailed, down to describing each individual expense, while others group expenses into broader categories. All P&L sheets track the relevant business figures of the past, while some also include projections into the future.

There is a certain political element to this kind of document: it shows where you're coming from, where you want to go, and where you will go if things continue to work the way they do right now. The projections, if sound, are particularly interesting for a potential acquirer. As the P&L is usually the first document a buyer gets to see, it is often used to anchor their expectations.

It is good business hygiene to have such a document from the beginning and to update it with the latest numbers once every month. This will allow you to have insight into the developments of your bottom line and give interested parties a quick and cursory glance into the current health and attractiveness of your business.

Internal Metrics

For the internal metrics of your business, I recommend using tools like ProfitWell or Baremetrics. Those business analytics services hook into your payment processor and use your subscription data to extract trends, key numbers, and aggregate numbers. While many payment providers have rudimentary dashboards and statistics pages, these business metrics tools are focused on obtaining the most meaningful numbers and making them actionable.

Often, since these services aggregate business data from many similar businesses, you can see how well you're doing compared to similar businesses that use those services. I always found it very reassuring to see that our churn rates were significantly lower than the average figures of businesses which had customers with similar lifetime values. We learned of a few parts of our business where we lagged behind, and that allowed us to focus on improving neglected areas of the business like the number and value of failed credit card charges.

All the business analytics services have slightly different ways of calculating values like your Monthly Recurring Revenue, and they may not be completely accurate—in fact, they probably won't be as accurate as a tax report would need them to be. For example, this happens because, at some point, the developers who built those analytics tools made a choice about when a charge should be counted as "completed": either when the customer subscribes, when their credit card is charged, or when the money actually hits your bank account. The same is true for unpaid but outstanding invoices: do they count? At a certain scale, this will make quite a difference in the final calculation. Every business analytics tool makes different choices here, so the numbers say a little.

However, you get a lot of insight into customer segmentation, retention, churn, and other relevant SaaS metrics, for free or for a low price. Actionable information that allows you to make smart business decisions is worth a lot more than just having accurate numbers. It's the actionable insight that you'll be using these tools for, and it won't make a difference if your churn is reported at 24.8% if it really is 24.5%—you have to do something about it either way.

These services offer read-only accounts with anonymized data that you can share with interested parties, so they have immediate insight into the metrics of your business without being able to see who your customers are.

The Power of Forecasting

Where analysis tools look into your past, forecasting tools look into your future. A tool like Summit will hook into your payment processor's data as well, and then give you projections and forecasts into the future of your business. You will be able to set goals and simulate how your growth would be affected if specific goals were reached or missed.

Forecasting will allow you to explore several scenarios of where your business could go if you made certain decisions that are hard to reverse and would be very risky to attempt in reality: hiring a number of people, switching to another audience completely, or pivoting to another kind of product. It's business experimentation powered by statistical models that are at least less biased than your hopeful entrepreneurial perspective. It's a projection of your ambitions into the future.

Being able to share this kind of projection will give your acquirer the confidence that you have thought about these things, and there is a statistically significant chance that the goals you have set may be reached in reality. If you have been using forecasting tools for a while, it will also show your buyer how well you've been able to reach the goals you have set. This will be very helpful in conveying your expertise as a founder and industry expert.

Becoming Aware of Liabilities

When it comes to legal tripwires, make sure you have your software licenses under control. Use tools that extract all the licenses used in your codebase, and turn this into a living document. When you use software that has no license attached, you may need to replace or modify it to comply with legal requirements. The same care should be taken with intellectual property rights and any trademarks you may own. In general, everything that touched a lawyer's hands at some point should be part of your digital documentation.

Are you currently involved in any litigation or lawsuits, or have you been threatened with that? Disclose it immediately. If there are any customers, ex-employees, or partners that may cause you trouble, point it out. Mention and list all past legal actions by or against your company, too. These things will be found out, and unless you're proactive about disclosing them, they will be the biggest red flags for buyers. Usually, at the first sign of legal trouble that was not mentioned immediately by the seller, a buyer will retreat from the acquisition. Be honest, forthcoming, and clear about the realistic consequences of those legal issues.

Codifying the Secret Knowledge

Finally, there are things that only you know: trade secrets, unfair advantages, insight into the industry that no one else has. How can you transfer that knowledge? You will need to find a way to put your insight into writing or another permanent and shareable form.

I recorded an 11-hour video walkthrough of the Feedback-Panda codebase before we sold the business so that my replacement would understand why the code was structured the way it was. That kind of information will differ for you, I am sure, but it needs to be ready to be transferred eventually, so it's better to start early.

Prepare for Controlled Handholding

The due diligence process will require a lot of work and focus from you. While the buyer will ask for insight, just sending documents to them won't do you any good. You will need to guide them to the information they seek, because the entire due diligence process is a trust-building exercise, and your involvement in building the relationship in this process will set the tone for years to come.

Start by explaining your documents and what they contain in an overview document. Provide a master document that gives your buyer quick access to the data they're looking for at a glance. If you're storing all of your documents in cloud storage like Google Drive, you can cross-link between documents easily. Anything you can do to speed up information retrieval will make the due diligence process less stressful.

While the due diligence phase usually comes with certain legal guarantees, don't be naive: there will be bad actors in the field, and some people will just promise more than they're willing to do. While most buyers are serious, some may just want to take a look under the hood of your business. For that reason, I recommend staging the release of information, starting with the least sensitive (like an accurate yet not too detailed P&L sheet), and keeping the most critical information (like your internal roadmap documents) until the very end. Don't share secrets. Never let your buyer access the account details of your customers without anonymizing them. Imagine what could happen if a competitor, disguised as a potential acquirer, gets their hands on your customer data. Don't make this possible.

Finally, make a checklist for yourself long before you ever get into the due diligence process. Your acquirer will likely also have one, and the more similar they are, the less you will have to scramble to prepare. Many serial acquirers will have a checklist that has been developed over many years, and they will make sure that all their bases are covered. You can help them develop that trust for you and your product by being meticulous about keeping your documents and affairs in order. The more organized you are, the less extra work will come your way. After all, you will still have a business to run during all of this.

SO YOU GOT AN OFFER: DUE DILIGENCE ON YOUR POTENTIAL ACQUIRER

THERE IS ALMOST NO BETTER and, at the same time, terrifying feeling than when you receive an email from someone who wants to acquire you. There was great joy when that happened to us at FeedbackPanda. Immediately after, we started to think about the level of risk to which we were about to expose our company.

The moment you allow a third party into your company, you lose a little bit of control. Someone is checking out if you're an exciting business for them to purchase, and they will require some information that you've never shown anyone before. Making sure that you don't get into trouble from that is paramount.

In a company acquisition, it's usually the acquirer who conducts thorough due diligence. We believe that before that happens, you, the seller, should do an equally exhaustive due diligence of your potential acquirer.

When Do You Need a Lawyer?

This is a question many founders often ask at this point. They have received an email or a phone call from a party expressing interest in buying their company or product. At this point, most founders wonder if they need to talk to a lawyer immediately.

I don't think that a lawyer is required at this point. Lawyers are expensive, and if you were to engage one for every party that expresses interest, you would soon be poor. Usually, you will want to hire legal professionals when you start signing documents that lock you into things that can't be reversed, like complicated non-disclosure agreements or agreements that forbid you from talking to other parties.

Once you are presented with such a document, I would suggest finding a lawyer and have a cursory talk about the process. If you feel that anything may limit you beyond the scope of mutual due diligence between the prospective buyer and you, intensify the conversation with your legal counsel.

The moment you are ready to sign a Letter of Intent, you should definitely involve a lawyer. From here on out, you'll be entering the selling process, and you will need to make sure that you're protected. You can anticipate that the buyer has a lawyer on their side, as it's probably not the first time they have purchased a company or product.

In the bootstrapped world, the first document to change hands is usually some sort of Profit & Loss sheet, and many transactions happen without any non-disclosure documents existing at this point. I recommend reaching out to other founders who have sold to your potential acquirer before and ask them for their experience and recommendations. With FeedbackPanda, we did just that, and it worked out well, as it allowed us to align our expectations with the reality of the whole acquisition process. We felt good the whole way, from first contact throughout the due diligence process. But when in doubt, consider reaching out to a legal professional.

Research the Company, Research the Person

The first and most important question you will need to answer is if this is a real person with the intent to actually purchase your business. Many bad actors are trying to scam business owners or extract sensitive information from companies. Good actors will have a track record of successfully buying businesses. Bad actors will not.

To verify the truthfulness of the offer, research the person that contacted you, and the company for which they work. Like real estate, acquisitions are mostly a reputation game. Parties who want to continue acquiring valuable businesses will need to present themselves as honest, respectful businesses. A botched acquisition or unethical behavior will cause a lot of damage to the brand, and bad news travels fast.

Look for traces of bad behavior and complaints both for the person reaching out and their company. That's quickly done with a Google search with something like "<company name> acquisition problem."

Look for public appearances by the person reaching out to you or the CEO of the company that has expressed intent to acquire you. See how you feel about dealing with this person. If you feel an instinctive attraction, great. If you don't like them, make a note. While an acquisition is a deal between companies, it's transacted between people. If the relationship doesn't work, the deal could sour.

Research the Portfolio and Make a List

Next, look into the companies and products that the acquirer already owns and operates. Are these businesses with which you want to be associated? Do you think they could benefit from your business strategically? Or is it just a financially motivated acquisition? You'll have a much clearer understanding of this once you figure out what your acquirer is already doing.

This is most easily done through Google search as well. You can usually find portfolio companies and products by googling for the full legal name of the acquirer, as it will be in the Terms & Conditions, which are often the same for all portfolio companies.

At this point, you should make your first list. Put down the name of the company or product, and find out who sold it to your acquirer. That will require some exploration and research, as pre-acquisition names are usually removed from the properties after they are purchased.

You can likely find traces of the names of the original founders in these locations:

- old company blog posts
- source code of the website
- old commits in public open-source code repositories
- public interviews about the sale of the company

Finding public information about the sale and the conversations that often happen around it will give you some insight into the process, as founders who have sold their businesses are frequently asked about the details of the process. I talked about this on Indie Hackers a few months after going through the sale of FeedbackPanda.

If you can't find public information about the sale, ask yourself why that is. It doesn't have to be sinister, as some founders like to keep their privacy, mainly when they just sold their business for many millions of dollars. Being too public can lead to a lot of stress, so many founders keep it a secret. Finding those founders will take more work, but it's worth it.

Request a List of References from Your Acquirer

Once you have a reasonable list of at least five founders who have sold to your acquirer before, I suggest asking the person who contacted you to give you a list as well. Ask them for a list of founders you can contact and ask about the process. Most acquirers are prepared for this and will present you with a few names and email addresses, and they may even make introductions.

While this is an excellent sign of trust and transparency, I advise you to be careful. The list an acquirer gives you will likely only include references that will be very positive and supportive of the acquirer. In most cases, that is because the acquirer is doing honest and reputable work, so their references will reflect that. However, there is a chance that a few people had less-than-optimal experiences, and they are likely not on that list.

Due Diligence Calls

To find the most interesting people to talk to, take your list, take their list, and make a shortlist with the founders that are on your list, but not theirs. Your chances of finding potential red flags and problems are highest here. Call those founders first, or send them an email explaining why you are interested in talking to them. If they have warnings to give, they will reach out quickly, provided that they are allowed to talk about their experience.

Then, call the founders on your buyer's list. While those founders are pre-selected for you, they will still give you great insight into the process and what to look out for.

In our case, the introductions from this list gave us the chance to talk to people we had only ever interacted with on Twitter. Having a personal connection to people who went through the same thing makes selling a company much less scary.

Here are the questions that we would ask in every call, to anyone on our list and on theirs:

Question 1: How Was the Transition Period? Was It Frantic, Was It Professional?

You'll want to learn about the amount of work that will be ahead of you once you hand over the reins. Some companies make it extremely easy, as they may already have a team in place to take over the operations. Others may need you to stick around and help them get on their feet. Ask which steps your reference had to take while transitioning the company and if there were any surprises.

Question 2: Do You Feel the Acquirer Served Your Business Well? Are Their Goals Similar to Yours?

Alignment is incredibly hard to predict. It's a mindset problem, and you can't expect to know how compatible you'll be before you're working with the acquirer. But you can ask the founder you're calling how well they were aligned: were there differences of opinion? Where did the business go during their transition? They won't be able to give you details, but they will be able to express their sentiments.

Question 3: Did They Trap You in Some Way? Did You Need to Stay on Longer than Required?

This is really about clarity and expectation management. You're likely selling your company with future plans in mind; you may have other projects to take care of, personally or professionally. Ask the founder you're calling if the acquirer made an effort to be truthful, clear, and precise in their communication. Ask how well they responded to questions about these things as well.

Question 4: Did They Take Care of the Team?

If you have employees, they will likely migrate to your acquirer. Ask the founder you're calling about how smooth that transition was for them (if they had employees). Ask if people were let go, and how well the ones that stayed were integrated into the team. Were there incentives for their employees to stay? Were there guarantees?

Question 5: Do They Understand the Businesses They Run? What Is Their Ultimate Goal with Them?

Some acquirers have been around for a long time and may have dozens of similar businesses in their portfolio. Others may just be starting. Ask your reference how well the acquirer understood the business they bought, and how much work went into non-operational knowledge transfer. If they had to explain to their acquirer what a SaaS business is, that may be a problem.

Question 6: Figure Out If They Acquired for Financial or Strategic Reasons

If your business is acquired for financial reasons, the acquirer may have different expectations of your involvement than if they bought your business for strategic reasons. Get a feeling for the kinds of acquisitions made by your acquirer.

Make Notes on What Stands Out

What is your reference talking about, what are they not talking about? Are there topics they don't want to talk about, where they change the subject of the conversation? Are there things they are very passionate about? Put those notes on your list.

Do a Background Check on the Finances

Ask for and do a background check that indicates from where the money in the company that acquires you comes. Are those clean sources? Is your acquirer willing to talk about the origin of their funding? Is it publicly available information, or are they secretive about it? Private Equity is often, well, private, but that should not mean that you have to be completely in the dark. When asked for in confidence, an ethical businessperson will give you at least some information about the funding they use to invest.

Red Flags

Here are several things that should raise the alarm in your mind when doing your own due diligence on your potential acquirer:

Red Flag 1: There Is No Public Information About the Acquirer

It's relatively easy to create a presence on the internet. If your acquirer does not have this, you should wonder why they would want to stay in the shadows. A company blog or at least a landing page should be present for any serious business. If there is none, this points at severe information asymmetry. In the end, that makes an interaction with such a potential acquirer very risky for someone like you: a founder who has to both run their business and research another one at the same time.

Red Flag 2: You Ask for a Specific Reference, and They Ignore that Request or Try and Dissuade You

If there is a person that someone does not want you to talk to, that should make you very wary. As I said, the acquisition business is a reputation game. If there is dirt that a company wants to sweep under the rug by making it inaccessible to you, that shows a lack of transparency and professionalism.

Red Flag 3: They Ask You to Sign Extensive NDA Constructs Before Talking to You

The more complicated the legal documents you're presented with, the worse off you'll be. Acquirers have legal teams to deal with Mergers & Acquisitions (M&A) while you have to run your business, grow your business, and deal with the acquisition offers. There is much more risk to your business in these talks than to theirs, so why would they need to annoy you with a time-wasting legal requirement? After all, it's just a conversation. At best, this is wasting your time. At worst, it could be an intentional attempt at distracting you from doing your work.

Red Flag 4: They Demand Access to Very Sensitive Data

If an acquirer asks you to give them access to things like your customer contact information, stop and think immediately. What could someone do with this information? Is the acquisition offer an attempt to grab your data? Make sure that they only have access to read-only data, limited views, and can't easily export all of your sensitive information.

Red Flag 5: They Want to See the Real Data (Instead of Just Reports)

If an acquirer asks to see the data of individual customers before you sign a Letter of Intent and start the real due diligence, be careful. Even after signing the Letter of Intent, which is a non-binding agreement, you should make efforts to restrict access to this information. The acquirer can always back out of the transaction later, but you stand to gain nothing. If you must, give them partial access, but don't give them everything just yet. That is what happens when you actually sell the business, not before.

Red Flag 6: They Decline to Sign Your NDA But Still Want to See the Real Data

If your acquirer truly needs to see sensitive data, you have the right to demand that they sign a non-disclosure agreement. Provide a simple one, that categorically states that access to your information is for exploration purposes only. If you feel like you need to protect your data at this point, reach out to a lawyer with M&A experience and have them draft an NDA for you. You have to feel comfortable throughout this experience. No serious buyer with a reputation to protect will be surprised by you being protective with your business information. They may even expect it. It's safe to say that no acquirer with good intentions ever wants you to feel uneasy about any part of your interaction.

Red Flag 7: They Are Not a Culture Fit

Working the transition will be very hard if they're not on your level. During the transition period, you will effectively be colleagues. You'll be spending a lot of time with people inside your acquirer's organization. If you feel that everyone you've been talking to interacts awkwardly, you may want to consider backing out of the deal.

At FeedbackPanda, we made sure we checked for all of these red flags when talking to potential acquirers. When we interacted with SureSwift Capital, we were pleasantly surprised to find how professional and transparent they were from the beginning. But we still checked for every single potential issue, and we found no problems.

Trust is earned. That's why doing your own due diligence on your acquirer is essential and needs to be conducted with care. Try being realistic about the transaction. There will be small obstacles and conflicts of interest. But you can talk these things through. In the end, both businesses want to benefit from an acquisition, and an optimistic perspective will make this an enjoyable process.

How to Prepare for Your Due Diligence

Finally, now that you have taken an in-depth look at your potential acquirer, here are a few things you can do to prepare for their due diligence on you.

Follow the scene. Listen to podcasts and read blog posts by the funds and Private Equity companies and brokers in your industry. That way, you will understand not only what multiples businesses are selling at, but you will also get to know the people who are involved in those businesses. I had been aware of SureSwift Capital long before they reached out to us since they had been present in the bootstrapper scene for a long time, providing blog content and being on podcasts and interviews.

Always have a Profit & Loss sheet ready, and keep it current. This is just good business practice. If you're tracking your business metrics, you also want to use several analytic tools like ProfitWell and Baremetrics. If you're among the emerging group of founders who are using planning and forecasting tools like Summit, having your forecasts and plans available for acquirers to look into will also give you an edge when negotiating the sale. Set up read-only accounts with these tools so you can quickly provide them to interested parties.

I recommend reading *Built to Sell* and listen to the *Built to Sell Radio* podcast. John Warrillow offers hundreds of episodes about people selling their business, mostly as interviews. I listened to almost all of them in preparation for our due diligence, and the recurring themes in those interviews gave me valuable insight into what questions I should ask.

And most of all, relax. I know this is an exciting time, and the thoughts of life-changing amounts of money are just as prevalent as the thoughts of dangers and risks of such an important transaction. Talk to your spouse, talk to your parents, talk to trusted friends. Don't rush things, and most importantly, keep your business running. Sometimes, what sounds like a dream opportunity turns into a risky gamble, and you will back out. That is perfectly fine, maybe even necessary. You will know when the time is right. And now you also know what you'll need to do.

EARN-OUTS: STICKING AROUND
AFTER YOU SELL

IN SOME CASES, you may be able to sell your company with a transition period where you are expected to be reachable and support your team and the people who replace you when they need help. This could last anywhere from three months to a year or more, but in general, it doesn't involve you working full-time for your acquirer.

In other cases, you will be expected to keep running the business like before, with the only difference being that you're not an owner anymore: you are now an employee.

Why Earn-Outs?

Earn-outs are usually considered when the seller is required to keep the business running due to their direct involvement. It's needed for companies that don't yet have a team in place to take over all the visible and hidden tasks of said business. It is a risk-minimization strategy for the buyer. It de-risks their acquisition by making sure that someone capable will be available to deal with the unexpected events that can occur in any business.

But it can be a risky move for the seller. Instead of handing over your business and taking the money, you're binding your-self to another business for a set time period without being able to enjoy the same level of entrepreneurial freedom as before. Particularly if you're committing to a year-long relationship as an employee, you will now be under completely different limi-tations than before.

The Risks and Limitations of an Earn-Out

There are many very real risks and limitations that you should be aware of if you're considering selling your business with an earnest clause attached. I'm not advising against taking this option, as it is quite a common thing for certain kinds of acqui-sitions, but a solid awareness of what could go wrong and how to prevent that will give you clarity into what you can expect.

The biggest risk is that an earn-out will lock up a large portion of your compensation in reaching a number of goals. Often, growth goals need to be reached to get the full amount. Unlike with a complete sale where you exit the company as soon as possible, you will need to stay on in a position where you have no control over the course of your business and the economy it's in. If a recession hits a year into your two-year earn-out, you may not be able to hit your goals, and a portion of the money you were promised becomes unavailable. That is a lot of risk, particularly if all your wealth is locked up in your business.

It's not like you wouldn't have been exposed to industry and economic risk if you had not sold the business, but this time, your hands are at least partially tied. One thing that will be noticeably different is that your actions will need to be signed off, or at least discussed with the owners. Gone will be the day of just randomly trying out new services or products to see if they fit. You may get a budget for this, but every purchase will require some sort of approval. Changing a feature or wording on your landing page will require approval. You'll need to justify all your choices.

The goals you signed up for could become unattainable when funding for the project dries up, or strategic changes are implemented. Some acquirers have been found to use this legally questionable sabotage to pay their sellers less than they had promised. It doesn't happen often, but it happens. That's why doing seller-side due diligence on your acquirer is such an important step in this process. The moment you learn of this behavior, step back from the deal.

Another thing you'll have zero control over is a rare but ground-shaking event: the company that acquires you may also get acquired. At that moment, every agreement you may have had before becomes a negotiable liability. When this happens, the risk that your agreement may not be honored anymore increases substantially. Goals may change, budgets may shift, permissions could be restricted, key employees may not be transferred to the new owner. Any organizational structure you may require can evaporate from one day to the other.

Handling the Risks of an Earn-Out

You can protect yourself from these risks by asking for the most substantial part of your money up front. Then, understand that the remaining portion that's in limbo has a chance of never reaching your bank account. If you reframe it as a bonus on top of the guaranteed portion, you won't feel as much pressure to reach it no matter what or regret the loss if things don't work out.

Also, getting an M&A lawyer with experience in earn-outs to look over your purchase documents will allow you to remove dangerous clauses. In addition to having your legal counsel inspect your contracts very closely, I recommend taking some time to listen to the Built to Sell radio podcast hosted by John

Warrillow, who interviews founders who have sold their business. Many guests on that show had earn-out experiences, and the majority ran into an issue along the way. In preparation for selling FeedbackPanda, I listened to more than 100 episodes of this podcast to make sure I knew about every possible problem I could encounter. While our acquisition process with SureSwift Capital was extremely painless, it was good to understand where things could have gone wrong.

The best way to not get these kinds of earn-out-based offers in the first place is to build a great business that gets so many competing acquisition offers that you can choose the ones that will allow you to walk away with as much cash and as few commitments as possible.

WHAT'S NEXT? THE SURPRISING CONSEQUENCES OF HAVING SOLD A BUSINESS

IT IS A STRANGE THING. We started a business from nothing. Danielle and I grew FeedbackPanda to an incredible size—one we definitely didn't expect ever to reach. And then we sold it. Fanfares! Victory! Life-changing amounts of money. A lot of high-fiving and cheers. We eagerly watched our bank account every day, and one day, the number just jumped. It was an ecstatic moment, and we knew that things would be different from here on out. I was incredibly happy, and I had just accomplished the greatest success of my life.

We started migrating over the company to our acquirer, handed over the reins, and trained our successors. It was a fun, professional, and rewarding experience for anyone involved. We had done it. We had built a business, and we had successfully exited it. Now we could direct our attention to new and exciting things.

And then, out of nowhere, despair. From one moment to another, I got a sinking feeling in the pit of my stomach.

We always talk about the valley of death that threatens SaaS businesses. We don't talk about the valley of despair that you are likely to fall into the moment you hand over the keys to your business. I've felt it for myself, and I have heard other founders talk about it, both in public and even more in private. Every founder who has sold their business has a desperation story.

The better you built your company, the harder it will be on you. Here is what I experienced: all of a sudden, I was wandering around without anything to do. Before, I would get up every single day, ready to throw myself into work, but there was a void now. Other people now did all that work. They asked for my help from time to time, sure, but the responsibility for the work was ultimately on them. I was just a source of support in their transition of the business to the acquirer.

I had no roles anymore. I couldn't "just do things" any longer. Another developer was in charge of the code. Another customer service agent was in charge of helping the customers. Another product manager took over the product and started making decisions. I was an ex-founder.

That hit me hard. When you are used to working seven days a week, being an entrepreneur almost every waking hour, it will come as a shock that, within a day, your whole life comes to a grinding halt. All of a sudden, there is a profound change in what you have control over. Your business isn't yours anymore.

Routines you built for years are pointless. I felt disoriented and confused. If you're not prepared for this change, it can hit you pretty hard. I had to consciously prevent myself from opening my Intercom dashboard to see who had created new customer support tickets during the night. I had to stop checking the error reporting tools and infrastructure health dashboards as I had done every morning over the last two years.

It was just so unexpected. And that is pretty ironic, considering that I had read up on the potential issues that being acquired may cause. I knew that many founders had expressed trouble reorienting themselves. I had dismissed those claims, thinking that, unlike them, I could adapt to this easily. But it was very hard to adapt to this change. It just came too abruptly, upsetting a balance that had been carefully constructed over the years.

I am aware that this is complaining at a very high level, and to any entrepreneur who struggles to find their first paying customer, it may even sound insultingly arrogant. We had just sold our business and had elevated ourselves into a whole new state of being, into a post-economic state of mind. That is what life-changing amounts of money can do. So, instead of continuing to grumble about how hard the change was, let me share what I did to avoid the post-sale emptiness.

First off, Danielle and I took a vacation. After years of only leaving the country on business-related trips, we finally forced ourselves to disconnect. That worked really well, as a change of scenery opens up your mind, and seeing how everyone just goes through their own lives doing what they want to do will make you think about your own future. This kind of thinking allows you to reset your mind from the routines and preconceived notions that you may have built up over the years.

I then reflected on what had just happened. Over the last few years, we had built a thriving business that helped teachers become better at what they do, and we were rewarded handsomely. At that moment, I understood that it was my time to teach. I started writing about my experiences, about the things we learned, and how we failed. That was my path forward.

We made sure we built a network before we quit. Keep in touch with your team, with the people you met along the journey. Many opportunities come from these kinds of connections. Don't think you have to sever ties with anyone just because you sell the business. You're still the person who made it possible, the founder who built something valuable from nothing. That makes you a very desirable contact and a peer to many successful founders.

If you must, look for a new project soon after. Some founders just have to work on something. They can't take a break. That's fine as long as you take care of your mental and physical health. A sale gives you the opportunity for a break. Once you have had some time to reflect on what you need to live a healthy and happy life, you can jump right back in. Without taking this time, you'll just run on auto-pilot, which will limit the scope of what you could accomplish now that you are in such an improved position.

The great thing about having worked in a SaaS business for years is that you will have encountered dozens of little problems that needed to be solved inside your business. Any of those could be turned into another business. Reflect on where you built a dirty quick fix to get things done and see if that points at a critical problem for other founders as well. This kind of awareness will also help you detect other audiences that have unsolved critical problems, which could make for great research subjects for your next entrepreneurial adventure.

But it's still important to take a moment to reflect on how fortunate you are. The work has paid off; the thing you built mattered enough for others to take notice, and they made you an offer you couldn't refuse. Take it in, and look at how you can have an impact like this again—or do something even greater in the future.

KEEPING YOUR COMPANY

LET's be quite clear here: I don't have much experience with keeping a large company running. We sold FeedbackPanda when we reached the point of continuous growth. I've certainly worked for larger companies but never held more than a fraction of the shares, so my ownership perspective is limited. I will still give you my opinion on the topic because I feel that there is more than just advocating selling your business.

I understand that you can retain ownership in a business and never sell it, generating constant income through a salary or dividends and bonuses. You won't be able to have a big payday like you would have if you sold your business, but you will be able to grow both the value of your business and your personal wealth steadily, at the same time.

And more often than not, founders really like their work. They build a business because of a vision they have, and they want to continue making it a reality for as long as possible. They enjoy showing up every single day, throwing themselves at problems and opportunities. It's not surprising that even after selling a business, most founders turn into serial entrepreneurs and jump at every opportunity that would allow them to get back right into the thick of it.

If you like your work, work. Continue with your business, grow it further, make it help more customers. Take it as far as it will go. Every day will surface new challenges for you to overcome. The value of your business will grow consistently, and new learnings will level up your expertise over time.

If you start disliking your work, delegate. Remove yourself from the operational parts of the business by hiring a director, as many late-stage founder-CEOs do. Hire someone good at leading a company and making sure it stays on track. Then, leave the main stage and just be an owner, a shareholder. Maintain the vision, make sure the company does what you think it should be doing, but do it through guidance instead of leadership.

It's quite likely that you will see changes you never expected to see in your business. You have your own idea of how things should be done, and you have been successful in seeing it applied to your business. Overcoming this confirmation bias will be essential when you hand over the reins: other leaders will lead differently. Preparing for those changes will make the transition much more comfortable. The goal is to continue growing the company, not growing complacent.

If you follow the methodology in Michael E. Gerber's book *E-Myth Revisited*, you will have created a fictional organizational chart before you started your business. Over time, you will have hired people into the positions on that chart, and your name will have moved more and more to the top. There will be the day where you strike your name from the operational part of that chart so that it only remains on top of the page where the owners are listed. Celebrate that day, as this is the ultimate entrepreneurial accomplishment: you have taken the final step of creating a business that works for you.

To step back from your CEO position with confidence, you will need to find someone to replace you. They will need to replace you as a leader, as a manager, and as the source of truth and vision. Start looking for that person early, and make sure they care about your business and your customers as much as you do. This person will have to maintain and expand a culture of collaboration and support. Technical skills can be acquired, but they will need to bring a longing for building tribes and communities from day one.

And you can still have your financial windfall: there is always the option of selling a minority stake in your business. The buyer of that stake would get all the benefits of owning parts of a sustainable and lucrative business without needing to put much effort into the operational or even strategic work. You, as the owner, would still have full control over the company. If you are left with a substantial amount of cash from selling the minority stake, you will always be able to draw dividends from the business, and you will have the freedom to continue to run the business as you please.

I sold FeedbackPanda because, among other reasons, I felt the need to diversify my assets. Having the biggest fraction of my wealth locked up in one business seemed more and more dangerous, and it kept me from experimenting and taking certain risks. If you want to keep running your business without projecting your personal risk tolerance onto it, consider the minority share sale or start investing your dividends in unrelated assets.

Keeping the business and growing it into an even bigger enterprise is something that many founders who have been through it describe as an intensely rewarding and incredibly taxing experience. The great thing about increasing the value of your business every single day is that should you ever decide to sell it, the amount of money you will walk away with is growing as well. That motivation alone will make it worthwhile, and the entrepreneurial experience you're amassing will guarantee that if you ever want to do it again, you'll know exactly what to do.

BEYOND BOOTSTRAPPING

FINANCING FOR THE HESITANT:
INVESTMENT OPTIONS

I'M a big proponent of looking at things from multiple points of view. That includes the central assumption we have made throughout this whole time: that bootstrapping is the most desirable form of building a sustainable SaaS business.

I still believe that to be true. Bootstrapping is a great way to build and own a fantastic business. It's a great way to stay in control and retain all of the value of your company. But it's not the only option.

Sometimes, financing can make a difference. Even though we never took any money when we ran FeedbackPanda, I never considered it to be wrong to imagine what would happen if we did. Funding is not the enemy of a bootstrapper. A lot of people in the indie business sphere have spoken very negatively about funding in the past, mostly due to the fact that whenever people talked about funding, they were thinking of venture capital. But this has changed. There are now a number of alternative ways of injecting money into your business, and most of them don't involve complicated ownership arrangements.

While makers and solopreneurs generally tend to avoid financing, there are opportunities for external money to do great good. It's just a matter of carefully weighing the pros and cons. There is wisdom in knowing what's possible, even when you don't want to use it. If you decide to never take any more, that's awesome. You'll learn how to create a business from nothing, a truly bootstrapped company all the way. If you decide at some point that you want some non-VC cash, you can do a lot of good without giving up control of your business. Even if you choose to raise some serious venture capital later down the road, that can be great. As long as your decision helps you reach your goal instead of just copying the choices and actions of others, it will be the right one.

As long as you're conducting your business with a focus on sustainable growth, being smart and conservative in your use of available resources, and forging long-term relationships with your customers, you are running a bootstrapped business. After all, bootstrapping is the mindset of using heavily constrained resources to their maximum potential.

That doesn't change if you get funding. Adding outside capital makes your business a semi-bootstrapped business, provided you retain control and ownership in the majority of the business, and your goals don't change from slow, sustainable growth to hockey-stick hypergrowth. Bootstrapping is about measured growth and realistic expectations.

The venture-capital-centric assumption that, if you burn through enough cash, you will capture the whole market may work for aspiring unicorn businesses who can spend hundreds of millions of dollars and not generate a single cent in revenue. Throwing millions of dollars at a lot of companies to see which one sticks makes sense if you expect the winners to outperform the losers dramatically. But bootstrapped businesses are different.

Several players in the market have understood that bootstrappers want both funding and to remain a sustainable small-scale business. They generally require the business to have clear validation, which is often called "post-revenue": you need to make money from your business. What has been a no-brainer for enterprises over the last few millennia now needs to be made explicit in a time of hypergrowth ventures.

Accelerators and Incubators

TinySeed is an accelerator for early-stage SaaS founders, helping with a cash injection and mentorship while focusing on a bootstrapping approach at the same time. Since there are dozens of businesses in the same batch, shared access to mentors and resources creates strong synergistic effects between the businesses that are all at the same stage. It's a community of founders, building their businesses together. This may even be more important than the monetary component.

Be careful when joining conventional accelerators and incubators. Many of them still operate intending to make you ready for the world of venture capital. This could create severe misalignments between what you need as a bootstrapper and what they think you should want. While getting money and guidance is enticing, being "accelerated" wrongly will create a dynamic of dependency and misalignment that can severely inhibit your future prospects.

Earnings vs. Equity

Funds have been started that use Income Sharing Agreements instead of shares to create returns from investment. Earnest Capital does this, and its Shared Earnings Agreement is publicly available. Understanding that a long-term profit-sharing relationship is more compatible with the sustainable business processes of a bootstrapped business makes this kind of agreement very interesting for founders who want to keep control and benefit from external funds at the same time.

Similarly, some VCs such as Indie.vc wants to support founders on their journey beyond initial profitability similarly. They take an initial percentage of ownership, which can be redeemed through a portion of the monthly revenue. Should you want to raise further money, the ownership will be converted into traditional equity.

Traditional Sources of Funding

I recommend staying away from bank loans. Banks still live in the non-digital past. They don't yet understand the world of SaaS businesses as well as they know the numbers of farms or factories. They require a lot of collateral, and have very rigid requirements like business plans and long-term commitments that don't work in the fast-paced, pivot-focused world of bootstrapping small SaaS companies. If you take a loan, you will likely be personally impacted if the business doesn't work out, and that is both added stress for you and a liability for the business.

And it's likely you won't get a loan in the first place. Many banks and institutions won't invest in software businesses. You will have a lot of conversations that end in, "We would love to, but we just don't give out loans for these kinds of businesses." Very rarely will the attempt to secure such a loan be worth your time. You'll be better off reaching out to the kinds of investors that understand and prominently support bootstrapped founders.

INTO THE THUNDERDOME: TAKING VENTURE CAPITAL

SOMETIMES, companies that have been bootstrapped for years take a seemingly surprising detour: they accept a large amount of venture capital funding. Almost always, this is met with bewilderment and criticism, as it was in the case of 1Password. There seems to be a common belief that once you're bootstrapped, you have to be bootstrapped forever. Why is that?

The VC world has expectations and goals that are opposed to the idea of bootstrapping a sustainable business: if you make a lot of risky bets, you expect most of them to fail, and some of them to work out really well. This requires a peculiar mindset on the side of the founders. They need to be okay with failing spectacularly and risking everything to have a shot of becoming the biggest, most radically expanding business they can be. At the same time, profitability expectations are deferred until that point in the future when the business is huge and has captured all that juicy market share.

As a result, any business that is profitable but not explosively growing is not worth much to a VC who is looking for the next unicorn. This is true even in an economic downturn, as previous bets that won't work out still need to be cushioned by the winning few. While recessions bring profitability back into focus even for venture capitalists, the growth expectations are still very much front and center.

That's why the community is very skeptical of bootstrapped businesses taking on VC money after bootstrapping for many years. With a VC investment, the expectations are "rocket ship or bust," and people fear that the previously bootstrapped business won't be able to make the changes needed to switch from slow, sustainable growth to hypergrowth.

But all of that is guesswork. And venture capital isn't a one-size-fits-all investment vehicle. Most VC deals are made with the unique properties of the bootstrapped businesses in mind, and no VC would invest their money into something they couldn't envision having future success. The same goes for the founders. They have spotted an opportunity to take their business somewhere else, and they see venture capital as the means to get there. If they were capable of bootstrapping their business to this point, who are we to say that all of a sudden, their choice is a wrong one?

And in all honesty: if you own a business, you get to decide what to do with it.

If you want to bootstrap forever, great.

If you want to get indie funding, wonderful.

If you want to take your business to another level and use VC funds for that, that's good, too.

Many bootstrapped companies have gone the VC route, and they have been successful with it. There is no point in expecting businesses to stay the same over time. Every business needs to adjust to the reality of the market. Being a bootstrapping purist won't make your business any better.

If you're contemplating taking VC money, just be aware of the potential risks that come with investor expectations. Read about the experiences of other founders, talk to them about the good and the bad, and make a decision based on the experiences of their journeys.

CLOSING WORDS

THANK you for reading *Zero to Sold*. I've learned many of the lessons of this book the hard way, and I share them in hopes of giving entrepreneurs some insight into the reality of being a founder.

In all of my writing, I have always imagined my reader to be myself, just five years ago. I've been writing for someone who always liked the idea of starting their own business, who wanted to use their skills to empower others. I wanted to build something to allow me to grow every single day and find financial security through it.

That person from five years ago was an avid reader and consumer of podcasts. I can only recommend the same for you: learn from those who are in the thick of things as well as from those who are sharing their experiences after the fact. Having both perspectives side by side will allow you to judge how realistic advice is and how much bias comes with it. In this book, I have tried to merge the experiential with the instructional, yet for your specific situation, the advice may not fully apply. Entrepreneurialism is also about choosing *which* advice you follow.

If you have found *Zero to Sold* helpful and instructive, please recommend it to other founders or those you think should consider founding a bootstrapped business.

I am grateful that you have read *Zero to Sold*, and I wish you the very best for your own entrepreneurial journey.

Two Questions

I want to leave you with two questions. Both have proven to be thought-provoking in my consulting and mentoring work. Ask yourself these questions within the context of your entrepreneurial ideas, whenever you wonder if the path you're taking is the right one:

What life do I want to lead five years from now?

Visualize this life. Try to see yourself, your work, your daily routine. Imagine where you are, what you do, how you feel, who and what you are surrounding yourself with. Then look at the choice right in front of you and ask:

What will give me traction toward this future state?

If it will get you there, start today. If it won't, find something else, and start with that.

The journey to successful entrepreneurship starts with a choice. It starts with action.

NOW WHAT?

Please take a moment to rate and review *Zero to Sold* wherever you bought it. It really makes a difference, and it would be very helpful to me.

If you'd like more, head over to **zerotosoldbook.com**, where you will find a large amount of resources and links that will help you continue your journey from here.

Consider visiting The Bootstrapped Founder blog at **thebootstrappedfounder.com**, where you can read my past, current, and future articles. You can stay up-to-date on my writing by subscribing to the Bootstrapped Founder Newsletter at **thebootstrappedfounder.com/newsletter**. Finally, I publish new episodes of the Bootstrapped Founder Podcast regularly at **thebootstrappedfounder.com/podcast**

Now that you've finished the book, I would love to hear from you–after all, I've been mentioning the word "feedback" over 40 times.

Finally, please send any questions, corrections, comments, crushing criticism or words of encouragement to **arvid@ thebootstrappedfounder.com**. Every email is truly appreciated.

ABOUT THE AUTHOR

Arvid Kahl is a software engineer, entrepreneur, and writer. He co-founded and bootstrapped FeedbackPanda, an online teacher productivity SaaS company, with his partner Danielle Simpson. They sold the business for a life-changing amount of money in 2019, two years after founding the company.

He writes on **TheBootstrappedFounder.com** to share his experience with bootstrapping as a desirable, value- and wealth-generating way of running a company.

In the years of running FeedbackPanda (and throughout the many failed attempts before that), Arvid learned how to run a self-funded company. He learned that not every business needs venture capital to succeed, and Arvid claims that most businesses are better off without it.

He wants to encourage other entrepreneurs to see bootstrapping as a viable option.

twitter.com/arvidkahl
goodreads.com/arvidkahl

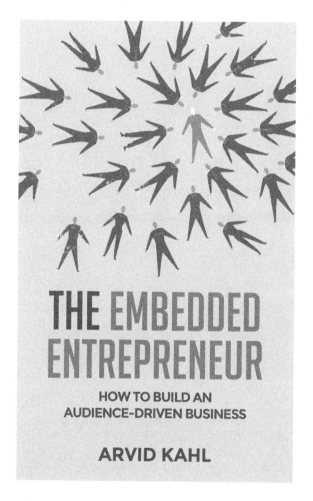

Find your Audience. Explore their Communities. Discover their Problem.

Build a Following. Build a Business.

Find out more at embeddedentrepreneur.com

Made in the USA
Las Vegas, NV
01 June 2022

49641595R00291